Sociological Perspectives on Aging

Laura Funk

OXFORD
UNIVERSITY PRESS

OXFORD
UNIVERSITY PRESS

Oxford University Press is a department of the University of Oxford.
It furthers the University's objective of excellence in research, scholarship,
and education by publishing worldwide. Oxford is a registered trade mark of
Oxford University Press in the UK and in certain other countries.

Published in Canada by
Oxford University Press
8 Sampson Mews, Suite 204,
Don Mills, Ontario M3C 0H5 Canada
www.oupcanada.com

Library and Archives Canada Cataloguing in Publication
Funk, Laura, author
Sociological perspectives on aging / Laura Funk.

(Themes in Canadian sociology)
Includes bibliographical references and index.
ISBN 978–0–19–900753–0 (paperback)

1. Aging—Social aspects—Canada. I. Title.
II. Series: Themes in Canadian sociology

HQ1064.C3F85 2015   305.260971   C2015-903455-8

Cover image: Rubberball/Mike Kemp/Getty Images

Oxford University Press is committed to our environment.
This book is printed on Forest Stewardship Council® certified paper
and comes from responsible sources.

Printed and bound in Canada

1 2 3 4 — 19 18 17 16

Contents

Preface

The sociology of aging is often difficult to distinguish from the more dominant field of social gerontology, and it is my hope through this book to help
restore and highlight the sociological contributions of the field. I was trained
as a sociologist at the University of British Columbia, and then in gerontology at Simon Fraser University. Following this, I pursued graduate degrees
in sociology at the University of Victoria, though I was mentored primarily
within the interdisciplinary Centre on Aging. There, I identified as a gerontologist and became interested in applied issues of practice and policy with
respect to older adults. The strong focus within gerontology, I observed, was
on the study of health and health care for older adults, in part because of the
many funding opportunities available in this area of inquiry, as well as the
concern of governments and policy-makers with reducing health care costs
associated with aging populations.

It was a significant turning point in my career when I was hired into
the sociology department at the University of Manitoba in 2011. There, I
was asked to teach introductory sociology as well as the sociology of aging.
Returning to teach the fundamentals of sociology helped strengthen my
approach to both research and teaching in the sociology of aging. For
example, concepts such as stigma, habitus, stratification, and of course
agency and structure open up a myriad of possibilities for their application to aging-related topics and issues. In addition, teaching the essentials
of a sociological perspective as applied to a variety of substantive areas (e.g.,
education, social movements, family, law) strengthened my motivation to
further explore the ways that aging too can be understood as more than a
private personal trouble, but as a public political issue (see Mills, 1959).

In this book, I have emphasized sociological research on aging, as well
as the contributions of Canadian scholars. I actively tried to set aside much
of the wide body of sociological research on health in relation to aging. In
doing so, I hope to address an imbalance in gerontological inquiry and to
foreground research conducted outside of a biomedical or public health
paradigm.

Chapter 1 provides an orientation to a sociological approach and dominant theoretical approaches in sociology. Following this, the rest of the chapter
introduces the core sociological theories of aging, including disengagement,
social exchange, and modernization theories; age stratification and the life
course perspective; social constructionism; critical approaches, including
political economy and feminist gerontology; and theories of postmodern
society. These theories are returned to in subsequent chapters in relation to
particular aging-related issues.

Chapter 2 opens with descriptive information regarding the aging of populations in Canada and around the world, followed by a caution against assuming that population aging will result in catastrophic consequences for society. Next, we consider the social position or status of older persons, including an exploration of ageism and how this can be understood in broader social, cultural, and historical contexts. The chapter concludes with attention to the issue of intergenerational relations and whether these are characterized by conflict or solidarity.

Chapter 3 draws attention to embodiment and aging, a topic not commonly covered in social gerontology textbooks. This includes but extends beyond the study of the effects of ageism on the body images and consumer behaviours of older persons, to a postmodern exploration of how we actively shape our subjective interpretations of our bodies and creatively expand the range of physical possibilities associated with old age. Following this, we address the ways that age is biomedicalized, and we explore the closely related emergence of the anti-aging movement. The final part of the chapter encourages discussion regarding how our society might change should the goals of the anti-aging (or prolongevity) movement become reality.

Chapter 4 introduces the study of health and older persons, but foregrounds a sociological approach that addresses the social determinants of healthy aging. The majority of the chapter examines the connections between the individual experiences of older persons, their family members, and paid care workers, and the broader demographic, organizational, political, and economic context of health care in Canada. The focus is on two dominant sites where care is provided to older persons: the home and the residential care facility.

In Chapter 5, we discuss the socio-economic security of older persons and how this is linked to the broader context of the labour market, retirement trends, and pension policies. The increasing reliance on private sources of income in old age, economic globalization, and labour market trends are examined as possible sources of widening income inequality among future cohorts of older Canadians. Lastly, we examine some of the explanations for the increased risk of poverty faced by both unattached older women and older adults who are new immigrants.

Chapter 6 addresses the wide body of research on social participation and older adults, although most existing research focuses on associations with health outcomes. In many ways, social participation is idealized and promoted as part of successful aging, often without adequate attention to the meanings behind participation or how choices about participation are constrained for some older persons. Attention then turns to the broader concept of social inclusion and how best to promote this among older adults.

In Chapter 7, we examine how and why family forms are changing in contemporary Western society, and the implications for older adults. Three emerging family forms in particular are addressed: late-life stepfamilies, living apart together relationships, and transnational families. Then, the chapter turns to the important contributions that older persons make to their families through providing child care. Lastly, we focus on how older persons' needs for support from their families, as well as family members' capacities to provide this support, are explained by broader social factors such as health care reform, demographic and labour market trends, and family change.

Chapter 8 traces cross-cutting sociological themes across chapters, as well as identifies fields of inquiry warranting greater attention by sociologists. We focus on core concepts such as social structure, individual agency, social change, and inequality, and on important and emerging issues such as the aging of Aboriginal peoples, globalization, and human rights.

As part of the *Themes in Canadian Sociology* series, this book is intended for second-, third-, and fourth-year undergraduate students at the college and university level. Though most appropriate as a core resource for sociology of aging courses, it could potentially be used in interdisciplinary courses addressing social aspects of aging in Canada. It is my intent that even without a foundational sociology course, you will find it understandable. The active use of this book in combination with class discussion and guided independent inquiry (i.e., your class assignments) will help you to (a) apply a sociological perspective to aging and age-related issues; (b) critically reflect on ideas and theoretical explanations; and (c) identify evidence-based approaches for improving the lives of older adults through policy and practice.

Acknowledgements

I appreciate the conscientious and skilled work of Jill Bucklaschuk in helping me pull together some of the research cited in this text. I also appreciate the University of Manitoba, for the start-up funding to assist in this regard. And most of all, I warmly thank Ray and little Natalie (for smiling as often as she can).

1

Choices and Constraints in Aging: Theoretical Approaches and Sociological Contributions

Learning Objectives

In this chapter, you will learn that:

◎ a sociological perspective on aging examines individual experiences and choices as connected to the broader ways we organize our society, including political, economic, cultural, and historical features of social structure.

◎ a sociological perspective can help us understand the intersecting inequalities—such as class, gender, sexual orientation, and race and ethnicity—that shape our experiences of old age.

◎ early sociological theories of aging were interested in the effects of societal industrialization on older persons; later theorization within age stratification and life course perspectives attends to the nature and implications of social change over time, more broadly.

◎ social constructionism and interpretive approaches consider how we actively construct the subjective meaning of age and use age-related ideas to interpret our lives.

◎ critical gerontology, political economy, and feminist perspectives examine how capitalist and patriarchal structures (including state policies) generate inequalities, and how ideological constructions perpetuate these inequalities.

◎ postmodern theories of aging and society address a range of ways that aging is being reshaped and reimagined in the contemporary cultural and post-industrial context.

Introduction

The study of aging and age-related issues is timely. Canada's population is "aging" due to social and cultural shifts that have led to increases in life expectancies and decreases in fertility rates. At least 15 per cent of Canada's population is now over age 65; this rate may reach 23 to 25 per cent by 2036 (Statistics Canada, 2010, 2013). These changes raise a multitude of issues for policy-makers and service planners, as well as public and media concerns regarding the assumed dependency of this population. A **sociological perspective** can make an important contribution in critically examining these issues. Despite this, the study of aging tends to be marginalized within the discipline of sociology (Morgan & Kunkel, 2011; Settersten & Angel, 2011).

Further, most social science research on aging occurs primarily through a multidisciplinary lens of **social gerontology**, which integrates knowledge from the social sciences and humanities, and tends to emphasize immediate problems of practice and policy (i.e., by generating **applied knowledge**). Though this approach has its merits, the uniquely sociological contributions to the understanding of aging and age-related phenomena tend to remain less developed in contrast to psychological and health service perspectives that aim to predict individual attitudes and behaviours. Social gerontological research has also been critiqued for being frequently **atheoretical**, resulting in general descriptions and few explanatory frameworks, particularly frameworks informed by a sociological perspective (Alley, Putney, Rice, & Bengtson, 2010; Bengtson, Burgess, & Parrott, 1997).

A sociological perspective understands aging and age-related problems as more than private, personal troubles faced by individuals, but as public, political issues faced by many and shaped by the socio-historical context (Mills, 1959). Sociologists examine the complex connection between the **micro level** of individual experiences and the **macro level** of social structures, processes, and forces—that is, how society and its political, economic, and cultural features are arranged (Settersten & Angel, 2011). Sociological theories of aging do not try to explain or predict aging itself, but address issues such as the following: how age-related social norms guide interactions; how age acts as a feature of social position and stratification; and how population aging changes society (Bengtson, 1996). Different theoretical lenses help us understand age-related phenomena as contextual and changing over time (Bengtson et al., 1997). Lastly, sociologists can and do use the knowledge they gain from studying aging to inform the broader understanding of sociological phenomena (Morgan & Kunkel, 2011).

In this chapter, we will look at the nature of a sociological perspective on aging, touching on concepts such as social structure, stratification, and inequality (individual agency will be covered in more detail in subsequent chapters, including Chapter 8). Following a brief review of core theoretical orientations in sociology—including structural functionalism, symbolic interactionism, and conflict theory—we will identify dominant sociological approaches to the study of age and aging societies. Considered as a whole, these various theories contribute to our understanding of a wide range of issues, including the following: the effects of social (structural and cultural) change on aging and life course experiences and identities; the effects of population and cohort aging on societies and social change; dominant interpretations of age and the life course and how these are shaped and given meaning by individuals; and the influence of broader capitalist and patriarchal political and economic structures on the construction of and applied responses to age and aging.

A Sociological Perspective: Examining Social Structure and Aging

A sociological perspective on aging will be emphasized throughout this book, as we examine how individual choices and experiences in old age are shaped by features of **social structure**: the ways in which a society is organized at a given point in history, including its distribution of wealth, political and economic system, cultural patterns, dominant social roles, and power relations between groups. Subsequent chapters will explore specific examples of a sociological perspective on personal choices in old age, including the following topics:

- From Chapter 2: An individual's choice to purchase a birthday card that pokes fun at older people may reflect cultural ageism that is in turn connected to social and historical change more broadly.
- From Chapter 3: The choice to use hair dye to hide graying hair can be influenced by the marketing efforts of the anti-aging industry and by cultural ageism.
- From Chapter 4: The choice to hire a paid companion to assist an older adult to live at home is related to broader trends in the erosion of health and social care services.
- From Chapter 5: The choice of when to retire from paid labour is influenced by government and employer policies that shape Canada's retirement income system.
- From Chapter 6: An older person's choice about participating in local community events may be limited by his or her access to socio-economic resources and community transportation.
- From Chapter 7: A divorced older woman's choice not to move in with a new romantic partner may reflect greater freedoms as more women have moved into the paid labour force.

A sociological perspective often tends to be obscured or difficult to see, however. For instance, in Chapter 3 we will explore how aging and various age-related conditions tend to be interpreted as medical diseases in need of treatment from a medical perspective. Biomedicalization makes it difficult to recognize the broader social, political, and economic forces and structural constraints in our daily lives—and that influences, for instance, how we interact with persons diagnosed with dementia. In addition, in several chapters (Chapters 2, 4, 5, and 7) we will address the individualizing focus of neoliberal ideology. Though Western societies have always been described as culturally more individualistic (e.g., in comparison to Eastern or other cultures), over the last several decades Western societies in particular have seen an expansion of individualistic thinking tied to neoliberal political and economic discourse that accompanies globalization and shifts within postmodern society. This perspective emphasizes individual responsibility for risk management (and, for example, successful aging); individuals are viewed as responsible for the outcomes of their actions, which are constructed as free choices between alternatives. From this perspective, it becomes difficult to view an individual's actions and decisions as rooted in forces beyond one's personal control.

Inequality, Stratification, and Exclusion in the Sociological Study of Aging

A sociological perspective, and in particular a critical gerontological approach (discussed later in this chapter), draws attention to issues of inequality, stratification, and exclusion. In Chapter 2, we will address the issue of ageism as one way to conceptualize age-related inequality. Later in this chapter, we will consider how more structured, patterned differences in access to power and resources between age cohorts affect our life opportunities as we age (see the section on age stratification theory presented later in this chapter). In this regard, a social exclusion framework (see Chapter 6) is helpful for examining the structural, geographical, environmental, and cultural factors that affect older adults' access to material resources, basic health care and social services, and supportive physical and cultural environments. Though some progress has been made by gerontologists seeking to promote more positive cultural images of successful aging, there is a concern that older persons who cannot achieve productive ideals due to cognitive or physical impairments or socio-economic disadvantage may be further marginalized or devalued.

Other dimensions of inequality and exclusion other than age are crucial to consider. In Chapter 5, we will identify poverty as an ongoing risk faced by some groups of older persons in particular, including unattached older women and older persons who have recently immigrated to Canada. We will also address how Canada's retirement income system has helped level out some socio-economic inequalities (class stratification) within older cohorts. However, there is uncertainty over whether these gains in economic security will be maintained, and there is cause for concern about the economic security of future cohorts of older Canadians. Income and socio-economic status can in turn shape the experience of aging; most of the gerontological research in this regard focuses on health outcomes, in response to income being a key social determinant of health (see Chapter 4). Other research we will cover in this book, however, highlights social class differences in perceptions of physical appearance (see Chapter 3); access to health care (see Chapter 4); and social isolation and participation (see Chapter 6). Economic security is not only a key determinant of health across the life course and into old age, but also a key dimension of social inclusion (see Chapter 6) and, as some argue, a human right (see Chapter 8).

Feminist scholars have helped to address some of the imbalance of attention in early social gerontology on men's experiences of aging, and to highlight the ways older women can be disadvantaged across the life course and into old age. In this book, for instance, we will explore the gendered experience of ageism as manifested in social norms of "beauty work" (see Chapter 3); the poverty often faced by unattached older women (see Chapter 5); and the disproportionate responsibility of family caregiving borne by women (see Chapter 4). Future research needs to attend to the ways in which both men's and women's experiences in old age are intertwined, and to explain the processes underlying gender differences (Calasanti, 2009).

There is remarkably little research on inequalities related to sexual orientation and the marginalization of lesbian, gay, bisexual, and transgender (LGBT) older adults (see Chapter 6). Indeed, sexual orientation was only added to the Canadian Human Rights Act in 1996. Research that does exist on LGBT older adults tends to focus on exclusion in health services and residential care settings (e.g., Addis, Davies, Greene, MacBride-Stewart, & Shepherd, 2009; Brotman, Ryan, & Cormier, 2003; Johnson, Jackson, Arnette, & Koffman, 2005). Further, medicalized discourses of sexuality in old age are based on narrow cultural definitions of gender and heterosexuality, as identified in Chapter 3, and these kinds of discourses perpetuate exclusion. More research is needed that explores other dimensions of both structural constraint and agency in this population of older adults, as well as a range of other issues such as age identity, late-life relationships and repartnering, and embodiment.

Inequalities related to ethnic minority and/or immigrant status are also of concern from a sociological perspective. The National Advisory Council on Aging (2005b) has noted the often unmet needs of **ethnocultural minority seniors**, defined as follows:

> seniors whose ethnicity, religion, race or culture are different from mainstream Canadians (including those born in and outside of Canada); immigrants who have aged in Canada; [and] seniors who immigrated to Canada late in life. Each of these sub-populations of ethnocultural minority seniors will have different issues and experiences that impact on their health and well-being. . . . Nevertheless, as members of an ethnocultural minority, these groups share the reality of being set apart from the majority, one way or another, and this reality can create barriers that leave them at risk for being marginalized. (pp. 2–3)

Ethnic and cultural background, migrant status, and experiences of **discrimination** influence aging and risk of marginalization, though there is considerable diversity related to life experiences, age of migration, Aboriginal status, language, employment history, and so forth. In Chapter 6, for instance, we will address social exclusion among older immigrants to Canada in relation to processes of migration and discrimination. Using 2006 census data, Ng, Lai, Rudner, and Orpana (2012) reported that the majority (around 75 per cent) of immigrant older adults had arrived in Canada before 1976; those who arrived more recently are more likely than those who immigrated prior to 1976 to originate from South or East Asian countries,

Figure 1.1 Intersecting forms of inequality have implications for aging experiences

and they are more likely to be at risk of poor health outcomes, particularly in the absence of strong social networks.

In this book, we examine what critical gerontology, political economy, and feminist perspectives can tell us about how capitalist and patriarchal structures generate inequalities. We also consider how certain ways of thinking about and responding to aging-related issues (e.g., apocalyptic demography, volunteerism, and aging in place or home) can further perpetuate inequalities, because they obscure the economic and political rationale behind certain policy actions (such as reductions in the public provision of formal health and social care services).

McMullin (2000) finds dominant sociological theories of aging, particularly age stratification, political economy, and socialist-feminist approaches, lacking in fully explaining inequality. As she argues, gerontologists need to go beyond the analysis and identification of group differences based on individual characteristics such as age, gender, class, and race and ethnicity

(McMullin, 2000). Rather, it is important to "show why and how group differences emerge in the first place" (McMullin, 2000, p. 517). To do this, McMullin (2000) suggests viewing each of these dimensions as part of one interlocking system of social relations characterized by power, organization, and regulation, through which powerful social groups maintain dominant positions over others through daily interactions.

For example, examining the many different aging experiences and outcomes among Aboriginal persons tells us little about why and how these outcomes exist. Canada is a settler society, in which the land and its original people were and continue to be colonized by others. This process displaces and disadvantages Aboriginal groups; as discussed in Chapter 8, this has created unique circumstances affecting the experience of aging among Aboriginal persons.

An Overview of Dominant Theoretical Positions in Sociology

In this chapter, we look at some of the dominant theoretical approaches in gerontology that have sociological relevance. If you have taken an introductory sociology course, you will notice that some of these approaches echo dominant theoretical positions in sociology: structural functionalism, symbolic interactionism, and conflict theory. First, **structural functionalism** generally assumes that **social norms**—guidelines that we learn and incorporate into our identities through socialization—influence our behaviours. These social norms, along with a strong consensus among different social groups, and the effective functions of various **social institutions** (e.g., family, schools, media, the law, government), help ensure a **social order** necessary for the balance of the system as a whole. For example, from this perspective, individual aging might threaten effective social functioning because aging disrupts social roles (e.g., a retired person is no longer an employee).

Symbolic interactionism, in contrast, focuses on face-to-face interactions between individual members of a society (i.e., at the micro level). It examines how individuals respond to each other on the basis of how they believe they are perceived by others and, in turn, how they want to convey themselves to others. Social norms and "rules" guide, but do not determine, patterns of interactions and are actively applied rather than passively followed. Further, the **symbolic meanings** of behaviours and events are influenced by broader, shared cultural frameworks, but with flexibility and implicit negotiation about meanings in particular settings. For example, research within this tradition has helped in understanding how the responses of friends, family, and care providers of persons diagnosed with dementia indicate a process of **social labelling** that can create a self-fulfilling prophecy.

Lastly, a **conflict theory** approach focuses on the macro level of broader social systems and in particular on stratification, hierarchies, social position, and power in societies. Conflict theorists view society as consisting of different groups that constantly struggle with each other to compete for scarce resources, with more powerful groups maintaining power and resources by marginalizing and oppressing others.[1] A system of inequality is thus maintained, and oppressed groups often willingly participate in the political and economic system in which they are disadvantaged. Conflict theorists are also interested in examining intersecting forms of social inequality and stratification (e.g., class, gender, age, ethnicity/race, and sexuality, as well as different struggles among nations[2]).

The theories that will be discussed in the rest of this chapter draw on elements of these dominant sociological perspectives. Though there was little explicit theorizing about aging prior to 1961 (Lynott & Lynott, 1996), sociological research on aging tended to reflect a particular way of thinking of aging as being a problem requiring individual adjustment—an idea that was later termed **activity theory** (e.g., Lemon, Bengtson, & Peterson, 1972; Longino & Kart, 1982). From this perspective, the loss of social roles due to aging means that individuals need to adjust their own lives by replacing these roles with new activities and continuing to be productive members of society (this perspective echoes structural functionalism). Activity theory and its close cousin **continuity theory** (Atchley, 1989) are also implicit in much of the current research into associations between participation in social activities and both life satisfaction and well-being (see Chapter 6). However, because the emphasis is on individual behaviour and coping (e.g., rather than on socio-cultural environments and structures that constrain individual choices to participate), these theories are more psychological than sociological. There were, however, some early theories of aging that devoted greater attention to the connections between individual aging and broader social contexts, in particular by seeking to explicate the effects of industrialization.

The Effects of Societal Industrialization: Theories of Disengagement, Exchange, and Modernization

The following three theoretical approaches examine aging as a social position or location, and they are united by a common interest in the effects of societal industrialization. Indeed, sociology itself, as a discipline of inquiry, emerged largely in response to rapid social changes and related problems associated with industrialization in the nineteenth and early twentieth centuries in Western Europe and North America. Early sociologists wanted to better understand and explain the impacts of industrialization on societies by using the scientific method. Although disengagement, exchange, and

modernization theories are rarely employed today, they represent an important sociological contribution to the theoretical landscape, particularly for
their consideration of the effects of industrialization on older persons.

The Disengagement of Older Adults

Disengagement theory (Cumming, 1963; Cumming & Henry, 1961) is
a milestone in the sociology of aging, because it was the first attempt to
explicitly theorize the social aspects of aging (Lynott & Lynott, 1996). The
theory hinges on an understanding of the history and impact of industrialization. Prior to industrialization, societies tended to have agriculturally
based economies and ways of life. With the Industrial Revolution, machine
technologies and new energy sources led to the centralization of work in
large factories, urbanization, increased specialization and division of work
tasks, and the emergence of waged labour and standardized work schedules.
Factories and cities became larger, more surplus wealth was created, and
large bureaucracies emerged over time. Populations grew, life expectancies
increased in response to public health gains, and in many societies, formal
education systems were introduced.

These changes had implications for the relative social position of older
age groups in industrialized societies. For example, longer life expectancies
generated larger available labour pools, increasing competition for paid work
between younger and older persons. Further, companies increasingly required
a workforce with up-to-date, highly specialized knowledge and skills, rather
than experience, wisdom, and general knowledge. Along with the fast pace of
technological innovation, these changes led companies to seek out younger
workers trained in the newest technology. As conflict theorists emphasize,
older workers also tended to be more expensive, with seniority being associated with higher pay, fueling a desire for younger, cheaper workers. Together,
these forces associated with industrialization contributed to the emergence of
retirement as an established institution, which tends to lower the income and
social status of older groups (see Chapter 5).

Disengagement theory is rooted in a structural-functionalist interpretation of this phenomenon, in which mutual withdrawal between the older
individual and industrialized society is viewed as natural and functional for
both the individual and society. Cumming and Henry (1961) proposed that
older persons will be happier and better adjusted when they disengage not
only from paid labour, through retirement, but also from other social roles
(e.g., segregation in nursing homes), because they are freed from social pressures to fulfill normative role expectations; this disengagement is also for the
greater good of society, because equilibrium is facilitated (e.g., older people
are removed from the workforce, thereby clearing the way for younger workers). This theory has been critiqued for its simplistic assumptions, a focus
on men's experiences to the neglect of women's experiences, and erroneous

logic (see Hochschild, 1975), and it is generally unsupported by research. However, disengagement theory still made an important long-term contribution in paving the way for theoretical development in social gerontology (Achenbaum & Bengtson, 1994).

Exchange Theory and Aging

Dowd's (1975) application of **exchange theory** to aging is often described as micro level in focus. Exchange theory proposes that each individual in a relationship or interaction possesses different resources or power (e.g., money, expertise, skills, or prestige). Generally, people hope the rewards they gain (e.g., approval or instrumental help) meet or exceed the costs of continuing these relationships. Dowd noted that industrialized societies produce age-related shifts in roles, skills, and resources; as a result, older persons (as well as youth) have fewer social resources, which contributes to imbalanced interactions (see Figure 1.2). Dowd argued that rather than being functional, this imbalance results in disengagement or isolation. To avoid being dependent within relationships and under-benefiting from exchanges, older persons withdraw from interactions. Dowd further abstracts exchange theory to explain relations between age groups in society and the effects of industrialization on older persons' status. Withdrawal is connected to broader social change:

> The amount of power resources possessed by the aged relative to other age strata is inversely related to the degree of societal modernization. Unlike the aged in more traditional societies, older people in industrialized societies have precious few power resources to exchange in daily social interaction. The net effect is an increased dependence upon others and the concomitant necessity to comply with their wishes. Mandatory retirement as a social policy is the most obvious result of this lack of power resources and consequent lack of power among the aged. (Dowd, 1975, p. 592)

Imbalanced relationships can take on a life of their own when they become "institutionalized and thereby [provide] a normative basis for future unbalanced exchanges" (Dowd, 1975, p. 589) with older persons, facilitating their economic and social dependence. Thus, whereas disengagement theory suggests that older persons choose to withdraw from society because it benefits them, Dowd argues that they are constrained to withdraw because of unequal exchange resources. However, the application of exchange theory to relationships between older and younger persons has been critiqued for representing human beings as overly rational and self-interested. For instance, one can consider intergenerational family relationships as guided more by solidarity and altruism than by a sense of calculated exchange.

→ critique of ex. theory

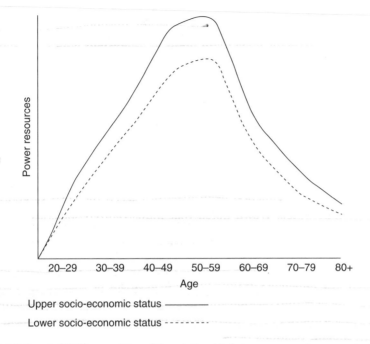

Figure 1.2 Dowd's (1975) proposition of the relationship between age, socio-economic status, and exchange-related power
Source: Dowd, J. J. (1975). Aging as exchange: A preface to theory. *Journal of Gerontology, 30*(5), 584–94. Reprinted with permission from Oxford University Press.

Modernization and the Status of Older Persons

Modernization theory (Cowgill, 1974; Cowgill & Holmes, 1972) as applied to aging proposes that with industrialization and urbanization, the status of older people declines.[3] Modernization entails the following:

> the transformation of a total society from a relatively rural way of life based on animate power, limited technology, relatively undifferentiated institutions, parochial and traditional outlook and values, toward a predominantly urban way of life based on inanimate source of power, highly developed scientific technology, highly differentiated institutions matched by segmented individual roles, and a cosmopolitan outlook which emphasizes efficiency and progress. (Cowgill, 1974, p. 127)

We will return to this theory in Chapter 2, when we examine ageism. Cowgill and Holmes (1972) drew attention to many of the processes described above (life expectancies, technologies, universal education, job competition, employers' preferences for younger workers, retirement patterns, and loss of income) as contributing to the declining status of older persons. In addition, they proposed that with urbanization and migration to large cities, families became geographically dispersed and older persons' roles within families (e.g., as grandparents) became more peripheral (the related idea that older people have been abandoned by their families is critically explored in Chapter 7).

Research examining modernization theory's propositions has noted that any association between societal-level modernization and the status of older persons is not simple or direct, but complex (e.g., Bengtson, Dowd, Smith, & Inkeles, 1975). For instance, government policies may mediate the impact of social change on attitudes towards older persons (Cherry & Magnuson-Martinson, 1981), and cultural features can preserve older persons' status in some modernizing societies (Rhoads, 1984). Logue (1990) argues that there has actually been little change in older persons' status (conceptualized as respect and positive attitudes towards older persons by others) over time, and that older people have not been highly valued or regarded even in the past. Research conclusions may vary depending on the measures of both modernization and status. Although modernization might initially decrease social status (measured as levels of employment, occupation, and education), "as societies move beyond a transitional stage of rapid modernization, discrepancies between the aged and non-aged decrease and the relative status of the aged may rise" (Palmore & Manton, 1974, p. 205).

Modernization theory has been critiqued in many respects, especially for idealizing older persons' situations in the past and in other less industrialized societies. The concept of modernization is also **ethnocentric** and does not address the complexity of social change, including diverse effects on social groups based on age, class, ethnicity, and gender.

Increasing Attention to Time and Social Context in the Study of Aging

Several theories and concepts share a concern with both time and social context in the study of aging. Gerontologists have pioneered this field, for example by drawing attention to social influences on subjective perceptions of the timing of age events and transitions, as well as by examining aging in successive groups of individuals to understand how social change occurs over time. In this section, we will consider attention to time and social context through the use of concepts such as generation and cohort, as well as more explicitly within the age stratification and life course perspectives.

Generation and Cohort

Gerontologists have long employed the concept of **cohort**, defined as a group whose members shared a common event (often, their birth) during a particular time. For instance, individuals born in the same year might comprise a cohort for longitudinal research studies. These cohorts are influenced by a variety of factors:

> Cohorts share a social and cultural history, experiencing events and cultural moods when they are at the same stage of life. Characteristics of a birth cohort and events that the cohort experiences combine to affect members in distinctive ways, influencing their attitudes, behaviors, and outcomes across the entire life course. Economic and political conditions leave lasting marks on those born in different historical periods. (Bengtson, Elder, & Putney, 2005, p. 495)

The term *generation* has often been used interchangeably with *cohort* to describe a horizontal social location based on individuals born around the same period of time[4] (Burnett, 2010; Pilcher, 1994). Used as sociological concepts, cohort and generation can help us understand processes of social change, social context, identity, and the life course (Burnett, 2010; Eyerman & Turner, 1998; McDaniel, 2001).

Generations can develop a sense of solidarity and shared identity, in part through commonly held memories of historical events, facilitated by media and communication technologies and representations of generations within popular culture (Burnett, 2010; Eyerman & Turner, 1998). However, strong stratification within a generation (e.g., by class or religion) can inhibit shared generational consciousness (Mannheim, 1963). Generally, generational identities can emerge when cultural, political, and economic events and changes create a need for younger groups to develop new ways of understanding the world (Burnett, 2010). This can facilitate the development of a distinctive consciousness and style for a generation. In this respect, Burnett (2010) draws on the work of sociologist Pierre Bourdieu (1977) to explain how the emerging generation's agency in response to social change in turn reshapes the society, creating new changes to be faced by subsequent generations.

From a conflict theory perspective, the concept of generation is viewed as ideologically constructed to benefit particular vested interests in society (Eyerman & Turner, 1998). For instance, Susan McDaniel (2001, 2004) explores how the idea of generational difference and generational inequities can become an ideological tool "to label, divide, and promote false perceptions of competing interests between birth cohorts" (Funk, 2011, p. 303). In Chapter 2, we will return to this area of inquiry.

Another concept that highlights the role of time in gerontological research is **age norms**, also known as **social clocks** (Neugarten, Moore, & Lowe, 1965), which refers to commonly held ideals about behaviours and life events that are expected and considered appropriate at certain ages. For instance, when I was a teenager, I assumed I would be employed, married, and have children in my twenties. However, because my path through university extended well into my thirties, my life course deviated from more normative patterns. Before I was hired in my current job, I watched many friends, who entered the paid labour force much earlier, advancing in their careers and establishing their homes and families well before me. Neugarten (1974) refers to this sense of being "off time" between one's real and expected life course. Though Neugarten's work (as summarized in Ferraro, 2014) was more psychological in focus (i.e., by considering how these norms shape life evaluations and satisfaction), she suggested these age norms reflected a broader **age grading** of society.

Age Stratification Theory

Riley (1971) extended these ideas in developing attention to how individual aging and cohort aging intersect with changing age structures in society. **Age stratification theory** progressed through various iterations, including the *aging and society paradigm* (Riley, 1971; Riley, Kahn, & Foner, 1994; Riley & Riley, 1999, 2000). From the perspective of age stratification theory, age is conceptualized as more than an individual characteristic—age is considered more broadly as a characteristic of society (Riley et al., 1994). Society is divided into **age strata**, differing in normative, expected roles (e.g., student, spouse, worker, retiree), behaviours, and privileges. Age strata are indicated in the left-hand axis of Figure 1.3 (young, middle, and old age). These strata result from age-related structural and normative constraints "that separate individuals into 'three boxes' of education for the young, work and family responsibilities for the middle aged, and leisure in retirement for the old" (Riley & Riley, 1999, p. 128). Cohorts move through these strata over time, which influences their behaviours and experiences: "over time, not only old people but people of different ages are *all* growing older, moving concurrently through a society which itself is undergoing change" (Riley, 1971, p. 80). As a result, each age strata has a distinctive character, because it reflects a group that not only is at a similar life course stage, but also was born during a similar historical period.

Changing realities in and behaviours of age cohorts can change age-related social norms and the broader social structures, though there can be **structural lag**[5] in this regard (see Box 1.1). For instance, as Riley, Kahn, Foner, and Mack (1994) note, an aging population suggests greater need for age-friendly communities, but this can involve a slow change in long-established and accepted values, policies, norms, and social institutions.

The overall system of age stratification is influenced by social, political, and economic circumstances, generates inequalities and social exclusion, and affects relations among age groups in society. Riley et al. (1994) suggest, however, that we are now moving towards an **age-integrated society** (refer to the right half of Figure 1.3), in which "age will lose its current power to determine when people should enter or leave these basic social structures (work, education, retirement), nor will age any longer constrain expectations as to how people should perform" (p. 110). The result is more flexible life

Age Stratification Theory.

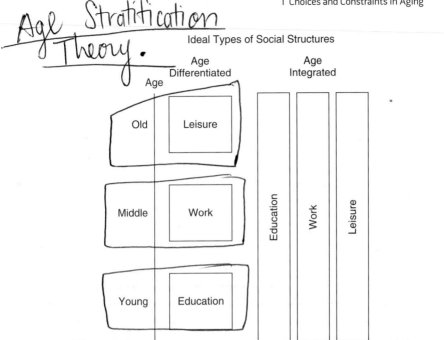

Figure 1.3 Age stratification theory's visual representation of two extremes: Age differentiation and age integration

Source: Riley, M. W., & Riley, J. W., Jr. (2000). Age integration: Conceptual and historical background. *The Gerontologist, 40*(3), 266–70.

journeys and variation within age strata; in this regard, Riley and colleagues draw on sociological theories of **individualization** and **postmodern society** (discussed at the end of this chapter).

Age stratification theory tends to assume that age norms influence everyone equally; it also devotes little attention to other forms of stratification, or to political or economic sources of age inequality. Age stratification theory has also been critiqued for its structural-functionalist understandings of norms and roles, and insufficient attention to individual agency (Dowd, 1987; see Chapter 8). Nonetheless, this approach, and the related life course perspective (discussed in the following section), represent an important endeavour to examine the interaction between individual lives and social structure over time.

The Life Course Perspective

The boundaries between age stratification theory and the **life course perspective** are blurred because they draw on similar concepts and ideas. Life course perspectives often draw more heavily on human development theories; this approach does not limit itself to the study of older populations, but rather it is relevant to all age groups.

> **Box 1.1**   A Description of Structural Lag

In society at large, lives have been drastically altered over this century—as a conse-
quence of increased longevity, advances in science and education, the gender revolution, improvements in public health, and other historical trends and events—but
numerous inflexible social structures, roles, and norms have lagged behind. There is
a mismatch or imbalance between the transformation of the aging process . . . and
the role opportunities or places in the social structure that could foster and reward
people at the various stages of their lives. While the twentieth century has experienced a revolution in human development and aging, there has been no compar-
able revolution in the role structures of society to keep pace with the changes in
the ways people grow up and grow old. The lag involves not only institutional and
organizational arrangements, but also the many aspects of culture that, in addition
to being internalized by people, are built into role expectations and societal mores
and laws. For the future, then, structural changes will be needed if people are to find
opportunities to spread leisure and work, as well as education, more evenly over the
life course, and to make room for family affairs.

Source: Excerpt from pages 16–17 in Riley, M. W., & Riley, J. W., Jr. (1994). Structural lag: Past and future. In M. W.
Riley, R. L. Kahn, & A. Foner (Eds.), *Age and structural lag: Society's failure to provide meaningful opportunities in
work, family, and leisure* (pp. 15–36). New York, NY: Wiley.

Originating most explicitly with the work of Glen Elder (1974/1999),
who examined the influence of the Great Depression on generations within
families, the life course perspective links micro- and macro-level considerations: "the personal and biographical level of human experience is examined
with simultaneous consideration of timing, social institutions/policies and
structural position (i.e., race, class, gender) within a historical time period"
(Phillips, Ajrouch, & Hillcoat-Nallétamby, 2010, p. 140).

The life course is a series of **transitions** or changes through statuses
and roles (e.g., marriage or retirement), which together constitute particular
patterns or **trajectories** over time depending on the individual. Transitions
and trajectories are historically shaped and structured by major social institutions (e.g., family, schools, labour market, religion, government) and their
institutionalized normative expectations (Bengtson et al., 2005).

The following list summarizes various principles of a life course
approach (Bengtson et al., 2005; Elder, 1974/1999, 1994, 1998; Grenier,
2012; Marshall & Mueller, 2003):

- **agency principle:** We have some **individual agency** or role in shaping
  our identities and the paths our lives take, as we navigate the constraints
  of social structure and historical conditions.

- **lifelong process principle**: Aging occurs over our entire lives; earlier experiences affect subsequent events and changes, and these affect our well-being and position in later life.
  - This principle has also been developed within **cumulative advantage/disadvantage theory**, which explores how advantages or disadvantages (e.g., in health or resources) at one stage of our life accumulate over time (Dannefer, 2003; O'Rand, 1996a, 1996b).
- **linked lives principle**: Because humans are interconnected, an event or change in our own lives will have implications for others with whom we share relationships, and vice versa. For instance, a woman experiencing a divorce who returns home to live with her own parents influences their lives as a result.
- **principle of historical time and place**: Our personal life course— including the opportunities and constraints we face, and our actions and decisions—is shaped by historical time, social context, and geographical place.
- **timing of transitions principle**: The causes and consequences of any particular key change or event in our lives depend partly on when it occurs to us in our life.

In empirical research examining change over time, gerontologists distinguish between age effects, period effects, and cohort effects. An **age effect** is a change that is explained by the individual-level aging process. A **cohort effect** is a change explained by membership in particular cohorts and the common experiences (such as historical events and structural features of society) that cohorts faced at particular times (Bengtson et al., 2005). Lastly, a **period effect** reflects environmental change in social and historical conditions, an effect which is experienced by all cohorts, although different cohorts react in different ways. Disentangling age, period, and cohort effects can be challenging, even with longitudinal data. Examples of hypothetical research topics and potential age, cohort, and period effects are provided in Table 1.1.

The life course perspective has potential for understanding individual and cohort aging within social and historical contexts, although the sociological features of the perspective remain to be better developed (Dannefer, 2011; Riley & Riley, 1999). Further, Settersten and Angel (2011) express concern that growing attention to this perspective may be to the detriment of the sociological study of aging because "there are questions about aging that do not entail the life course" (p. 11).

Social Constructionism

In mapping out the theoretical profile of social gerontology, Lynott and Lynott (1996) identify an **interpretive shift** in theorizing about aging,

Table 1.1 Examples of age, cohort, and period effects in explaining change over time in selected research topics

Hypothetical research topics	Age effect	Cohort effect	Period effect
Older persons' deference in interactions with their doctors	As people age, they feel less able to assert themselves with doctors, because they internalize ageist stereotypes	Older cohorts were socialized into the "sick role" and deference to medical authorities	A lack of general practitioners in Canada has developed over time, and members of all cohorts are worried that if they assert themselves, they might lose their doctor
Older persons' voting behaviour in provincial and federal elections	As people age, closeness to death makes them more concerned about ensuring a strong future for other generations	Older cohorts today were raised at a time when patriotism was emphasized (e.g., during the First and Second World Wars)	There was some political event, issue, or candidate that increased the turnout rates of all voters
Obesity prevalence and age	Physiological changes associated with age cause muscle loss and make it more difficult to lose weight	Older age cohorts became accustomed to diets that were higher in fat and calories	Over the decades, changes in our lifestyles (e.g., less physically demanding jobs; more access to vehicle transportation; television sets) made populations less likely to be active

representing the influence of both social phenomenology and political economy approaches. In this section, we focus on the former. Many of the theories described earlier in this chapter stem from a broader worldview known as **positivism**. That is, they view aging and age-related phenomena as objective facts of reality, and they imply that one accurate truth can be known about these facts through scientific inquiry. In contrast, a social phenomenological (or social constructionist, or interpretive) approach views age and age-related phenomena as social constructions—they are given meaning when they are constructed, and they are often unconsciously negotiated in social interactions, including interactions between researchers and participants. This tradition overlaps with and draws on some principles of symbolic interactionism. **Social constructionism** is therefore an interpretive theoretical and methodological approach that highlights the processes through which humans create meaning and interpret their world through language and social interaction.

Phenomenology directs attention to these processes of construction and to the dominant bodies of knowledge that people draw on to interpret their worlds and construct meanings. Phenomenologists examine the use of language in talk and interaction: "language has an intentional quality . . . such that its use serves to construct a reality" (Lynott & Lynott, 1996, p. 753). For example, phenomenologists might examine how people use or employ age-related explanations in their conversations, actively producing the realities they talk about (Lynott &

Lynott, 1996). From this perspective, age is something that is "accomplished" as we provide meaning to age in our actions and interactions (Laz, 1998).

Social phenomenology can help us learn about the social construction of aging and the nature of identities as we age (see Box 1.2). There is an emphasis on human beings as actively producing their worlds, rather than

---

Box 1.2   *The Ageless Self* and Social Constructionism in Gerontology

In *The Ageless Self*, Sharon Kaufman emphasizes that the construction of self is an ongoing process as we draw on particular events and experiences from our past when talking with others. We select those experiences that have symbolic value for how we want to present ourselves to others. Kaufman draws on three case examples from interviews with older nursing home residents.

First, Millie has just moved into the nursing home. She views herself as constantly improving and learning, and she has a strong need for relationships with others, particularly family. She emphasizes how other people tell her that she looks better than she did before moving to the home, and she explains that she moved because she was lonely (her physician might suggest the "cause" was functional decline due to a stroke). Though she does not see her children as often as she would like, Millie nonetheless focuses on the ideal theme of her children as her primary, constant source of affection and reason for living.

Another resident, Ben, talks about feeling the same as he did when he was younger, and he does not identify with his chronological age. He remembers his college days and "yearns to become what he remembers about that self now"; however, to behave now like he did then, he believes, would be inappropriate. As such, "the conflict of feeling one age and being another age" creates frustration. Ben describes his expectation that aging will involve disengagement and isolation, though in fact his experience with unstable social relationships has been lifelong.

Lastly, Stella also lives in the nursing home but spends most of her time in an art studio. She does not think of herself as old "except when she cannot be active." She has long-term plans to continue to develop her artistic productivity and to preserve her studio after she dies (contributing to her sense of immortality). Stella spends a lot of time around younger artists and "their behaviour toward her reinforces her own view of self as ageless." With no children of her own, she views her artist friends as "these kids" (establishing a familial link).

Millie, Ben, and Stella do not view age as an important frame of meaning for their lives and identities, even though they are dealing with age-related changes. Rather, they "think of and describe themselves in terms of the themes they express as they reflect on their lives, rather than in terms of age." Kaufman concludes by highlighting how we "symbolically connect meaningful past experiences with current circumstances" to continually construct our identities as we age.

Source: Adapted from Kaufman, S. R. (2000). The ageless self. In J. F. Gubrium & J. A. Holstein (Eds.), *Aging and everyday life* (pp. 103–111). Malden, MA: Blackwell. (Original work published 1986.)

being influenced (in a deterministic way) by the surrounding society. In producing particular ways of understanding the world, people produce particular realities, even if they are unaware they are doing so.

Research using an interpretive or social constructionist perspective tends to be qualitative—focusing on the subjective meanings of experiences and behaviours for participants from their point of view. These meanings are examined through methods such as open-ended interviews and observation. In gerontology, a constructionist perspective is evident in a number of fields, including **biographical work** and **personal narratives** (de Medeiros, 2005; Starr, 1982–1983). Fitting with a constructionist view, the findings themselves are often viewed as co-constructed—acknowledging the role of the researcher, who can never be truly objective—and as representing a fluid, shifting world rather than one objective reality.

Gubrium (1988) draws on a social phenomenological approach in observing how family caregiver support groups discuss decisions about institutionalizing care recipients with dementia. Participants often compared themselves to the cultural exemplar of the "devoted wife" ideal, yet in one support group conversation, "the wifely martyr was transformed into a negative standard" (Gubrium, 1988, p. 200) as reflecting unrealistic denial. In this case, the interpretive framework was the devoted exemplar; however, the particular meaning of this exemplar can be redefined in social interaction (indicating agency).

In another study based on a social constructionist perspective, Van den Hoonaard (1997) examines the autobiographical narratives of older Canadian and American widows. The women's accounts present their experience as a transformation rather than a recovery; though at first these women spoke of struggling with a loss of identity—reflecting a process of **identity foreclosure**—they also developed new identities that aligned with dominant North American ideals (e.g., confident, brave, independent, responsible).

In one of my own studies, I examine how adult children construct the support they provided for aging parents (Funk, 2012). For the most part, participants rejected the idea that they were or should be "paying back" their parents, a notion reflecting the principle of **delayed reciprocity**. Delayed reciprocity can imply that the relationship is or was imbalanced, and in contrast, participants emphasized that they provided support because they loved their parent(s). An interpretive perspective considers what this kind of talk accomplishes for participants' identity. For instance, some participants believed that children *should want to* provide support because of love (by emphasizing this motivation they affirm their identity as a good daughter or son). In addition, "by prioritising affection as a motivation for support, adult children can continue to interpret their parent's own care for them as a similar manifestation, reinforcing publically and privately that they were loved by their parents" (p. 650). Lastly, participants may simply have been emphasizing the role of affection in their behaviour because it is imbued with a greater sense of choice than the expectedness of debt repayment, helping them maintain an independent identity.

Additional examples of a constructionist approach in gerontology can be found in Chapter 3, within the discussions of research addressing the connection between aging bodies and identity. Although social constructionism has overall not been well developed (or understood) in gerontology, this is one area where it has made a considerable impact (Longino & Powell, 2009).

Social constructionism is often critiqued for being overly focused on the micro level of individuals and interactions, with less attention to broader issues of social structure and power. The latter issues are more often addressed using approaches drawn from political economy and critical theoretical approaches, which are addressed in the following section.

Political Economy, Feminism, and Critical Gerontology

Political economy theory springboards from social constructionism, going further to ask questions, informed by a conflict theory approach, such as the following: Who defines the problems and issues of aging and why? What are the vested interests that benefit from certain constructions of aging? Theorists using a political economy approach examine how particular forms of capitalism, and the governmental systems that support capitalist goals, shape how old age is constructed and generate age-related and other forms of inequality (Estes, Swan, & Gerard, 1982). From this perspective, "the 'facts' of aging, in a capitalist society, are part and parcel of the work requirements of a labour market controlled by the needs of industrial development" (Lynott & Lynott, 1996, p. 754). Capitalist political and economic structures generate the problems and dependency of older persons, constraining their choices and contributing to loss of social position and resources. State policies in social welfare, health, and pensions, though intended to ameliorate inequality, can actually reproduce it, as they are often inadequate to redistribute wealth (Kail, Quadagno, & Keene, 2009). Further, social policies reflect **ideologies**: "belief systems that enforce, bolster, and extend the structure and advantage in the larger economic, political, and social order" (Estes, 1999a, p. 30).

Political economists have examined the role of businesses and economic interests in implementing mandatory retirement policies that pushed older persons out of paid labour into poverty, accompanied by ideological constructions of their "alleged incapacity" (Lynott & Lynott, 1996; Phillipson, 2005). Mandatory retirement (discussed further in Chapter 5) attempted to address the unemployment that was generated by the market, and it helped employers seeking to hire cheaper (i.e., younger) labour. The relatively low level of public benefits for older persons in retirement, as well as social stigmatization, age-discriminatory policies, and inadequate health, housing, and long-term care all contribute to their **structured dependency** (Estes, 1999b; Phillipson, 2005; Walker, 1981). Political economists argue that the process of structured dependency becomes obscured because the dominant ways of thinking about aging (e.g., as a disease requiring treatment, or as an individual-level problem of isolation and inadequate social support requiring targeted services) render the structural sources of these problems invisible (Estes, 1999b).

Political economists also direct attention to how the "crisis" of an aging population is socially constructed by the state to rationalize politically motivated health or pension reform agendas (Estes, 2011; Walker, 2012), such as the erosion of public services and the expansion of private providers (e.g., of pensions, home care, or residential care). The state also minimizes collective opposition to such reforms by justifying the reforms as being an inevitable and necessary response to demographic realities. The social construction of the negative effects of population aging for political purposes is also discussed in Chapter 2, while drawing on contributions of Canadian sociologists.

Political economists also critically assess how profit-making industries and service providers benefit indirectly from particular constructions of age. Carroll Estes (1979, 1999b) argues that an "**aging enterprise**" has arisen because of the construction of older persons as a problem requiring individual-level, age-specific services. This aging enterprise encompasses private corporations as well as professionals and state-supported businesses, programs, and organizations providing services to older populations. Providers benefit from certain constructions of older persons (e.g., as being victims, at risk, or incompetent), as these constructions perpetuate older persons' dependence on their services (Lynott & Lynott, 1996).

More recently, political economists have directed attention to international and global political and economic processes (Phillipson, 2005; Walker, 2005) and the expansion of **neoliberalism** across the world. Neoliberalism encompasses the ideological beliefs and associated practices and policies supporting the expansion of free trade, market competition, privatization, and restricted government involvement in both markets and social welfare. The effects of globalization on policies and on individual aging experiences will be addressed in Chapter 8.

The political economy approach is one of several approaches that constitute **critical gerontology** (Phillipson, 2005). Political economists do not neutrally observe the effects of capitalism on aging; instead, they identify capitalism as problematic and seek to change the effects by advocating for changes at the structural level. All research, they argue, is political, even if it intends to be objective. This is because much gerontological research and theory only reproduces certain constructions of aging that support the status quo (i.e., the established way of doing things); the status quo supports powerful vested interests in maintaining a system of inequality.

Critical gerontology, therefore, is a theoretical approach that influences how we view research knowledge and the methods we use to study aging. Rather than focus on objective "prediction" of outcomes taken as fact, or on understanding subjective meaning, critical gerontologists conduct research designed to **emancipate**, through challenging existing societal arrangements, highlighting the voices of marginalized older persons, and advocating for social justice (Baars, Dannefer, Phillipson, & Walker, 2006). Some forms of critical gerontology even try to directly create change through research, by using methods that actively engage and empower disadvantaged groups in all aspects of the research process—for instance, **participatory action research**.

Much of what is considered **feminist gerontology** is also critical gerontology. Feminist scholars have helped in strengthening the attention to gender within political economy theory (Walker, 2005) and more broadly in sociological theories of aging that tended to focus on traditionally male careers and retirement trajectories (Calasanti, 2009; Davidson, 2011). Feminist gerontologists have explicated how the gendered division of labour (women's disproportionate role in unpaid, domestic labour across their life course, such as child care, elder care, or housework) and other structural inequalities shape the aging experiences of women. For instance, the gendered division of labour affects women's experiences in the paid labour force, which tends to be more intermittent and in lower paid work, with direct implications for their retirement incomes, especially in situations of divorce or widowhood (Gazso, 2005). Women are often referred to as "doubly disadvantaged" in old age, reflecting structured inequalities across their life course—inequalities that are generated by capitalism and patriarchy (Estes, 2006). Aging itself has been described as a feminist issue, because the majority of older persons are female (due to longer life expectancies) who disproportionately face disadvantages in old age, such as the risk of poverty (Russell, 1987).

Other feminist gerontologists (Calasanti, 2009) emphasize a need to move beyond viewing gender as only an individual characteristic to be contrasted against men's experiences, but rather to examine the broader forces explaining gender differences. In this regard, **gender relations** are taken-for-granted, invisible, "dynamic, constructed, institutionalized processes by which people orient their behaviours to ideals of manhood and womanhood, influencing life chances as they do so" (Calasanti, 2009, p. 472). The term *relations* highlights how women's experiences and disadvantages are inextricably intertwined with men's experiences and privileges—one cannot understand women's or men's experiences without understanding the other. For instance, men's greater retirement income has long been dependent on the

unpaid domestic labour of women that supports their involvement in paid
labour, but has implications for women's situations. This is also a key concept underpinning the **gender lens** approach—a way of looking at issues,
policies, and programs with the consideration of gender equality and gender
relations in mind (Calasanti & Slevin, 2001).

Aging in Postmodern Society

Several gerontologists—including scholars such as Jason Powell, Stephen
Katz, and Simon Biggs—have drawn on a sociological understanding of a
post-industrial and/or postmodern society to examine aging in contemporary Western contexts. Issues explored by gerontologists in this regard range
from the deinstitutionalized life course, to embodiment and new biotechnol-
ogies, to transnational aging families. Many of these issues will be discussed
in greater detail throughout this book.

Some life course researchers have also drawn on sociological understandings of postmodern society to consider the ways in which the life
course itself has changed. Specifically, new technologies have proliferated,
characterizing the "information age," and the post-industrial economy has
become increasingly dominated by the service industry and professional,
white-collar occupations. Over time, there has been greater social tolerance
of diversity and increased female participation in both post-secondary education and the labour force. Business is also increasingly conducted in global
markets. With all of these changes, life course theorists and postmodernists
suggest that we are witnessing the **deinstitutionalization** or destandardization of the life course from the age-normative, expected linear structure
discussed by Neugarten (1974), towards more fluid and flexible pathways
and patterns that are more variable and self-directed (Bengtson et al., 2005;
Heinz & Krüger, 2001). This is seen most frequently in the timing of family,
career, and educational pathways—for instance, instead of the expected
transition to retirement at age 65, we see more variability in retirement, and
a person might retire early but then return to some form of work or even to
university. Or, because of increases in divorce and women's greater financial
independence, a woman might marry early but delay having a child, and
then divorce and remarry, eventually having a child with her second partner. Lastly, a smooth linear transition from post-secondary education to one
lifelong career is now less common, and many people will work in a number
of different jobs throughout their life course.

In general, a postmodern perspective on aging highlights the fluidity
and expanding possibilities of age identity, yet this increased opportunity is
accompanied by growing forms of surveillance as well as the imperative to
self-manage personal risk across the life course (Powell & Hendricks, 2009).

Conclusion

In this chapter, we have reviewed many of the early and more established sociological theories of aging. Early theories were interested in the effects of societal industrialization on older persons and were often influenced by structural-functionalist understandings of society. Attention was directed to how features of social structures shape individual lives and the actions of cohorts over time. Social constructionism drew on the principles of symbolic interactionism to shift our focus to how we actively construct the meaning of age and use age-related ideas to interpret our experiences. Critical gerontology, political economy, and feminist perspectives extended social constructionist ideas to consider how these constructions function as ideologies to obscure inequalities related to capitalist and patriarchal structures. Lastly, postmodern theories explore the dynamics of new constraints and possibilities of age identity in a changing cultural and global context.

By examining how age is influenced by historically specific features of society and its organization, sociological perspectives imply a need to address age-related problems or concerns at the societal level rather than at the individual level. For instance, the remaining chapters will discuss a variety of societal-level concerns, such as the following:

- Addressing ageism requires more than changing negative individual attitudes, but changing taken-for-granted ways of organizing society based on the standard of younger persons (see institutionalized ageism in Chapter 2).
- Enhancing the quality of care for persons with dementia requires a holistic, person-centred approach to practice that challenges biomedical frameworks (see Chapter 3).
- Improving the well-being of older adults requires attention to change in key social determinants such as housing and income security (see Chapter 4).
- Reducing the increased risk of poverty in old age for women requires ameliorating the patriarchal structures (e.g., workplace and family policies) that generate economic instability over their life course (see Chapter 5).
- Increasing older persons' participation and integration within society requires changes in broader structures, such as developing age-inclusive communities (see Chapter 6).
- Supporting the well-being of families who are providing care to an older adult at home requires attention to home care policies that equally address the needs of family caregivers alongside those of the care recipient (see Chapter 7).

In reading through this book, you are encouraged to consider how the apparent individual choices we take for granted across our life course and in our old age are shaped by the social structures around us. Identifying how older persons express individual agency and create change within the limitations of social structure is also a key task of sociology. In reflecting on the interplay between agency and structure in relation to aging, you will develop your own sociological consciousness and your ability to create positive social change.

Questions for Critical Thought

1. Dowd (1975) suggests that the withdrawal of older persons from society might change if future cohorts of older persons gain more formal education and economic resources. Do you think this has occurred today or does an imbalance of exchange persist?

2. Modernization theory claims that retirement decreases the social status of older persons. Do you think this is the case today? Why or why not? Draw on a sociological understanding of the concept of "social status" to explain your answer.

3. From a life course perspective, can you think of additional examples of the ways in which our life pathways are increasingly becoming more fluid, flexible, diverse, and unstandardized?

4. What do you expect that your own future life course will look like? Do you expect to start a career, find a partner, have children, buy a house, and retire, and if so, at what ages? Draw on the concepts of "age norms" and "social clocks" in explaining your beliefs.

Suggested Readings

Bengtson, V. L., Burgess, E. O., & Parrott, T. M. (1997). Theory, explanation, and a third generation of theoretical development in social gerontology. *The Journals of Gerontology, 52B*(2), S72–88. The authors lament a relative lack of explicit use of theory in articles relevant to the sociology of aging. They review the most commonly used theoretical traditions, distinguishing between positivistic (i.e., traditional scientific models seeking to predict and control features of the world) and interpretive (i.e., focused on elaborating complex subjective meanings) perspectives. The authors further classify theories as first, second, or third generation, and as focusing on micro-level analyses, macro-level analyses, or both.

Lynott, R. J., & Lynott, P. P. (1996). Tracing the course of theoretical development in the sociology of aging. *The Gerontologist, 36*(6), 749–60. This article outlines how sociology of aging theories developed over time, including "two transformations" in theorizing. The first transformation represents a change from implicit theorizing about successful adaptation to aging, to theoretical self-consciousness and explicit statements of theoretical positions. The second transformation represents the emergence of meta-theoretical, interpretive perspectives that problematize the "facts" of aging as social constructions that can obscure and perpetuate larger vested interests.

Marshall, V. W., & Bengtson, V. L. (2011). Theoretical perspectives on the sociology of aging. In R. A. Settersten Jr. & J. L. Angel (Eds.), *Handbook of sociology of aging* (pp. 17–33). New York, NY: Springer. This chapter provides an overview of perspectives commonly used to understand "the *how* and the *why* behind the social manifestations of aging we observe" (p. 17). Theoretical perspectives in the sociology of aging are classified as focusing on either macro-level structural explanations or micro-level social psychological explanations. They are also classified as either normative (viewing behaviours as influenced by social norms) or interpretive (viewing individuals as actively constructing more flexible, general guidelines). Newer theoretical perspectives are also reviewed.

Relevant Websites

Canadian Association on Gerontology
http://cagacg.ca

This is the official website of the primary professional organization for gerontologists in Canada. Members present at an annual conference, and you can review abstracts for upcoming presentations—this will familiarize you with some of the issues being addressed by Canadian gerontologists. Try to identify those that address theoretical topics or employ a sociological perspective.

Canadian Sociological Association
http://www.csa-scs.ca

This website will orient you to some issues currently being examined by sociologists. Canadian sociologists meet annually at the Congress of the Humanities and Social Sciences. You can review available abstracts for upcoming presentations—try to identify the presentations that address aging-related issues.

American Sociological Association, "Section on Aging and the Life Course"
http://www.asanet.org/sections/aging.cfm

This web page outlines the American Sociological Association's "Section on Aging and the Life Course." The association meets yearly, and when abstracts for presentations are available, you can review these for an overview of current research on aging from a sociological perspective.

Population Aging, Ageism, and Intergenerational Relations

Learning Objectives

In this chapter, you will learn that:

◎ Canada's population includes a growing proportion of older persons, as a result of declining fertility rates and increasing life expectancies.

◎ overstated assumptions about the negative, catastrophic, and inevitable implications of population aging for public services tend to serve particular political and economic goals.

◎ meanings of old age are shaped by more than individual beliefs—they have origins in wider social and cultural forces, such as the demographic composition of populations and changing political and economic contexts.

◎ ageism not only implicates particular attitudes and beliefs about aging, but also becomes institutionalized within taken-for-granted practices and policies.

◎ ageism is only one way of thinking about age-related inequality—we also want to consider how more structured, patterned differences in access to power and resources between age cohorts affect our life opportunities as we age.

◎ research on intergenerational relations tends to focus on the quality and extent of interactions between generations in a family, but can also examine the quality and extent of relations between generational groups in society.

Introduction

If you have ever felt uncomfortable about or laughed at the idea of older people having sex; if you have found yourself thinking that an older person was "too old" to be dressing or acting in a certain way; or if you have complained about a slower driver in front of you in traffic ("Come on, grandpa!"), you might admit that, at times, some of your beliefs about older persons reflect a form of ageism.

Now, think about the following possibilities. If you have ever told an older person how well she looks despite her age, you might have thought you were giving her a compliment (and indeed, she may have been pleased). If you have given an older person a birthday card that joked about his age, you might have hoped to make him laugh (and indeed, he may have laughed). Or if you have heard an older person complain about a physical ailment, such as a sore back, you might have tried to reassure her that this is "normal at your age" (and indeed, she may have agreed). Although we do not often consider these situations to be ageist, these instances, too, can be far more subtle reflections of ageist beliefs, being ultimately rooted in an understanding of aging as negative (e.g., unattractive, comical, unhealthy).

In this chapter, we will examine ageism and relations between age groups in society from a sociological perspective—one that seeks to understand how our changing social context shapes and is shaped by the social and cultural meanings of old age and aging. In particular, we move beyond an understanding based on individual attitudes or beliefs (i.e., a psychological perspective) to consider the role of an aging population, neoliberal political and economic forces, and other features of contemporary society (e.g., modernization and postmodernity), in relation to ageist attitudes and their institutionalization within dominant practices and policies. By way of introduction, in the following section we will examine evidence of aging populations, before turning to consider how this demographic change informs one powerful ageist ideology: apocalyptic demography.

Population Aging in Demographic, Global, and Historical Perspectives

In Canada and in other industrialized countries, it is well publicized that populations are aging. For instance, the percentage of Canadians who are over age 65 was estimated to be 14.4 per cent in 2011 (see Figure 2.1); historical trends show that this percentage has been increasing, and it is projected to continue to increase, for reasons that will be described in this section.

There is variation in population aging trends among different geographic regions, however. In Canada, geographic areas with higher concentrations of Aboriginal peoples, such as in Nunavut or Northern Manitoba, have relatively low proportions of persons over age 65. In these areas, there are higher **fertility rates** (i.e., more children being born) and lower life expectancies (i.e., fewer people living to old age) in comparison to non-Aboriginal populations. A similar trend is evident globally—although most countries are "aging," areas and countries with lower life expectancies and higher fertility rates (trends generally associated with higher poverty) have smaller proportions of older adults.

Indeed, population fertility rates, and to a lesser extent life expectancies, are key determinants of the age structure of the population. From a sociological perspective, we are interested in identifying even broader-level social changes driving population aging. Historically, as societies industrialize, they experience an aging population as they move from patterns of high fertility and mortality to low fertility and mortality—this is referred to as a **demographic transition** (LaPierre & Hughes, 2009). How does this occur? Declines in

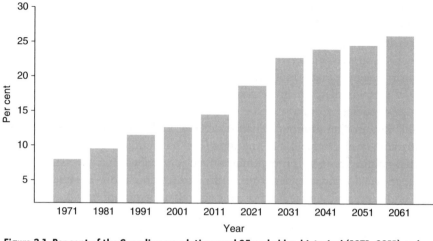

Figure 2.1 Per cent of the Canadian population aged 65 and older, historical (1971–2011) and projected (2012–2061)
Source: Employment and Social Development Canada. (2015, January 21). Indicators of well-being in Canada: Canadians in context—Aging population. Retrieved from http://www4.hrsdc.gc.ca/.3ndic.1t.4r@-eng.jsp?iid=33

fertility are connected to social forces associated with industrialization, such as urbanization, the decline in the "family wage" and rise in dual-earner couples, increased access to and acceptability of contraception, and the women's movement. More women are pursuing higher education and career pathways that delay partnership and child-bearing decisions to later ages, which often results in fewer children per partnership. The high costs of and difficulties accessing child care may also be a deterrent for some couples.

In Canada, population aging is related in part to the historical "baby boom" that occurred after the Second World War. This relatively sudden spike in fertility rates was followed by relatively low and then progressively declining fertility rates. From this point onwards, the "baby boomers" (people born between 1946 and the early 1960s) have been aging, with the first of this cohort turning 65 in 2011. The baby boomer group has accentuated the trend towards population aging in Canada.

Although fertility rates are the dominant cause, population aging is also affected by trends in **mortality rates** (death rates).[1] The demographic transition is also accompanied by a shift in the rates and patterns of disease within populations. In this way, increases in life expectancy, and declines in mortality, are connected to rising standards of living and socio-economic circumstances in many population groups, including access to universal education; improved housing; developed public health infrastructure; access to clean water and sanitation; access to nutritious, healthy food sources; and advances in medical technology and access to health care services. Over time, the expansion of these forces within a geographic area leads to lowered risk of infectious diseases and, as such, people in these areas tend to live to older ages, which "ages" the population. Another effect of the epidemiological transition is that the primary causes of ill-health and death shift towards chronic and degenerative conditions more common in older age groups—for instance, the current major causes of death in Canada are circulatory system diseases, respiratory diseases, and cancer.

The percentage of the population over the age of 65 is one of three common ways to represent the **demographic** trend of population aging. One of the problems with relying on this statistic is that it is very simplistic and can lead us to assume that every person over age 65 is the same; that is, reliance on this statistic "homogenizes" older persons and tells us little about the variation that exists within the older population (e.g., by gender, socioeconomic status, or ethnicity) or between older age groups (e.g., people aged 66 to 75 may be considerably different than people aged 86 to 95). Further, given current and potential future advances in health and life expectancy of the older population in industrialized societies, 65 may no longer be a meaningful indicator of old age—indeed, it is a socially constructed indicator developed in the past with the introduction of retirement policies, when our life expectancy as a population was lower.[2]

Another common way to describe the age composition of a population is by relying on visual summaries in the form of **population pyramids**. Generally, these represent more complex demographic data, including proportions in particular age categories after age 65. As illustrated in Figure 2.2, population pyramids are visual representations of the age structure in a population (in this case, the population of Canada), including the proportion of males (as shown on the left) or females (as shown on the right) occupying each age category (refer to the vertical axis) within a population (refer to the horizontal axis for the population count per thousand). Figure 2.2 provides historical estimates (represented by the solid line) and projected estimates (represented by the dotted line), along with 2011 data (represented by the grey fill).

Finally, it is also common to depict population aging using the **old-age dependency ratio**: the proportion of dependent older adults compared or relative to the rest of the working-age population. The proportion of older adults can also be combined with the proportion of children to create the **total dependency ratio**. Historical and projected dependency ratios are illustrated in Figure 2.3. Both ratios tend to utilize statistics of the proportion of the population over age 65; as such, they suffer from the same problem of oversimplification and homogenization described earlier in this chapter. In particular, dependency ratios can lead to overstated assumptions about the extent of older persons' dependence on the rest of society, and to conclusions that the "burden" of older populations is reaching the point of crisis. However, many older persons continue to work in the paid

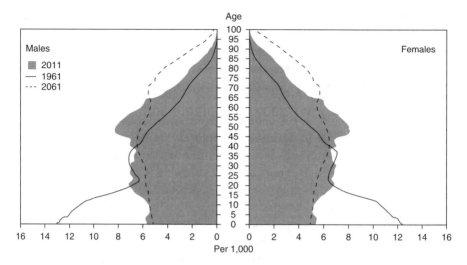

Figure 2.2 Comparison of Canadian population pyramids for the years 1961, 2011, and projected 2061
Note: Persons aged 100 and over are included at age 100.
Source: Statistics Canada, Demography Division. (2014). *Canadian demographics at a glance* (2nd ed.) (Catalogue No. 91-003-X). Retrieved from http://www.statcan.gc.ca/pub/91-003-x/2014001/section01/05-eng.htm

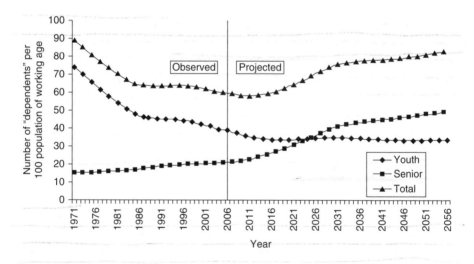

Figure 2.3 Historical and projected dependency ratios (youth, senior, and total) in Canada, 1971 to 2056
Source: Statistics Canada. (2010). *Healthy people, healthy places* (Catalogue No. 82-229-X). Retrieved from http://www.statcan.gc.ca/pub/82-229-x/2009001/demo/dep-eng.htm

labour force after the age of 65, as well as participate in a variety of activities that contribute to Canada's society and economy (e.g., through child care or volunteering).

In sum, although statistics representing age composition can provide a useful starting point for understanding population aging, they need to be accompanied by an understanding of the broader historical and social contributors to these demographic trends. Further, we must be cautious of jumping to conclusions based on these statistics, which can obscure more complex realities and can lead to and fuel crisis thinking about population aging, as well as ageism; these concepts will be discussed in the remainder of this chapter.

The Concept of Apocalyptic Demography and Myths of Population Aging

Social gerontologists have contributed in a significant way towards "debunking" some very pervasive assumptions about aging populations. In particular, they have sought to expose and counteract a phenomenon present in policy, media, and public discourse known as **apocalyptic demography** (Gee, 2000), also referred to as *demographic alarmism* or *demographic scapegoating*. Many well-known Canadian gerontologists have been leaders in drawing attention to this concept (see Chappell, 2011; Gee, 2000; Gutman, 2010; Katz, 1992; McDaniel, 2003).

Apocalyptic demography refers to overstating the negative effects of demographic trends for society—in this case, a construction of the effects of population aging, and the resulting numbers and proportions of older persons, as catastrophic for society—in particular, for our health care and pension systems. Michael Prince (2000) describes this as a "Chicken Little" reaction.[3] For example, one study (Martin, Williams, & O'Neill, 2009) examined descriptions of population aging in the influential *Economist* publication, which is read by many political and financial leaders, and found that 64 per cent of the articles portrayed population aging as a burden or "time bomb" for society. Although the researchers of this study conclude that the *Economist*'s portrayals might result in apocalyptic thinking among its readers, it is equally possible to view these articles as already reflecting the presence of such thinking among its readers. Apocalyptic demography has been traced in other contexts, including the following: Swedish newspapers (Lundgren & Ljuslinder, 2011a, 2011b); government discourse in Australia (Johnstone & Kanitsaki, 2009); and public opinion in Canada (Northcott, 1994). For another example, see Box 2.1.

One of the concerns with apocalyptic demography is that because of its narrow focus on population composition (i.e., demography), it can promote a view of population aging as "separate from the socio-economic circumstances which produced it" (McDaniel, 1987, p. 332). Indeed, it can perpetuate such a negative view of the "problem" of population aging that we fail to realize how population aging actually results from quite positive

---

Box 2.1   Apocalyptic Demography in the News

Foner (2000) notes that in the 1960s and 1970s, the strong social and political ideals typical of younger generations, often expressed through protests and rallies, contributed to a sense of age conflict—for instance, with older generations seen as barriers to progressive social change. During the more recent 2012 Quebec student protests, which began in response to proposed university tuition fee increases, John Moore wrote an editorial for the *National Post*, in which he supports the students and responds to claims that they are "entitled"—claims he believes originate from older persons in particular. Specifically, Moore argues that the older generation, "having already been afforded a plum goodie" throughout their younger years (e.g., low tuition rates, job security, employment insurance, family allowance, and a more robust medicare system) and into their old age (e.g., Old Age Security program, Canada Pension Plan), "is now wagging his finger at the first generation that will be asked to pay the tab. So who really is entitled here?" Moore further suggests that the benefits enjoyed by these older generations will no longer be available to younger generations. In sum, he states the following:

> Today's youth face a grim future not of their own making. Is it any wonder that they're angry about it? What they are asking for is what previous generations so eagerly gobbled up for themselves. If those generations now believe their entitlements were too generous, then, perhaps, in the spirit of sharing the burden, they might want to give some of them back.

In essence, Moore reinforces apocalyptic demography, along with the idea that intergenerational inequity is created by older generations. From an alternative perspective, the problem is not with an older generation that has "gobbled up" benefits and social programs, but rather with the ideology that suggests that cutting back on such services is the inevitable result of our demographic and economic circumstances, rather than neoliberal policy goals.

Source: Summary of Moore, John. "It's the older generation that's entitled, not students." *National Post.* May 24, 2012. Material reprinted with the express permission of: National Post, a division of Postmedia Network Inc.

---

societal changes, including increasing standards of living, gains in health, and increasing recognition of women's citizenship rights. McDaniel (2007) effectively summarizes this idea in the title of one of her works: "Population aging: Better than the alternative."

Catastrophic assumptions about the effects of population aging are often unfounded based on existing evidence. For instance, concerns about supporting older Canadians overlook the fact that the composition of the support burden has and will change substantially over time—in the past, and especially during the baby boom, Canadian society was heavily invested in social supports for families and children (McDaniel, 1987). Statistical analyses by F. T. Denton, Feaver, and Spencer (1998) suggested that the total dependency burden of an older adult population will most likely remain below the level experienced during the baby boom. Many other factors are far more important than population aging in influencing the viability of our health care, pension, and social welfare systems (McDaniel, 1987), including modifiable factors related to political, organizational, and financing decisions (Chappell, 2011; Gee, 2002; Shaw, 2002).

For instance, a recent report from the Canadian Institute for Health Information (2011) indicates that over the past 10 years in Canada, "although population aging contributed to [health care] spending increases, its impact to date has been relatively modest" (p. 37), adding only 0.8 per cent growth in public-sector health spending each year. Numerous studies have demonstrated the sustainability of the Canadian health care system and suggested that rises in health care costs are only minimally driven by the aging population; rather, it is necessary to examine the rising costs of prescription drugs and increases in potentially inappropriate over-servicing of older patients, who tend to receive more specialist referrals and surgeries (some of minimal benefit) than in the past (Barer, Evans, & Hertzman, 1995; Evans, McGrail, Morgan, Barer, & Hertzman, 2001; Morgan & Cunningham, 2011).

Similar arguments have been made in relation to Canada's system of economic supports for older persons. Countering the perception of a crisis, for instance, the sustainability and affordability of both the Old Age Security program and the Canada Pension Plan have been confirmed in recent years (see Chapter 5 for more details; also see R. L. Brown, 2011; Fitzpatrick, 2012).

Apocalyptic demography constitutes the discourse on aging as a negative experience for both individuals and society. This thinking not only contributes to ageism (discussed in the following section), but homogenizes the health of the elderly and obscures heterogeneity (e.g., at-risk groups of older persons may be hurt the most by the service cutbacks that apocalyptic demography is used to justify), and further detracts attention from social and structural factors that influence our aging experiences at the individual and population level (Carrière, 2000; Estes & Binney, 1989; Gee, 2002; Stahl & Feller, 1990).

Apocalyptic demography can also contribute to the construction of generation as an identity signifier that pits groups against one another, fueling intergenerational conflict (and a sense of injustice among younger groups who believe they are faced with paying for the "burden" of older generations; see Box 2.1) rather than emphasizing and revealing the many ways that different generations are interconnected and have common interests (Binney & Estes,

1988; McDaniel, 2000; Robertson, 1997). International governmental organizations (see Chapter 8) contribute to this phenomenon through promoting the belief that the provision of social services to older persons is at the expense of younger generations—an idea often used to legitimate cuts to these services by national governments (Estes & Phillipson, 2002).

Lastly, critical gerontologists have raised concerns that apocalyptic demography can serve an ideological purpose to justify the erosion of publicly funded services in aging countries, particularly health care systems and pension systems (e.g., Walker, 2012). In essence, reforms to these systems that seek to reduce public contributions are viewed as an inevitable result of demographic trends—trends that threaten the sustainability of publicly funded services. What is concealed beneath this argument is that these cutbacks are motivated by more than concern about population aging, but are politically and economically motivated in a context of neoliberalism and globalization. In other words, apocalyptic demography conceals political and economic motivations for policy changes to health care and pensions. In doing so, the discourse also inhibits collective resistance in response to these reforms, as the public generally accept and become resigned to the "inevitable" need for increasingly limited service. For instance, in one research study, my colleagues and I identified an example of one family member who had been frustrated with the long wait his dying father faced in receiving care in the emergency department; however, this participant resigned himself to these long waits, viewing it as a necessary reality: "That's probably just something we're all going to have to get used to as we get older, being the baby boomer group" (Funk, Stajduhar, Cohen, Heyland, & Williams, 2012, p. 1019).

In sum, even though population aging is occurring, we must be careful not to overstate its potential impact on Canadian society relative to other forces, such as political and economic decision-making. Although Canadians will need to adapt and adjust to an increasingly aging population, we should be cautious of claims suggesting that aging populations will bring devastation to our social system (Chappell, 2011; Cheal, 2000).

Conceptualizing Ageism

Ageism was originally defined by Butler (1969) as "systematic stereotyping of and discrimination against people because they are old, just as racism and sexism accomplish this with skin color and gender" (p. 243). This definition reflects the most commonly accepted conceptualization of ageism in gerontology, and it integrates both attitudinal and behavioural dimensions: in other words, not only what people think, but what they *do*. A similar definition has been advanced more recently by Bytheway and Johnson (1990):

> Ageism is experienced both through the negative valuation of the ageing process throughout the life course, and through the consequential stigmatising and institutional identification of "special" groups on the basis of chronological age. (p. 33)

Byteway and Johnson's definition is broader and allows for the possibility that some young persons may experience ageism, for instance for being viewed as "too young" (e.g., as too inexperienced to do a good job).

As Butler (1975) further noted, ageism involves constructing older persons as different from the rest of the population—older persons are seen as "others" who are different than ourselves, but all older persons are seen as constituting a homogenous (i.e., similar) group. The notion that the variability and diversity evident among younger and mid-life persons actually carries on into later life is obscured when we consider older persons in this way.

Most existing research focuses on attitudinal aspects and measures of ageism, primarily from a psychological perspective. However, negative attitudes towards and beliefs about older persons are frequently expressed in and reinforced by broader societal **stereotypes** and constructions of older people (e.g., as forgetful, resistant to change, complaining, slow, bad drivers, unhappy, passive, socially inappropriate, asexual, lacking usefulness). We also tend to associate older adults with particular social roles (e.g., grandparent, volunteer, cruise ship passenger), yet not with other roles (e.g., parent, worker, activist).

Some seemingly less harmful stereotypes also exist. For instance, when we see two older persons sitting together on a park bench and holding hands, we might exclaim, "How cute!" Although "cute" might suggest a harmless, even positive descriptor, it is a paternalistic characterization that suggests powerlessness in the other. Another example stems from one of my own analyses of how resident care aides (RCAs) coped with bereavement in long-term care facilities (there are frequent resident deaths in these settings). Funk, Waskiewich, and Stajduhar (2013–2014) describe how RCAs reminded themselves, and each other, that the deceased resident is "better off." In some cases, this was tied to beliefs about dying, old age, disability, and dementia, as illustrated in the following quotes from two RCAs: "Most of them are old and have dementia so I know it's their time to go. There's really nothing but suffering for them in their lives"; and "They're not just going to be turning from side to side and looking at walls anymore" (Funk et al., 2013–2014, p. 33). Though this type of thinking might help the RCAs feel better after a resident dies, it can inadvertently reinforce stereotypical beliefs that view misery and suffering as an inevitable part of aging—and the idea that it is better to be dead than it is to be old and with limited functioning.

We will refer to some of the broader sources of these kinds of social and cultural stereotypes later in this chapter. Ageist attitudes and beliefs are concerning because they can serve to legitimate discriminatory behaviours or practices towards older people, including systematically denying them access to certain resources and opportunities (McMullin & Marshall, 2001). In 2009, the Canadian Association of Retired Persons surveyed more than 4,000 of their members about their experience of ageist behaviours. Although this was a self-selected sample,[4] the organization reported that 62 per cent of survey respondents believed they had experienced forms of ageism, such as being demeaned by others (35 per cent), receiving poor service (32 per cent), or being laughed at or joked about (29 per cent) because of their age. Analyses of the European Social Survey held in 2008 and 2009 (Age UK, 2011), which included data from 54,988 respondents in 28 countries, indicated that 35 per cent of respondents reported experiencing age discrimination as unfair treatment based on age, including experiencing lack of respect or being treated badly because of their age.

A telephone survey of a non-random sample of 1,501 Canadians in four age groups was conducted in 2012 to assess ageism in Canada (Revera & International Federation on Ageing, 2012). In total, 63 per cent of those over 66 years of age responded that they had been treated unfairly or differently because of their age. Most commonly, this occurred in interactions with younger people, although other sources are identified in Figure 2.4. Reported forms of ageism included being assumed to be incompetent, ignored, or treated by others as if they are invisible or have nothing to contribute. Respondents also noted that they sometimes felt their physical symptoms were dismissed by their health care professionals (i.e., as an inevitable part of aging), or they

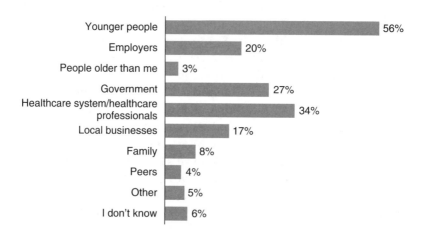

Figure 2.4 Reported sources of age discrimination towards older adults (aged 66 and older)
Source: Revera & International Federation on Ageing. (2012). *Revera report on ageism*. Retrieved from http://www.reveraliving.com/About-Us/Media-Centre/Revera-Report-on-ageism/docs/Report_Ageism.aspx

felt that they had experienced government programs or policies that did not take older persons' needs into account.

It is noteworthy that the survey by Revera and the International Federation on Ageing (2012) was based on an extended definition of ageism that included the failure of some programs or policies to consider the needs of older persons. Indeed, ageist outcomes do not always result from the actions of particular individuals who hold ageist attitudes, but can be the result of ageism that becomes embedded into established and taken-for-granted policies, procedures, and practices in our culture, social institutions, governments, or particular organizations (Calasanti, 2005). This is **institutionalized ageism**, which includes not only explicitly discriminatory programs, but more broadly, "a tendency to structure society based on an assumption that everyone is young, thereby failing to respond appropriately to the real needs of older persons" as noted by the Ontario Human Rights Commission (2001, p. 15). Examples include retirement policies that require individuals to stop or limit their participation in paid work at a certain age (see Chapter 5), government programs such as job retraining that restrict eligibility to those under age 65 (McMullin & Marshall, 2001), and even the taken-for-granted cultural practices of giving birthday cards with age-related humour (Hagestad & Uhlenberg, 2005). Institutionalized ageist policies and practices such as these can further reinforce ageist beliefs in the population—and in older persons themselves.

When older persons begin to accept negative views of aging as part of their own self-concept, this is described as **internalized ageism**. The sociological tradition of symbolic interactionism, for instance, would focus on how we might, once labelled old, begin to be treated differently by other people, which can then affect our own concept of self. Dobbs et al. (2008) draw on this approach in their focus on **stigmatization** as a process wherein age-related cultural beliefs label older persons as a separate category of persons, resulting in differential treatment (i.e., discrimination), loss of status, and "spoiled" identities. For instance, older persons who are continually viewed as and treated as inferior and incapable may, over time, begin to exhibit passivity and learned helplessness.

Harbison and Morrow (1998) hypothesize that ageism, and in particular a focus on older people as burdens, can work to "discourage their participation in political demands for service, especially those services that emphasize their vulnerability" (p. 696), such as programs and initiatives to address elder abuse. Further, older persons may resist defining themselves as old and may try to maintain a youthful appearance (Calasanti, 2005; Hurd Clarke & Griffin, 2008); they may view their physical bodies as a kind of mask or as a betrayal (Hurd Clarke, 2000; Morell, 2003). The internalization of ageism in relation to bodies will be discussed further in Chapter 3.

Sociological Perspectives for Explaining Ageism in Canadian Society

Social Psychological Theories of Socialization

Why do negative attitudes about and discrimination towards older persons persist in Canada? From a psychological perspective, it has been suggested that ageism is rooted in a pervasive, cross-cultural existential fear of death, because older people are a symbolic reminder of our mortality (Martens, Goldenberg, & Greenberg, 2005). Dominant explanations, however, draw on social psychological theories of **socialization** and **social learning**, primarily at the individual level. Essentially, this perspective focuses on how negative age stereotypes are learned through socialization—especially in childhood, but across the life course—and how this shapes our beliefs and behaviour towards older adults.[5]

More broadly, we might consider some of the sources of these stereotypes in wider society and culture (see, for example, Figure 2.5). We might, for example, highlight the absence or negative portrayal of many older adults in Hollywood films, which tend to exaggerate the burdens and fears involved in aging and loss (Chivers, 2011). Other researchers have examined negative depictions of aging—and constructions of older persons as a distinct

© Photos 12 / Alamy

Figure 2.5 Scenes on the animated television series *The Simpsons* that contain the character Grampa Simpson feature a lot of ageist humour. Do you think the show uses humour to expose and challenge ageist stereotypes, or does it reinforce them?

other "group"—in birthday cards (Ellis & Morrison, 2005); social media (Levy, Chung, Bedford, & Navrazhina, 2014); products and marketing of the anti-aging industry (Calasanti, 2005; see Chapter 3); and political, government, and lay media discourse (Bytheway & Johnson, 1990), including public discourse depicting older populations as a burden (as noted earlier in this chapter).

North American culture in particular, as with many modern industrial cultures, tends to idealize youth, health, and independence, which may further bolster negative views of aging (Calasanti, 2005). Indeed, it is commonly assumed that other (non-Western, more collectivist) cultures have less ageism, as well as less neglect and abuse, and more respect and reverence for older generations. Traditional Chinese cultures, for example, have tended to emphasize the importance of **filial piety** within families—this concept extends beyond the idea of caring for parents to include obeying them, showing deference, and honouring one's ancestors. As another example, those socialized within Greek and Brazilian cultures may view the institutionalization of an older adult as a form of abuse (Daskalopoulos & Kakouros, 2006; Patterson & Malley-Morrison, 2006).

In fact, the assumption that other cultures are less ageist often relies on considerations of familial values towards older family members and the extent of family-based care they would provide. For instance, a participant I interviewed for one study stated the following:

> It's a real shame that people don't hold the same standards as Japanese people. My daughter spent a year in Japan and said it's unbelievable—the family stays together! They live together and they have it dead-on right! She said here we're screwed up about it, and stick our elderly people away! (Funk, 2010, p. 81)

In other words, we tend to draw conclusions about attitudes towards older persons based on whether or not families provide support for them and to a lesser extent based on whether or not our society supports them (e.g., through public programs).

It is also commonly assumed that many Aboriginal cultures share a common emphasis on respect for older persons. However, although Elders in Aboriginal cultures such as First Nations communities in Canada are well respected, this is not necessarily because of their old age but rather due to other characteristics they possess, such as spiritual leadership—not all Elders are old (see Chapter 8). There tends to be, however, a high value placed on collective responsibility in First Nations communities in Canada, yet there is a lack of research on caregiving interpretations in this population (see Chapter 8). One exception is a study by Crosato, Ward-Griffin, and Leipert (2007), who reported that a group of Aboriginal women they spoke with viewed care for the elderly as an expected part of their culture and life course, and the women felt honoured to assume the role; however, these women also emphasized the importance of additional sources of support.

Caution is needed to avoid drawing erroneous conclusions or overly idealizing the status of older persons in other cultures. Older persons in non-Western cultural groups can still experience family abuse or neglect, for instance (Dong, Simon, & Gorbien, 2007; Lai, 2011; Yan & Tang, 2001). Several studies have explored attitudes towards and stereotypes of older persons across different cultural groups, generally reporting more consistency of these stereotypes and perceptions across cultures than we might normally assume (Cuddy, Norton, & Fiske, 2005; Eyetsemitan, Gire, Khaleefa, & Satiardama, 2003; Huang, 2013; Musaiger & D'Souza, 2009). Much of the misunderstanding about ageism in other cultures and in the past is in part due to our tendency to conflate "caring for" (and co-residence in multigenerational households) with "caring about." Even where differences in cultural values are noted, the actual practice of supporting older adults (within families, at least) often differs less than we might assume (Sheng & Settles, 2006). Additionally, to the extent that cultural ideals of family relationships and responsibilities are shifting in both Western and Eastern cultures, this may be less related to the influence of individualistic cultural beliefs and ageism, and more related to how families adapt to actual changes in the capacities of individuals to meet the needs of older family members (see Chapter 7). Similarly, research by Lan (2002) suggests that filial norms, though not necessarily weakened when Chinese families immigrate to America, are renegotiated and redefined by adult children who are faced with a restricted ability to fulfill the traditional norms (e.g., due to employment).

From the dominant social psychological or social learning perspective, eliminating ageism requires changing the social and cultural norms and stereotypes about aging—and thereby attitudes and beliefs about aging— through increased circulation of positive ideals and images of aging. For example, this approach is advocated in a recent report by the Special Senate Committee on Aging (Carstairs & Keon, 2009), which proposes a public relations campaign that portrays healthy older persons active in volunteering, educational activities, and physical exercise. In fact, a review by Zhang et al. (2006) of advertising images of aging in the United States, United Kingdom, China, Germany, and India suggested that such images are increasingly becoming more positive, albeit in limited representation overall.

Although it is important to challenge negative attitudes towards aging and older adults, K. E. McHugh (2003) cautions against **positive ageism**: an overemphasis on positive images of aging, which can inadvertently devalue and actually stigmatize older persons who cannot meet this ideal (i.e., as being a failure). In other words, a more diverse representation of the realities of later life may be needed. For instance, Stephen Katz (2012), in writing about the relatively negative images of aging in Hollywood films, suggests that audiences must demand more varied representations of old age, "more than just pity, comedy, derision, decline, sadness, and horror" (p. 255).

Social learning theorists have also suggested a need to change the beliefs of children and young adults in particular, through early socialization processes; in this respect, promoting positive interaction and socialization experiences between older and younger generations may be another means of reducing ageism. Authors of one study (Allan & Johnson, 2009), for instance, suggested that contact with older persons reduced younger persons' anxiety about aging, which in turn reduced ageist beliefs. This idea aligns with broader-level theories that connect individual ageism to a societal-wide tendency to separate or segregate younger and older generations, an idea that will be returned to in the following sections (Hagestad & Uhlenberg, 2005; Riley, Kahn, & Foner, 1994).

Modernization Theory and Social Change

Modernization theory suggests that declines in the status of older persons— and increases in ageism—are connected to various processes associated with societal industrialization. This reflects a structural-functionalist approach in sociology, because the value of older persons is conceptualized as being directly related to whether they contribute to the appropriate functioning of society. Current discussions about modernization theory (e.g., Aboderin, 2004) tend to focus on the ways that industrialization affects family-level exchanges of support, which are often viewed as reflecting the status of older persons or ageism in particular societies.

Cowgill and Holmes (1972) explained that new technologies and increased standards of living contribute to increased life expectancy, which in turn leads to intergenerational competition for jobs. The societal response was to develop the institution of retirement, yet this had the ultimate effect of lowering the status and income of older persons. As job requirements increasingly required the development of new skills, universal education was introduced, which further devalued older persons' knowledge (e.g., because everyone could obtain this knowledge). With industrialization, companies also reorganized their work practices and introduced technology to increase profits, which meant that particular jobs became obsolete—younger people were introduced into the new jobs because they were the most recently hired, and obsolete jobs tended to be those in which older persons worked. With increasing urbanization and the development of large cities, families became more dispersed geographically, leading older persons to have more peripheral family roles. Modernization theory has been critiqued in many respects, especially for idealizing older persons' situations in the past and other less industrialized societies. For instance, Rhoads (1984) concluded that despite modernization within Samoan society, traditional cultural values of age as enhancing social status persisted. Nonetheless, modernization theory remains an important example of a sociological perspective, in that it seeks to examine how the nature of society and social change shape our beliefs about and behaviours towards older persons. However, it provides little in the way of productive solutions for changing ageism in industrialized societies.

Further, contemporary sociologists suggest that countries that have already moved through the industrial era are now moving into a distinct **post-industrial society** (or postmodern society). Generally, this is said to be characterized by the loosening of traditional social and cultural (and age-related) norms along with expanding choices available for individuals across their life course (as a result, for example, of new technologies, rising affluence, and changing norms), whether in family relationships and child-bearing, leisure and lifestyle, occupational and retirement trajectories, and so on. In this context, older persons may have greater freedom from aging-related cultural and biological constraints; old age may no longer have meaning for identities. What are the implications of this kind of society for ageism? Higgs and Jones (2009) note the potential, from this perspective, for positive implications: "age could be released from the negative status that currently blights it and ageing identities could be constructed and reconstructed in playful and self-conscious ways" (p. 61).

Riley, Kahn, and Foner (1994) would agree that technological innovation and social change have increased the capabilities of older persons and enhanced life-course possibilities. However, their perspective differs in maintaining that our society, as it is currently structured, still offers few meaningful social role opportunities for older persons in society, and that social norms, expectations, and existing social institutions have been slow to change: this, they maintain, represents a kind of societal inflexibility or structural lag. Indeed, we noted earlier in this chapter how ageist ideas can become institutionalized into existing policies and practices; these in particular can be difficult to change. The Ontario Human Rights Commission (n.d.) suggests that existing institutional barriers to older persons should be identified and removed, and that to fully address ageism, "the age diversity that exists in society should be reflected in design stages for policies, programs, services, facilities and so forth so that physical, attitudinal and systemic barriers are not created."

Critical Gerontology and Political Economy

From a critical theoretical perspective, ageism is not simply the result of ageist attitudes and their subsequent institutionalization, but is in fact rooted in and generated by broader social structures—in particular, within our political (neoliberal) and economic (capitalist) systems. Historically, for example, mandatory retirement policies that required older persons to retire at age 65 were created in part to help employers remove a segment of their workforce that tended to be more expensive because the older workers were more experienced (e.g., cumulative pay raises over time; this will be discussed more in Chapter 5). By institutionalizing retirement in this way, these policies "constructed a social group of people termed 'the elderly' who have been systematically denied certain rights and privileges including the right to participate in paid employment" (Bytheway & Johnson, 1990, p. 29).

McMullin and Marshall (2001) examined workers' reported experiences of age discrimination within Montreal's garment industry, which had been under considerable pressures to increase profits in the global market. From the authors' perspective, employers' intimidation of workers, which appeared to be based on their age, was in fact motivated more by their desire to push out certain workers that were viewed as problematic for company profits (e.g., they filed too many union grievances). The authors further suggest that older workers in many ways themselves inadvertently reinforced ageist beliefs about differences between themselves and younger workers. For instance, older workers referred to their age as limiting their ability to be more productive, often without realizing the broader forces increasing their workload pressures—garment industry companies have increasingly contracted out easier work to save costs, such that the work that remains is more complex and time-consuming (McMullin & Marshall, 2001).

A critical gerontological perspective tends to reverse the commonly held assumption that ageism creates age-based stratification or inequality in society. Rather, the perspective is one that begins with the existence of social stratification and then suggests that to justify inequality and hold onto their dominant positions, more powerful ("ruling") social groups influence existing systems in a way that constructs and reinforces difference to their own advantage. This process excludes and oppresses others, including older persons, women, ethnic minorities, and workers. Further examples will be provided in Chapter 6, when we discuss the concept of social exclusion. From a critical gerontological perspective, addressing ageism requires broad changes to our political system and even to our economic system; at the very least, public programs, policies, and collective action to address class and other inequalities may be required. In the next section, we will expand on some of these ideas as we address the contributions of two particular concepts to understanding the status of older persons: age relations and age stratification.

From Ageism to Age Relations

A sociological perspective would encourage us to look beyond ageist beliefs and attitudes as a source of age-related inequality in society. In sociology, *status* refers to more than just how we are regarded by others, but to our positions within structured status hierarchies that have as much to do with power and resources as they do with prestige. Calasanti (2005) writes that to really understand ageism, we need to understand the broader context of societal power relations based on age, or **age relations**: that is, how "societies organize on the basis of age" (p. 8). In sociology, age relations refer to more than the quality and nature of social interactions. Rather, the concept is meant to direct attention to how "age serves as a social *organizing principle*" in society; how "different age groups gain *identities and power* in relation to one another" (e.g., age often results in a lack of power); and how "age relations *intersect with other power relations*" (Calasanti, Slevin, & King, 2006, p. 17)—in other words, how old age can exacerbate other sources of inequality. These phenomena influence our lives, including our health and economic well-being (Calasanti et al., 2006).

Many of you may recall from your early sociology courses a disciplinary focus on class stratification—in other words, how wealth, power, and privilege are unequally distributed in society. In 1971, a similar idea was proposed by Matilda White Riley, who developed age stratification theory (discussed in Chapter 1). She proposed that age is a major source of this inequality in resource distribution and that age cohorts have different access to societal resources.

In sum, there has been considerable concern about ageism in Canadian society, as it can generate discriminatory behaviours towards older adults, and it can become institutionalized within policies and practices that limit older adults' opportunities and access to resources (this is known as patterned social exclusion; see Chapter 6). There is further concern that older adults themselves will internalize ageist beliefs, with negative implications for their well-being and quality of life. More broadly, ageism may be used as justification for neoliberal political and economic interests (e.g., the erosion of the welfare state, as with apocalyptic demography; or justifying discrimination against older workers that has more to do with the pursuit of profit). Many are also concerned that ageism reinforces an age-segregated society and intergenerational conflict (this will be discussed in the following section). A sociological perspective on ageism reminds us that ageism is not just a characteristic of individuals, but that it has broader origins in the way our society is structured—as such, it may be useful to draw on concepts such as age relations and age stratification.

Intergenerational Relations: From Families to Cohorts and Generations

Ageist beliefs and practices, including the construction of age as a source of difference, can contribute to reinforcing both age conflict and segregation more broadly in society. Whereas the concept of age relations in the previous section highlights issues of power and inequality, the concept of **intergenerational**

relations tends to focus more narrowly on interactions and exchanges between age groups, and attitudes towards each other, either within families or at a larger scale. For instance, dominant perspectives seek to describe these interactions and their positive or negative dimensions, as reflecting solidarity, conflict, or ambivalence.

Most of this research focuses on the micro level of younger and older generations within families; often, trends in these within-family inter-actions are assumed to reflect broader societal bonds between older and younger cohorts. This topic is reviewed in more depth in Chapter 7, when we counter the myth that older persons were more respected—and better cared for—in the past. Briefly, in that chapter we will emphasize the following: families continue to provide the majority of help for older family members, even when formal services are available; historical patterns of co-residence were not necessarily reflective of higher levels of affection or concern, or better family relationships; families are, in fact, now faced with increasing responsibilities at a time when their capacity to provide support and care is more limited.

Other scholars move beyond the family level to examine how age cohorts develop distinct identities in relation to one another and to consider the degree of conflict or segregation between cohorts at a societal level. For instance, earlier in this chapter we noted how apocalyptic demography can promote a sense of intergenerational inequity between generations, when younger groups feel unfairly burdened by growing proportions of older persons. Gilleard and Higgs (2005) further explain how individuals who are born at a similar point in historical time, and experience similar major historical events, can become culturally distinctive from other groups and may even develop a conscious sense of collective identity. Drawing on the theoretical work of Bourdieu (1977), Gilleard and Higgs (2005) posit that conflicts between generations stem from conflicting lifestyles, values, and tendencies of thinking and acting, "which have been produced by differ-ent modes of generation . . . [that] cause one group to experience as nat-ural and reasonable [those] practices or aspirations which another group finds unthinkable or scandalous" (Bourdieu, 1977, as cited in Gilleard & Higgs, 2005, p. 70). For example, older cohorts who grew up in depression-era Canada are often said to have developed particularly practical, thrift-conscious ways of living; later cohorts who grew up in a time of relatively greater prosperity and a cultural emphasis on consumerism tend to view older cohorts as overly "cheap." There is, further, a tendency for younger groups to view the traditional social values more common in older groups as obstacles to transformational social change.

The quality and extent of interactions between generations in a family does not necessarily reflect upon the quality and extent of relations between age cohorts or generational groups at a societal level (or vice versa). However, some gerontologists suggest that intergenerational relations at micro (i.e., within family) and macro (i.e., between young and old groups in society) levels are in fact tied closely to each other. For instance, Hagestad and Uhlenberg (2006) argue that strong within-family generational bonds mitigate broader trends towards **age segregation** in Western societies and promote integration. This segregation is generated, for instance, when entry into particular social institutions, like school or work, is normatively or formally restricted to certain age groups (institutional segregation); when age groups tend to be funnelled into different physical spaces (e.g., older persons in retirement communities), reducing the likelihood of interactions (spatial segregation); and when age groups tend to live within distinct cultural domains (cultural segregation).[6] Segregation, through limiting between-group interactions, can generate a sense of distinctness and even conflict.

Foner (2000) likewise argues that when we interact with and form bonds across generations within our own families, this promotes intergenerational cohesion and solidarity more broadly; indeed, she suggests this is one reason that younger cohorts actually tend to support the provision of public programs for older persons. Similar sentiments were expressed by participants in one of my own studies. One adult child, for instance, expressed that respecting and feeling responsible for your parents is one of the basic ways in which you learn to be socially responsible, more broadly, to all older persons (Funk, 2010). Another participant suggested that when children are socialized within their families to respect older family members, this learned value "spreads to the view of society" (Funk, 2010, p. 84).

The dominant assumption tends to be that population aging, especially in the current political and economic context, will fuel societal-level generational conflict. In contrast, Foner (2000) draws on the premise described in the preceding paragraph to argue that "age integration will offset tendencies to age conflicts" (p. 272) between generations at the macro level. She further emphasizes the ways in which families themselves are interdependent, such that public supports received by older family members benefit younger generations indirectly (i.e., the benefits might circulate within the family, as older family members help out younger ones; public benefits also offset potential costs otherwise faced by younger family members to support older family members). More broadly, Robertson (1997) suggests that we turn the debate from "inequity" between cohorts towards acknowledging the fundamental interdependence between all individuals in society, as well as our own moral obligations for collective responsibility.

Conclusion

Gerontologists have helped to challenge overstated assumptions about the negative, catastrophic, and inevitable implications of population aging, although more work is needed to counter these quite pervasive beliefs. Personal views on the most appropriate way to address ageism, intergenerational relations, and the position of older persons in Canadian society depend highly on an individual's theoretical assumptions about the causes and origins of these phenomena. Although a variety of ideas exist in this regard, social gerontological work tends to focus most heavily on the role of social psychological factors and social learning. From a sociological perspective, we might also consider features of our society that perpetuate ageist practices, promote intergenerational conflict, and generate inequalities in older persons' patterned access to resources. An aging population, neoliberal political and economic forces, and processes of societal change and industrialization could all be considered for the ways they shape both the cultural and structural positions of older persons. In particular, more macro-level research is needed that explores the intersection between ageism, power structures, and the complex dynamics of intergenerational relations between age cohorts in Canadian society.

Questions for Critical Thought

1. With the increasing progression of globalization and neoliberalism, will ageism and age inequality likely increase or decrease? Why?

2. What evidence exists to indicate whether we are currently facing "age wars" in our society?

3. After identifying three newspaper articles that are good reflections of "apocalyptic demography," can you explain how and why these articles represent this concept?

4. What do you believe are the best practices and/or policy responses that could help address (a) ageism, (b) intergenerational conflict, and (c) age segregation? Can you identify the theoretical assumptions behind each practice or policy?

5. Consider one of your favourite movies or television shows from the past year that included an older character: How was that character portrayed? Did the character fit in with or break from established stereotypes? What ideas did the character, movie, or television show reinforce about aging?

Suggested Readings

Foner, A. (2000). Age integration or age conflict as society ages? *The Gerontologist, 40*(3), 272–6. Foner takes a structural-functionalist stance in this article as she examines the potential implications of population aging for the quality of relations between young and old age groups in society (i.e., whether age conflict might destabilize social functioning). Rather than assuming that public policies supporting older persons will generate a sense of conflict or inequity for younger generations, Foner argues that we should consider that the strong evidence of age integration at the micro level of families will serve to mitigate conflict over public policy, such that younger persons generally support such policies.

McDaniel, S. A. (2003). Toward disentangling policy implications of economic and demographic changes in Canada's aging population. *Canadian Public Policy, 29*(4), 491–510. In this article, McDaniel articulates the ways that dependency ratio statistics, apocalyptic demography, and economic concerns intersect to influence policy decisions in Canada. A comprehensive critique of dependency ratios is presented, and McDaniel explains how policy responses based on apocalyptic demography further reinforce this thinking, as well as contribute to societal views towards older persons.

McMullin, J. A., & Marshall, V. W. (2001). Ageism, age relations, and garment industry work in Montreal. *The Gerontologist, 41*(1), 111–22. In this critical gerontological approach to the study of ageism, McMullin and Marshall draw on research conducted in Montreal's garment industry. The authors challenge an individualistic view of ageism (i.e., that individuals hold ageist attitudes, which cause them to discriminate), and explicate the complex ways that broader social structures (political and economic forces) contribute to ageism in a paid work setting. In their analysis, apparent age-based discrimination by employers conceals employers' ultimate goal of increasing profits and reducing costs in a globalized marketplace.

Relevant Websites

Aging Watch, "Elder Stereotypes in Media and Popular Culture"
http://www.agingwatch.com/?p=439
> Jessica Walker, the founder and director of the US-based think tank Aging Watch (a group targeting ageism and the social marginalization of older persons), wrote this post in 2010, which identifies five dominant negative depictions of older persons in popular culture and media, while drawing on specific examples.

Hans Rosling's "200 Countries, 200 Years, 4 Minutes," from The *Joy of Stats* for BBC
http://youtu.be/jbkSRLYSojo
> This portion of Hans Rosling's lecture is an entertaining visualization of the demographic transition throughout the world since 1810 and the connection between living standards, wealth, and life expectancy. Inequalities between (and within) countries are illustrated.

Population Pyramids of the World from 1950 to 2100
www.populationpyramid.net
> This interactive website provides population pyramids for different countries and geographic regions, as well as for the world overall, in five-year intervals. The website is useful for comparing and contrasting populations in different regions and countries, as well as for examining historical demographic trends and projected future trends.

3 The Aging Body, Biomedicalization, and Life Extension

Learning Objectives

In this chapter, you will learn that:

◎ the concept of embodiment in the sociology of aging draws attention to how we experience age within and through our physical bodies, and how we actively shape our subjective interpretations of our bodies.

◎ although ageist cultures prioritize youthful physical appearance, individual-level perceptions of aging bodies are particularly complex.

◎ older persons' use of anti-aging products, services, and technologies helps them actively manage ageist norms and stigmas of physical appearance and function, yet can further reinforce these norms and stigmas more broadly in society.

◎ aging and age-related conditions such as dementia and osteoporosis tend to be interpreted as medical diseases of the body in need of medical treatment, generating limitations in how we view and respond to these issues on a societal level.

◎ the "anti-aging" movement includes an industry of consumer products focused on aesthetic appearances, and it also involves a more organized study directed to extending the human lifespan.

◎ sociologists are interested in how advances in extending the human lifespan might change the future of society.

Introduction

When people begin to approach mid-life, they may start to experience more aches, pains, and physical symptoms of decline that are often interpreted as signs of "getting old." These physical experiences, when interpreted as aging signs, shape our age identities. In turn, our sense of our chronological age, when we live in an ageist society, can influence our interpretations of our physical symptoms (see Chapter 2). These and other phenomena are relevant for the concept of **embodiment** in sociology, which draws our attention to the ever-present and immediate ways in which we experience age within and through the physical realities of our bodies (Hurd Clarke & Korotchenko, 2011).

In this chapter, we begin by extending the study of ageism to examine how commonly held negative perceptions of aging physical bodies might shape the body images and self-perceptions of older persons. This process, alongside technological developments, can (but does not necessarily) limit our experience of our aging bodies, and in gendered ways. A booming **anti-aging industry** focuses on offering products and services to slow, stop, or reverse the biological aging process, primarily in terms of physical appearance. You do not have to look far these days to find a variety of print, audio, and video advertisements that communicate the importance of changing one's appearance to prevent oneself from "looking old." Moreover, a phenomenon called **biomedicalization** contributes to the perception that the physical appearance of aging bodies is a reflection of inner health; from this perspective, older bodies tend to be viewed as diseased (Kaufman, 1994). Within the biomedical model, aging is seen as something that can be "cured"; as such, anti-aging researchers seek not only to distinguish this field as a legitimate science, but also to address the question of how to extend the human lifespan. This chapter ends with a discussion of some of the recent debates regarding this controversial endeavour.

Cultural Ageism, Individual Body Image, and Beauty Work

Bodies are a highly visible site for physical markers of aging that can be stigmatizing—wrinkles and decreased skin elasticity, age spots, grey hair, weight gain (or loss, at advanced ages), thinning hair, bunions and joint changes due to arthritis, receding gums and chins, enlarged noses and ears, decreased physical stature and curving backs, and so on. Gerontological researchers have examined how older adults perceive their aging bodies, often with consideration to the broader context of societal ageism and cultural preoccupation with physical appearances. With respect to the latter issue, Lewis, Medvedev, and Seponski (2011) conducted a content analysis of images in eight fashion magazines, confirming the fashion industry's ongoing focus on youthful images to the exclusion of older women. Coupland (2007) similarly examined how lifestyle magazine articles and skin care advertisements convey visible signs of aging as problematic and as requiring (purchased) solutions.

The anti-aging industry can be seen as capitalizing on, and further reinforcing, this phenomenon. Indeed, a key aspect of this industry is the focus on aesthetic anti-aging—communicating the message that we must work on our physical bodies to make them more beautiful and younger-looking, "to minimise, reverse, and even prevent signs of aging altogether" (Brooks, 2010, p. 251). This **beauty work** (also known as *youth work*) can become a kind of moral imperative in a context in which individuals are held responsible for maintaining their physical appearance across the life course.

Some research has sought to connect the macro level of ageist cultural ideals of bodies and physical attractiveness with the micro level of negative individual body image and dissatisfaction among older persons (Hurd Clarke

& Korotchenko, 2011). Cultural ageism may be one reason why older adults tend to distance themselves from identifying as "feeling old" and view their aging bodies as betraying or masking their true selves (Gubrium & Holstein, 2003; Hurd Clarke & Korotchenko, 2011). Hurd Clarke and Griffin (2008) and Calasanti (2005) further argue that women face more social pressure to attain a youthful physical appearance than men do, and they argue that this difference is crucial for understanding the gendered experience of ageism.

Empirical research, however, suggests the connections among age, gender, and body satisfaction are incredibly complex. Consideration of social norms might lead one to assume that older women are more dissatisfied with their physical appearance than older men are. However, some research suggests that body dissatisfaction in both men and women tends to be fairly stable across the lifespan (Kaminski & Hayslip, 2006; Roy & Payette, 2012; Tiggemann, 2004; Webster & Tiggemann, 2003), and to some extent, women's body satisfaction may even become more similar to that of men in old age (Granzoi & Koehler, 1998; Green & Pritchard, 2003; Wilcox, 1997). Further, the importance of physical appearance for one's self-evaluation may decrease with age for both women and men, perhaps in part due to developing cognitive coping strategies as people age (Roy & Payette, 2012; Tiggemann, 2004; Webster & Tiggemann, 2003). In other words, physical appearance—and thus dissatisfaction or satisfaction—becomes less important with age to both men and women as a source of their overall well-being (Dumas, Laberge, & Straka, 2005; Hurd Clarke & Korotchenko, 2011; Roy & Payette, 2012; Tiggemann, 2004).

Algars et al. (2009) examined body image in adults and concluded that "it is insufficient to merely study how age affects general body image because adults might become more satisfied with some aspects of their bodies as a function of age and less satisfied with other aspects" (p. 1112). For example, in a study comparing body image attitudes of 142 older adults and 132 younger adults, Granzoi and Koehler (1998) reported that older adults were less positive than younger adults about their bodily function and facial attractiveness; older women were, however, more satisfied with their weight than younger women were.

Overall, there may be considerable variability and flexibility in body images and satisfaction in old age, and this variability is in part influenced by our social positions or circumstances. Dumas, Laberge, and Straka (2005) applied the work of Pierre Bourdieu to understand social class variability in relation to **embodied habitus**—cultural tastes and practices related to the body, including ways "of treating it, caring for it, feeding it, maintaining it" (Bourdieu, 1984, as cited in Dumas et al., 2005, p. 885). Affluent older women interviewed by Dumas et al. (2005) tended to place more emphasis on their bodily appearance than lower-income women did. In part, this was because the affluent women could afford to purchase anti-aging remedies.

The high-income women in this study appeared to view their physical appearance as distinguishing their social position from that of others. However, older low-income women tended to be satisfied overall with their appearance, perhaps because they valued it less.

Older persons can also exhibit agency in redefining and challenging traditional ideals of physical appearance in their old age. For instance, although age-related weight gain may decrease older women's body satisfaction, those interviewed by Tunaley, Walsh, and Nicolson (1999) tended to reject social pressures, viewing their old age as a time of relative freedom from sexist and ageist norms associated with youthful physical appearance. Likewise, older women interviewed by Dumas et al. (2005), though expressing some unease about age-related physical change, began to accept this change over time and to reassess the dominant ageist norms, even criticizing older women who continued to try to conform to these norms.

In fact, empirical research has documented what might appear as a paradox: older women tend to explicitly reject or express discomfort with ageist beauty norms, while often conforming to them, for instance through the use of anti-aging products and technologies (Brooks, 2010; Hurd Clarke, 2000; Muise & Desmarais, 2010). Hurd Clarke and Griffin (2007, 2008) interviewed 44 older women about their use of cosmetic surgery and products such as hair dye and anti-wrinkle creams. These women were often critical of such products and procedures, praising those who aged naturally, yet most of the women themselves participated in these forms of beauty work. The authors suggest that older women's complicity can be explained by their need to manage gendered ageist stigmas and further suggest that their use of anti-aging techniques can be seen as a sign of agency. Ironically, however, the authors also conclude the following:

> The women's beauty work efforts and acceptance of social norms concerning feminine beauty further entrenched the stereotypes concerning older women and physical attractiveness, and ultimately reinforced the loss of social value that they fought so fervently to maintain. (Hurd Clarke & Griffin, 2008, pp. 669–670)

In a later project, Hurd Clarke, Griffin, and Maliha (2009) noted that older women also similarly used clothing and fashion to compensate for physical realities of aging and to manage ageist stigmas (Twigg, 2007, also considers how clothing can be used to redefine the cultural meaning of age). Their research demonstrates a point made by Gubrium and Holstein (2003), who discuss how "the aging body's objective presence and its meaningful visibility can be socially managed" (p. 209) as part of the presentation of self.

These studies are not alone in suggesting that beauty work can reflect individual agency. Garnham (2013) suggests that receiving cosmetic surgery does not mean denying aging; participants in her study argued that they did not use cosmetic surgery to look younger, but rather they wanted to look better. Drawing on a sociological understanding of a postmodern society, Garnham concludes that cosmetic surgery is actually transformative in that it can serve to challenge overly narrow beliefs about what an older body looks like and to express individual freedom. Similar findings were reported by Brooks (2010), while again drawing on a postmodern understanding of American society. Brooks interviewed women who purchased anti-aging products and services designed to help them look younger and found that these women viewed themselves as fighting the aging process and resisting death and the invisibility of aging. The women viewed these products and services as empowering them to reconstruct themselves, enhancing their sense of control and self-esteem (Brooks, 2010). However, Brooks (2010) also highlights how this aesthetic anti-aging practice can have the unintended effect of reinforcing ageism and a cultural obsession with external appearance. In addition, some older women feel personally responsible, even penalized, for not using these products or services; from this perspective, "aging becomes *their fault*" (Brooks, 2010, p. 247). Brooks (2010) further notes the following:

> Realising the potential for new freedom with age (a freedom, that, in part, can be attributed to the release from the admiring/objectifying male gaze) becomes more difficult as anti-ageing surgeries and technologies gain ground and offer more and more avenues for older women to continue to comply with, and conform to, the normative and disciplinary practices of femininity. (p. 251)

To date, issues of body image and satisfaction have tended to dominate social gerontological research on the aging body. Ageism, and the double standard of aging for women, alongside consumer developments in the anti-aging industry, can shape our experiences of our aging bodies, though empirical research indicates nuance and complexity in this regard. Many older women critique the purchase of products and services and reject the goal of beauty work oriented to youthful physical ideals. However, most women appear to engage in beauty work to varying degrees, further perpetuating these normative standards.

Embodiment and Aging: Towards a Postmodern Understanding of Bodies

Existing research on the topic of aging bodies extends beyond beauty work and aesthetic anti-aging, as Hurd Clarke and Korotchenko (2011) observe. A postmodern understanding of aging bodies infuses much of this research. Whereas a critical gerontologist would focus more on the negative effects of ageism and the double standard of aging, those drawing on a postmodern theoretical approach emphasize agency and the variability and fluidity of individual identity. For instance, as noted in the previous section, Garnham (2013) and Brooks (2010) argue that older women can actively use anti-aging products or services in empowering ways to challenge ageist restrictions on identities in old age. Postmodernist scholars generally critique the one-sided idea that older persons' experiences of and interpretations of bodies are solely the product of social influence (i.e., ageism). The concept of embodiment foregrounds the ways in which older persons also actively shape their own experiences and interpretations of their bodies (Gubrium & Holstein, 2003; Higgs & Jones, 2009; Twigg, 2004; Waskul & Vannini, 2006).

Higgs and Jones (2009) and Gilleard (2005) discuss how we purchase and use anti-aging strategies and technologies to achieve more control over our bodies and exert agency across the life course. They view this process as best understood by examining the culture of postmodern society. Postmodern societies tend to have longer life expectancies and more diverse social norms and individual freedoms; the effect is one of "destabilizing" and diversifying traditionally chronological, age-based expectations about the life course (Jones & Higgs, 2010) and creating space for creative self-construction of identities in old age (Katz & Marshall, 2003). These scholars further imply that ageism is no longer as straightforward as in the past and that older persons have more freedom in shaping their identities in old age.

However, postmodern societies are also increasingly neoliberal and consumer-oriented, and they are characterized by an emphasis on individual choice and responsibility (Gilleard, 2005), including self-control over and maintenance of one's body as an internalized moral imperative (Higgs & Jones, 2009). At the same time, technological advances make a wider number of anti-aging products and services available for purchase by consumers (Gilleard, 2005). This can limit the ways we think about and experience the aging body—that is, as something to be managed or controlled in its physical state. Given the ever-increasing diversity of life course possibilities in postmodern society, Gilleard (2005) argues that old age is increasingly viewed by the public as an individualized experience rather than as a shared experience of a group of people requiring collective solutions.

Moreover, as noted earlier in this chapter, another concern is that the aged body is increasingly seen as a symbol of failure for which one is morally responsible (Higgs & Jones, 2009). Jones and Higgs (2010) further describe how the body is seen from this perspective:

> The postmodern body is a privatized, individualized concern that, while drawn by the promise of escape from modernist notions of normality, is simultaneously caught up in an imperative to attain the unattainable. . . .

[W]hile these may have beneficial outcomes deriving from a rejection of "ageist" assumptions about the older person, they also risk labelling individuals as failures within this new somatic culture. (p. 1518)

We see this phenomenon when considering older women's use of anti-aging strategies as part of beauty work. As a further example, Long (2012) explored how frail older Japanese people use everyday assistive "technologies" (e.g., wheelchairs, hearing aids) not just passively, but creatively "to accomplish personal goals, alter the devices to make them more suitable to their own needs, and negotiate identities" (p. 121). Older persons use these devices, for instance, to resist dependence on other people and maintain both function and status; however, many older persons also express ambivalence or discomfort with relying on these devices, because they serve as reminders or symbols of weakness and loss of independence. The devices themselves can both enhance independence while subtly reinforcing narrow ideals of successful aging. Similar points are made by Joyce and Loe (2010), who emphasize the ways in which older persons creatively use everyday assistive technologies to enrich their lives—making them **technogenarians**.

Social gerontologists—in particular, Canadians Barbara L. Marshall and Stephen Katz—are also interested in new medical and pharmaceutical technologies to address age-related changes in sexual function. Through historical analyses of cultural material (such as advertising) and interviews with older persons, these authors describe how the biomedicalization of aging bodies and the anti-aging movement have contributed to viewing sexual difficulties (such as erectile dysfunction) as a marker of old age and decline (e.g., Marshall, 2009; Marshall & Katz, 2012). A focus on age-related sexual function can also be understood in the context of post-modern society, which "opened the aging body to new forms of intervention based on modification, improvement and enhancement" (Marshall & Katz, 2012, p. 227).

Marshall and Katz (2012) discuss potentially positive outcomes of this attention to sexuality in late life—for instance, it helps counter negative stereotypes of older persons as non-sexual and undesirable, representing a "post-ageist" discourse to "liberate bodies from chronological age" (p. 222). However, this new discourse of sexualized old age also reinforces medicalized views of aging bodies (and the use of drug treatments) and the neoliberal agenda of individual responsibility to manage aging bodies; lastly, it is based on narrow cultural definitions of gender (masculinity, femininity) and youthful heterosexuality that do not always fit with older persons' experiences of intimacy, gender, and sexuality in late life (Katz & Marshall, 2003; Marshall, 2012; Marshall & Katz, 2012).

Embodiment and Aging: Contributions of Symbolic Interactionism

Other research on embodiment and aging bodies draws to a greater extent on the sociological traditions of symbolic interactionism and social constructionism. Indeed, Higgs and Jones (2009) highlight the need for greater integration of sociologist and symbolic interactionist Erving Goffman's work on non-verbal behaviours in face-to-face interactions. Examining these forms of communication can help in understanding how older persons use their bodies to "perform" certain social identities.

Also drawing on a social constructionist tradition, Cheryl Laz (2003) examines how older persons perform their age, albeit in ways that are limited by the physical realities of their bodies. For instance, when Laz asked older persons to reflect on their age, participants responded with frequent claims of being in good health and having active, functioning bodies (e.g., they were able to engage in physical activities such as exercise). The pervasiveness of this kind of response, Laz argues, reflects participants' awareness of activity and function as the normative ideal for older adults in their age range (fifties to seventies), and further reflects the use of this normative ideal in the context of the social interaction of the interview to accomplish or perform age.

Symbolic interactionist frameworks have also drawn attention to how the concept of frailty is socially produced in interactions (Kaufman, 1994). Further, Grenier and Hanley (2007) examine how older women challenge the application of the "frail" label to their bodies, for instance by rejecting it as having meaning for their own personal identity, or even subverting the concept (and its implication of helplessness) by using it strategically in their interactions in order to secure needed funded services to remain independent.

There has also been research on the symbolic, social meanings of incontinence in old age (Brittain & Shaw, 2007; Isaksen, 2002; Mitteness & Barker, 1995). For instance, the loss of control and the bodily disorder associated with incontinence pose a symbolic risk to individual identity, are associated with stigma (for older persons as well as their caregivers), and signify declines associated with aging.

Sociological research on aging bodies also has relevance for the study of formal care work in a variety of settings. Julia Twigg (2000, 2004; Twigg, Wolkowitz, Cohen, & Nettleton, 2011) examines how paid care providers (most often immigrant women) and older persons themselves negotiate the symbolic aspects and power dynamics involved in hands-on, intimate, and "dirty" work done to older bodies, such as bathing and toileting. In addition, Kontos (2005) describes how dementia care tends to be premised on a view of Alzheimer's disease in which the body is treated as passive. Kontos

(2005) argues for an understanding of selfhood as extending beyond the mind to include "the body's power of natural expression" (p. 561) and non-verbal movement, including culturally acquired mannerisms, habits, and gestures. Lastly, Whitaker (2010), in a study of embodiment among dying nursing home residents, reports that the body is an important tool for com-munication—for example, touch can be a way for people to confirm their understanding of what they have been told by another person, or it can be a way for the speaker to communicate in a non-verbal manner. Whitaker (2010) elaborates by stating the following:

> Through their bodies the residents call for a care consisting of bodily atten-tion, confirmation and touch that goes beyond the instrumental and task-oriented "bed-and-body work," but the body also performs the important function of a tool for communication, especially when language does not suffice. (p. 102)

Several researchers (Gubrium & Holstein, 1999; Lawton, 1998; Whitaker, 2010) have further examined how nursing homes and hospice environments shape interpretations and experiences of aging and dying bodies. For example, Gubrium and Holstein (1999) examine the ways that the physical signs of the aged body are monitored and interpreted within the nursing home environment—notably, they observed the use of language associated with decay or passivity (such as "vegetables"). Additionally, Whitaker (2010) analyzes how older nursing home residents speak about their aging and dying bodies. For instance, in the context of nursing homes, the idea of death is an ever-present reminder, and bodies are the focus of the majority of care work; residents describe their awareness that they are slowly dying in a physical sense.

Considering the intersection between embodiment and aging, both postmodern and symbolic interactionist perspectives serve to remind us that we participate not just as passive objects (i.e., as beings shaped by broader discourses and structural constraints), but as active subjects (i.e., as observ-ing beings with individual agency and fluid, diverse identities).

The Biomedicalization of Aging as a Disease

The physical appearances of aging bodies are often viewed as reflections of people's inner health, and older bodies tend to be viewed as diseased (Kaufman, 1994). A process called biomedicalization contributes to this way of thinking. The **biomedical model** views a disease as having one specific, physical, objective[1] cause that manifests in the body of the individual, and as requiring medical treatment or intervention to control or remove the cause, thereby curing the disease (Chappell, Gee, McDonald, & Stones, 2003).

This is the dominant paradigm of Western medicine and culture, which emphasizes rational control and technical solutions. The biomedical model shapes health care service delivery, which is founded on a reductionistic and curative, acute care approach—even though this approach is of questionable appropriateness for older populations, who tend to experience more chronic, incurable diseases and non-specific medical conditions with multiple causal factors (see Chapter 4).

Biomedicalization refers to a social process whereby a particular behaviour, event, or condition becomes interpreted and labelled as a medical problem that requires medical treatment (Clarke, Shim, Mamo, Fosket, & Fishman, 2003). This process has a historical dimension: more and more conditions that were not previously medicalized now tend to be interpreted from this perspective, such as childbirth, alcoholism, obesity, or dementia. The biomedicalization process tends to obscure attention to broader social causes of particular behaviours as well as social determinants of illness (see Chapter 4). For instance, homeless persons may exhibit behaviours that are considered unusual or socially inappropriate—these behaviours can originate to some extent from the context of their lives and daily challenges, and could therefore be seen as normal adaptation. However, from a biomedical perspective, such behaviours can become defined as mental illness indicating biological problems within the individual. Indeed, medicalization can be a societal response to controlling deviant or socially problematic behaviours in groups of people, through redefining these behaviours as requiring medical treatment and surveillance.

Critical gerontologists Carroll L. Estes and Elizabeth A. Binney applied the concept of biomedicalization to aging in 1989, when they described it as composed of two mutually reinforcing phenomena: first, the social construction of old age itself as a disease or sickness requiring medical treatment (e.g., a view of the problems of aging as primarily individual problems of biology and physiology); and second, the related behaviours, practices, and policies that result from this perspective. The latter can include an institutional emphasis on policies and research funding that support a biomedical view on aging, as well as a tendency in practice settings to treat older persons as if they are little more than their disease, as opposed to using a holistic or person-centred approach.

Many age-related conditions have been cited as examples of the biomedicalization of aging, including Alzheimer's disease and dementia (Bond, 1992; Robertson, 1990). Memory loss and related behaviours have been increasingly viewed as symptomatic of disease rather than a part of normal aging (Miller, Glasser, & Rubin, 1992). For example, drawing on a social constructionist perspective, Bond (1992) explains how the problematic behaviours associated with dementia were, over time, defined as a medical problem. Likewise, Moreira, May, and Bond (2009) trace a growing interest among clinicians, researchers, and drug companies in identifying earlier signs in those at risk of developing Alzheimer's disease, in order to target these populations for early treatment. These potential "early signs" or symptoms have now been termed **mild cognitive impairment**. Yet some researchers have suggested that the biomedicalization of dementia is problematic because of the considerable uncertainty surrounding the disease's clinical diagnosis, biological causes and trajectory, and the lack of an effective cure or clinical treatment (Bond, 1992; Miller et al., 1992). For instance, Miller et al. (1992) noted that this perspective creates situations in which "family expectations of medical intervention have increased beyond the capacity of the medical profession" (p. 135) to manage and treat the condition.

Drawing on a symbolic interactionist perspective and on labelling theory, Bond (1992) and Lyman (1989) also explain how a label of "dementia patient" facilitates control by medical authorities, for instance because patients' and families' perspectives regarding cognitive status are not accorded much weight in comparison to standardized clinical assessments. Further, the label affects how families, health care providers, and others behave towards the person in social interactions (e.g., social exclusion, infantilization), and how they interpret the behaviours of the person as "evidence" of their diagnosis. This in turn affects the self-concept of persons labelled as having dementia, which can shape their behaviours, becoming a **self-fulfilling prophecy** (e.g., generating dependency and learned helplessness) and promoting stigmatization.

These kinds of social or contextual contributors to the behaviours and cognitive symptoms of dementia tend to be obscured in the biomedical focus on physical pathology (Bond, 1992; Lyman, 1989). For instance, a family caregiver who is facing a number of competing responsibilities in his or her life and experiencing a high sense of burden may interpret certain behaviours as more problematic than another caregiver. In this way, societal factors shaping the resources and support available for family caregivers can have implications for family and system responses to the labelling, diagnosis, and treatment of older persons with dementia. Further, if the older person is institutionalized, the institutional care environment itself might be an external stressor that exacerbates cognitive and behavioural symptoms; in turn, these symptoms are interpreted as evidence of ongoing physical decline.

Another age-related condition that has been cited as an example of biomedicalization is menopause. Rebecca Utz (2011) describes how over time, menopause is less often viewed as a natural transition in late life, but as a hormonal deficit or problem that requires medical intervention. In her study, older women tended to talk about menopause as a developmental change that simply happened to them and was accepted as a fact of life; their younger daughters tended to talk about it as a disease requiring pharmaceutical treatment and delay (Utz, 2011). Utz (2011) describes this as an example of how the media and pharmaceutical industry shape women's subjective experiences of their aging bodies over time.

Salter et al. (2011) further explain how new emerging technologies are leading to the increased ability to identify those at risk of (but not having yet developed) osteoporosis; they suggest this diagnostic expansion reflects the extension of biomedical perspectives to include pre-disease states. There are important implications for the identity of older persons labelled in these new ways, even in the absence of physical manifestations or symptoms. These researchers interviewed older British women who had recently been notified that they were at increased risk of developing osteoporosis, and they documented the women's concern, surprise, and fear, as well as how "the detection of fracture risk brought to the fore socially resisted representations of ageing bodies" (Salter et al., 2011, p. 813).

The process of biomedicalization is facilitated by several factors, including physician dominance and profit motives, public faith in science, and fear of the biological realities of aging (Estes & Binney, 1989). For instance, Clarke, Shim, Mamo, Fosket, and Fishman (2003) outline how the increasing power of multinational corporations in the health care and pharmaceutical sectors contributes to and is further reinforced by cultural biomedicalization. Clarke et al. suggest that medicalization has a particular intensity given the increase in various technical and biological innovations in postmodern society, generating new possibilities and identities. This includes innovations such as the following: those helping to detect new "at-risk" populations for particular diseases; genetic therapies; information technology in health care management; hybrid and bionic devices; cosmetic surgeries; and other anti-aging technologies. Clarke et al. (2003) suggest that given the increasing possibilities, "human bodies are no longer expected to adhere to a single universal norm. Rather, a multiplicity of norms is increasingly deemed medically expected and acceptable" (p. 161).

Biomedicalization is essentially a **double-edged sword**, meaning that it has both positive and negative effects. In consideration to the positive effects, some researchers have suggested that biomedicalization challenges previous ageist beliefs that certain conditions (e.g., incontinence, dementia, erectile dysfunction) are normal and inevitable parts of aging, and thus individuals with these conditions do not require treatment or care (Lyman, 1989). However, Kaufman, Shim, and Russ (2004, 2006; Shim, Russ, & Kaufman, 2006) claim that old age has in fact been so biomedicalized that a medical approach to aging is the new "normal." Their concern is with a tendency to accept medical and life-saving interventions (e.g., cardiac procedures, kidney dialysis and transplant) without question at later and later ages. Such interventions also provide families and patients with much-needed hope, which facilitates the medicalization process. Kaufman et al. (2006) suggest that not only age-related conditions but aging itself is no longer seen as inevitable, which raises concerns about the cost implications for health care. The authors' claims of the normalization of medical treatment for older adults remain to be conclusively determined based on empirical data. Instead, for instance, there may be implicit **age-based rationing** in clinical decisions about medical treatments and interventions for older persons, whereby public health care services and treatment decisions favour younger patients and impose limits on the levels or types of services accessible to older patients. Concerns over the appropriateness of medical treatments and interventions for older persons have been expressed at the policy level in recent years with a strong emphasis on implementing policies requiring older persons to have **advance directives**—for instance, upon admission to a personal care home or long-term care facility (Gilleard & Higgs, 1998; Johri, Damschroder, Zikmund-Fisher, & Ubel, 2005; Kane & Kane, 2005).

As noted earlier, biomedicalization can promote a very narrow, limited view of age-related conditions and situations that limits our experiences and interpretations of aging bodies; it also promotes a reliance on pharmaceutical and technical solutions to these problems and ignores broader contexts—including social, cultural, economic, and political influences—that shape age-related concerns on a larger scale. For instance, negative assumptions that equate age with sickness, and result in fear about the needs and demands of the aging population, can function as political and ideological tools to facilitate particular policy actions such as rationing or the erosion of publicly funded health and social services (Estes & Binney, 1991; Gee, 2000). These policy actions, as critical gerontologists note, tend to serve private, profit-making interests; the effect is also to draw attention away from issues of appropriateness, effectiveness, and accountability in existing services (Evans et al., 2001). Biomedicalization, in other words, contributes to apocalyptic demography (discussed in Chapter 2).

Approaching aging as a medical problem can also erode older persons' own agency and autonomy, by consolidating power with medical professionals and service providers (Robertson, 1999). Aging is seen as treatable by medical services, and the dominant discourse is one of individual-level needs and risks, as defined by the economic interests of those who might profit directly and indirectly (Estes, 1999b). In a postmodern society, however, biomedicalization may take a slightly different form—that of **governmentality**, reflecting a society in which the interests of the neoliberal state are internalized and embedded within individuals who take moral responsibility for monitoring and preventing *their own* individual risk through the purchase of products and services (Clarke et al., 2003). Moreover, the ability to purchase these products and services depends on one's income, which generates new inequalities.

From a political economy perspective, the biomedicalization of aging reflects and further expands the power of biomedical professions and medical industries in society, by transforming "the health needs of the aging into com-modities for specific economic markets" (Estes, Wallace, Linkins, & Binney, 2001, p. 51). In the next section, we consider the anti-aging industry, which was developed for this purpose.

Life Extension: A Sociological Perspective

Earlier in this chapter, we discussed how one component of the anti-aging industry is the focus on aesthetic appearances of aging bodies—for instance, cosmetic surgeries. However, there are also anti-aging researchers seeking to distinguish themselves as a legitimate form of science, as well as those addressing the question of how to extend the human lifespan. The topic of life extension, and its potential societal implications, will be discussed in the following sections.

The Anti-Aging Movement

The **anti-aging movement** directly reflects the biomedicalization of aging, and it emerged in its current form most strongly during the 1990s in Western industrialized societies (especially the US). It has been strongly fuelled by the public's desire to extend life, which commercial markets and the mass media respond to and further promote (Moody, 2001–2002; Spindler & Streubel, 2009). The movement generally encompasses various private eco-nomic aims—including an anti-aging industry of products and services—and some more academic objectives, such as anti-aging science. As such, Vincent (2009) describes the anti-aging movement as incredibly diverse, consisting of established scientists, profit-seeking corporations, and "new-age entrepre-neurs selling herbal elixirs" (p. 197).

The academic field of anti-aging "draws heavily upon research into molecular, endocrine and cell activity and an array of technologies and theories such as nanotechnology, stem cell research, genetic enhancement, neuro-endocrine theory, and pharmacotherapy" (Kampf & Bothelo, 2009, p. 189). The field has long been trying to establish itself as a legitimate sci-ence, but it has faced harsh criticisms from gerontologists who critique this work, in part because gerontologists want to preserve their own power and to distinguish themselves from the anti-aging movement. There is a ten-dency to associate the field of anti-aging with its marketization and in some extremes with fraudulent claims and potentially risky products. Binstock (2003) cites this as a sociological example of how groups compete for power and boundaries, maintaining in-group and out-group status. In other words, the critique of anti-aging medicine, albeit a useful way to promote evidence-informed opinion, represents an example of **boundary work**. Boundary work occurs in this example because the anti-aging movement threatens the legitimacy of gerontological research due to some similarities between these fields—ultimately, the issue is "about defining the boundaries of the subject, who can count as a *bona fide* scientist of old age, and who can claim knowledge about old age" (Vincent, 2006, p. 683).

The anti-aging movement hinges on the idea that aging itself (i.e., as opposed to simply age-related disease) is a modifiable or even reversible disease that can respond to treatments and medical innovations—in other words, the movement argues that we can "intervene in the aging process to slow, stop, or reverse growing old" (Kampf & Bothelo, 2009, p. 188). As Gilleard and Higgs (1998) note, anti-aging can be seen as a continuum between the softest biomedical solutions to promote successful aging and the more extreme anti-aging proponents that seek to extend the human lifespan, or enhance **prolongevity**. Vincent (2006) similarly identifies one branch of anti-aging science focused on aesthetic or physical appearance, another focused on specific medical diseases associated with old age, and two others focused on increasing the human lifespan at a more biological level—at the most extreme, seeking immortality. The work of British biogerontologist Aubrey de Grey is an example of the latter perspective; de Grey claims that biological aging can be "cured" and that we can envision lifespans of up to 1,000 years old (for instance, watch his 2006 TED Talk, "A Roadmap to End Aging," listed at the end of this chapter). The issue of life extension continues to capture public attention; for instance, a May 2013 *National Geographic* cover story featured a baby's photo and the caption, "This baby will live to be 120" (Hall, 2013). In Box 3.1, we examine two contrasting ways in which life extension has been depicted within *National Geographic*.

Box 3.1   Life Extension Possibilities: Genes or Social Environments?

Geographically and/or genetically isolated populations whose members are particularly long lived—sometimes partly due to specific disease-protective gene mutations, healthy daily lifestyles, or health-promoting cultural values—are of particular interest to life-extension researchers. Examples of such populations include those of Molochio, in southern Italy; the province of Nuoro, in Sardinia, Italy; the Nicoya Peninsula, in Costa Rica; Loma Linda, in California; the island of Ikaria, in Greece; the province of El Oro, in Ecuador; and the prefecture of Okinawa, Japan, as well as the Old Order Amish in Pennsylvania and the Ashkenazi Jews. Researchers hope that these and other such populations provide clues as to the "keys" of life extension.

Some research focuses on genetic mutations that are protective against age-related and life-limiting conditions, such as cancer and diabetes (e.g., Hall, 2013). In

Continued

contrast, Dan Buettner (2012) highlights the importance of the ways of living that are strongly embedded within particular social environments. In an article for *The New York Times*, Buettner describes his work with *National Geographic* on studying populations around the world where people live the longest. From his research, he concludes that diet, rewarding activity, spirituality, and a sense of purpose and community are important for increased life expectancy, but he argues that these factors are nurtured through strongly rooted cultural traditions, social norms, communal ways of life, and geographic features. For example, on the Greek island of Ikaria, "the cheapest, most accessible foods are also the most healthful—and . . . your ancestors have spent centuries developing ways to make them taste good." Further, "It's hard to get through the day in Ikaria without walking up 20 hills." Buettner concludes by stating, "the power of such an environment lies in the mutually reinforcing relationships among lots of small nudges and default choices."

Ironically, however, Buettner's more recent work appears to emphasize individual responsibility for living a long life, as reflected in the following claim on the website for his company Blue Zones (http://www.bluezones.com): "80% of living longer is in your control. Learn how."

Source: Summary of Buettner, D. (2012, October 24). The island where people forget to die. *The New York Times.* Retrieved from http://www.nytimes.com

Anti-aging science has long been dismissed as lacking feasibility, in the absence of substantial or convincing evidence that aging can be delayed. For instance, some evidence suggests that drastic caloric restricted diets may be one means of effectively extending human lifespans, although this hypothesis has also been called into question—and no research has been conducted with humans (Heilbronn & Ravussin, 2003; Sohal & Forster, 2014). However, Mykytyn (2010) suggests the legitimacy of the anti-aging movement is increasing due to recent progress made in the field—even some previously skeptical gerontologists, for instance, are now cautiously optimistic about the potential for life extension. Nevertheless, public attitudes towards life extension are surprisingly complex: in one Australian study (Partridge, Lucke, Bartlett, & Hall, 2011), survey findings indicated that though the majority (65 per cent) of the public supported life-extension research, only 35 per cent of respondents stated that they would use a hypothetical life-extending pharmaceutical (e.g., to extend life up to 150 years) if it was available (see also Figure 3.1 for a humourous perspective).

As Vincent (2008) points out, the idea of aging as a disease to be avoided (and not part of the natural life cycle) may be inherently ageist, but anti-aging science can enhance the variety of physical possibilities in older age and may help to free older persons from structured dependency—that is, from the dependency generated by the internalization of ageist stereotypes (Gilleard & Higgs, 1998). In other words, in a postmodern society, bodies

"My goal is to die before there's a technology breakthrough that forces me to live to a hundred and thirty."

Figure 3.1 Aging humour: Not everyone is excited about the potential of life extension technology . . .
Source: Barbara Smaller/The New Yorker Collection/The Cartoon Bank

have fewer limits; however, there is also a tendency towards the individualization of life extension, whereby the onus is now on individuals to purchase particular strategies to delay their physical aging (Gilleard & Higgs, 1998).

Societal Implications of Prolongevity

If we were to radically extend the human lifespan, what would our society look like? This question is of particular interest to sociologists—as well as science fiction writers (see Box 3.2). In a survey of Australians by Partridge, Lucke, Bartlett, and Hall (2011), 47.8 per cent of respondents reported that life-extending technologies "would do more harm than good to society overall" (p. 78), although 42.3 per cent disagreed with this statement and 9.9 per cent were unsure.

> **Box 3.2**
>
> ### Science Fiction and the Sociology of Aging: Bruce Sterling's *Holy Fire*
>
> In the fictional story *Holy Fire*, Sterling explores issues of population aging and life extension, and their implications for society. The society he envisions is controlled by a cautious, paternalistic **gerontocracy** and medical-industrial professionals. Advanced biotechnologies have allowed life extension to become the norm. Individuals choose their particular means of life extension or "upgrades" from an ever-changing array of possible technologies: "the pursuit of longevity was declared a fundamental free-dom left to the choice of the individual. . . . [I]f you were smart or lucky, you chose an upgrade path with excellent long-term potential" (p. 59). Being "easily maintained" in one's old age, however, and not straining existing government resources, is viewed as an important virtue, resulting in an older generation that is incredibly responsible and cautious with their health. Younger persons themselves are marginalized and devalued within this society. The government is "a plague-panicked allocation society in which the whip hand of coercive power was held by smiling and stout-hearted med-ical rescue personnel. And by social workers. And by very nice older people" (p. 62). The main character, 94-year-old Mia Ziemann, has enjoyed her privileged position and life of routine until she decides she wants to recapture the pleasure and adventure of her youth and undergoes an experimental procedure to return to her youth, becoming a fugitive as a result.
>
> Source: Summary of Sterling, B. (1996). *Holy Fire.* New York, NY: Bantam.

Several moral and ethical concerns have been raised about the pursuit of prolongevity, and some researchers have suggested that societies require limits on the human lifespan (Gilleard & Higgs, 1998). Many of these pos-itions implicitly reflect a structural-functionalist perspective in their con-cern for how changes in the age structure of society could affect the function of its key social institutions and roles. Moody (2001–2002) raises several intriguing propositions: for instance, in a society with radically extended human lives, we would be able to envision our lives as leading farther into the future, which would promote a desire to preserve the environment and our personal health, and to build private savings. Moody (2001–2002) fur-ther notes that marriage would no longer be "a lifelong commitment but a 'renewable contract' in 50-year increments" (p. 34).

One of the most obvious concerns with prolongevity is the potential for global overpopulation and related social and environmental consequences (Hayflick, 2000; Moody, 2001–2002). From a structural-functionalist per-spective, longer lives might also result in societal imbalance, due to problems with housing, health care, and pensions (D. Callahan, 1987; Dumas & Turner, 2007; Moody, 2001–2002). This argument should remind you of apocalyptic demography (discussed in Chapter 2). For instance, there are claims that longer lives would overwhelm our "carrying capacity for healthcare and social support and [produce] imponderable consequences" (Moody, 2001–2002, p. 35). Further, it is argued that there would be "radical changes" in society to "virtually every social institution" (Binstock, 2004, p. 531), which would "[threaten] traditional institutions" (Dumas & Turner, 2007, p. 14). Alex Dumas and Bryan Turner (2007) argue that the current increases in life expectancy that are occurring in industrialized societies provide evidence that there will be negative outcomes for pensions and health care, and they assert that societal resource distribution would only be exacerbated if lifespans were dramatically increased.

Dumas and Turner (2007) provide further illustration of a Durkheimian structural-functionalist response to prolongevity by suggesting that extending lifespans would also threaten traditional societal values. They suggest that for older persons, disease and decline are normal because they are "timely," and that we should not expect health in old age as we do in youth; to do so is against the "universal order of the human maturation process" (Dumas & Turner, 2007, p. 10).

Another concern with a life-extended society centres on the existential and psychological impacts, including the loss of meaning and sense of purpose to life, as well as boredom (Kass, 2001). Moody (2001–2002) suggests that these factors may generate social pathology. This claim hinges on the idea that life would lose meaning without (timely) death.

It should be evident that many scholars have expressed concern that the effects of prolongevity would inevitably be negative. However, the actual effects are unknown, and proponents of the negative viewpoint often make sweeping generalizations with few specific details about the underlying mechanisms that would produce negative outcomes. Further, the effects of prolongevity may not necessarily be all negative.

Perhaps a more valid concern regarding prolongevity centres around the possibility that life-extending interventions might be quite expensive. As a result, it is quite possible that individuals would be responsible for incurring considerable private costs in order to extend their lives. For many gerontologists, this raises concerns of equity and social justice—in other words, it becomes necessary to consider who would be able to pay for a longer life, and who would be left out (Binstock, 2004; Dumas & Turner, 2007; Ehni & Marckmann, 2009). Stronger and more powerful countries, social groups, and individuals would be able to pay for this privilege, strengthening the gap between wealthy and poor. Dumas and Turner (2007) suggest that this inequality could contribute to increased conflict between social groups over existing resources. Further, given the already wide gap in life expectancy between developing and industrialized countries (e.g., due to poor living conditions and higher infant mortality rates in industrialized countries), they argue that "it is morally unjustified to value some lives more than others, to value the addition of extra years to already long lives rather than to add extra years to those whose lives are relatively short as a result of existing social inequality" (Dumas & Turner, 2013, p. 71).

In addition, there are concerns that the current anti-aging quest for pro-longevity contributes to the cultural devaluing of old age as a biological failure, and to ageism, with negative consequences for the ongoing experience of older persons in society (Vincent, 2006, 2009). Due to its reductionist focus on biology, attention to prolongevity contributes to the ongoing ignorance of other features—including behavioural, cultural, and socio-economic factors—that affect our life expectancies (Kampf & Bothelo, 2009) and our quality of life.

If one looks closely enough at discussions of life extension in the public sphere as well as in the research literature, a **boundary problem**[2] emerges (Moody, 2001–2002): it appears as though life-extending technologies become confused and conflated with life-saving, health promoting, and disease-curing technologies. For example, medical advances might, through reducing cancer rates, increase our life expectancies, but this is a distinct endeavour from trying to identify and change the biological basis of aging (or "senescence," as it is sometimes called). As Moody (2001–2002) notes, "we can't easily distinguish anti-aging technology (bad) from health promotion interventions (good), which most of us take for granted" (p. 37). Indeed, many of us may already be using some form of anti-aging technology, if anti-wrinkle creams and hip-replacement surgeries are included in our definition. The distinction is between the biology of aging itself and age-related physical changes, symptoms, and health conditions.

In sum, sociologists play an important role in research that examines the emergence of the anti-aging movement within its broader social context, including its relationship to the discipline of gerontology and its role as both a key driver and outcome of biomedicalization. Sociologists have also, though to a lesser extent, considered the societal implications of prolongevity and how a drastically long-lived population might change human societies.

Conclusion

Topics such as embodiment, biomedicalization, and life extension have tended to receive little attention in mainstream social gerontology textbooks, which devote little space to reviewing these concepts. Drawn together by a focus on aging bodies, however, these concepts are important for a sociological endeavour that seeks to link the micro level of experience and inter-pretation of aging bodies to the broader cultural and societal contexts in which we live. They are also helpful concepts for exploring how the ways we think about aging bodies are constrained by these contexts. For instance, an examination of how aging and dying bodies are interpreted and responded to in residential care environments reveals the shared symbolic meanings that can structure our experiences of and care for these bodies. However, individuals also seek to actively navigate social and cultural constraints, for example by resisting ageist ideals of youthful physical appearance and func-tion even as they reproduce these same ideals in their use of anti-aging prod-ucts, services, and technologies. This endeavour, though, generates new inequalities in a consumer society whereby one's ability to purchase these services is dependent on personal income.

The biomedicalization of aging and various age-related conditions is an important feature of our contemporary society, and it is concerning from a sociological perspective, which emphasizes the need to consider broader social, political, and economic forces and structural constraints shaping age-related processes and our responses to aging populations. Whether or not we might see a future in which aging is no longer viewed as a medical disease is a topic for speculation. For instance, just as there is a trend towards demedical-izing childbirth, we might see emerging interest in issues such as **palliative care** and **death doulas** that call for a return to an approach that views dying in particular as a natural feature of life that should not be avoided. Possibly, this could also influence perceptions of aging, although there is a risk that returning to a view of aging as "natural" could generate additional problems (e.g., limiting older persons' access to life-extending surgeries or procedures). Advances in biotechnology that might radically extend the human lifespan continue to spark hopes in the general population, however, suggesting the ongoing dominance of anti-aging in the near future. By moving beyond a simplistic view of the consequences of population life extension as "all good" or "all bad," sociologists can help us consider how life extension might change human societies in complex and nuanced ways.

Questions for Critical Thought

1. Do you believe that the use of anti-aging products reflects our freedom to redefine and challenge age-related expectations, or do these products reinforce ageist norms of beauty? What evidence supports your belief?

2. How does a sociological perspective lead one to critique the biomedical model as individ-ualistic and reductionist?

3. What evidence supports or refutes the idea that even today (including in Canada), the public is convinced that aging is primarily a medical problem to be managed by medical professionals?

4. What other changes could occur in a society with advanced prolongevism? Try considering the impacts on one particular social institution in detail. What are the assumptions behind your conclusions?

5. Moody (2001–2002) asks his readers to imagine that a new "magic pill" has become available that would extend your life with no side effects. Would you take this pill? Why or why not?

Suggested Readings

Estes, C. L., & Binney, E. A. (1989). The biomedicalization of aging: Dangers and dilemmas. *The Gerontologist, 29*(5), 587–596. This work is a classic for those interested in the biomedicalization of aging. Although the authors are drawing on a number of examples from the United States, the phenomenon also has resonance in Canada. The authors utilize a critical gerontological approach and clearly explain, alongside concrete examples, how aging has been socially constructed as a medical problem, as well as how this social construction has been in part driven by and further reinforces the development of scientific knowledge and professional practice in gerontology, health and research policy and funding priorities, and public attitudes towards aging.

Kontos, P., & Martin, W. (2013). Embodiment and dementia: Exploring critical narratives of selfhood, surveillance, and dementia care. *Dementia, 12*(3), 288–302. The authors examine the importance of the concept of embodiment for the study and care of those with dementia, including how we understand the social production of dementia and the meaning of "selfhood" for those with dementia. Further, they review the ways in which older, "chaotic" bodies are managed, regulated, and supervised in residential care environments, as well as the ways that innovative approaches to dementia care (such as music programs, dance therapy, and elder-clowning) are drawing on an understanding of embodiment and non-verbal expression.

Twigg, J. (2004). The body, gender, and age: Feminist insights in social gerontology. *Journal of Aging Studies, 18*, 59–73. In this article, Julia Twigg emphasizes the importance of studying how embodiment intersects with both age and gender, drawing on feminist theoretical insights and the work of Michel Foucault. In particular, she explores these theoretical ideas in relation, for instance, to how older people experience the receipt of intimate personal care in old age, and how paid care involves bodies as the object of a worker's labour.

Vincent, J. A. (2006). Ageing contested: Anti-ageing science and the cultural construction of old age. *Sociology, 40*(4), 681–698. John Vincent provides an overview of the field of anti-aging science and the biogerontological focus on life extension, as well as explores how, within the various debates on this topic, the language and rhetoric that is used can indicate the particular meanings of old age that are culturally constructed in these debates. For instance, a key issue of debate is over whether old age should be understood as a disease or as a natural process.

Relevant Websites

American Academy of Anti-Aging Medicine
http://www.a4m.com/
> Navigating this website provides insight into the field of anti-aging medicine and its key concerns, as well as how it seeks to legitimize itself as a discipline.

Mayo Clinic, "Aging: What to Expect"
http://www.mayoclinic.org/healthy-living/healthy-aging/in-depth/aging/art-20046070
> This website is a great example of the current trend towards governmentality, or the ways in which individuals are made responsible for delaying or preventing age-related conditions. This site provides a brief overview of common age-related changes to our bodies and then entreats readers to take steps now to prevent these changes. After reading through this website, reflect on how you feel about aging. What kind of view of aging is represented in this material? Consider the various structural constraints that may make it easier for some people, more than others, to implement the strategies mentioned here.

National Geographic Feature, "The Secrets of Long Life"
http://ngm.nationalgeographic.com/ngm/0511/feature1/index.html
> This accompaniment to *National Geographic*'s work with Dan Buettner on the keys to long life features a photo gallery, Buettner's field notes, related resources and websites, and a short video ("Sights and Sounds").

TED Talks, "Aubrey de Grey: A Roadmap to End Aging"
http://www.ted.com/talks/aubrey_de_grey_says_we_can_avoid_aging
> In this accessible 2005 TED Talk, biogerontologist Aubrey de Grey elaborates on his view that aging is a curable disease.

4 Health Systems and Care for Older Persons

Learning Objectives

In this chapter, you will learn that:

◎ declines in health that can accompany aging are not inevitable or universal, and we need to be cautious in equating age with illness.

◎ personal health and needs for care across the life course are influenced by social determinants, processes, and contexts, such as the distribution of income.

◎ over the last several decades, demographic, political, and economic changes have reoriented health systems with a focus on promoting and supporting older persons to remain and be cared for at home as long as possible.

◎ the needs of older adults who receive formal care services in residential or institutional care settings are becoming more complex.

◎ as older persons' needs for care increase, they draw on both informal and formal sources of support; the latter generally do not reduce the amount of care provided by family and friends.

◎ a sociological perspective can illustrate how the individual experiences and well-being of older recipients of care services, their families, and paid and unpaid care workers are connected to broader policies, practices, and contexts.

Introduction

From a sociological perspective, **health** can be viewed as the outcome of a reciprocal relationship involving mutual influence between micro and macro levels, or between *individual agency* and *social structure* (Robertson & Minkler, 1994). In other words, our health is shaped by structural forces at the macro level—such as the distribution of income in a society or the organization of the health care system—but the concept of health is given personal meaning at the individual level, for instance in how individuals subjectively interpret their symptoms.

In Chapters 2 and 3, we discussed the problems with a narrow view of old age as equated with illness, the biomedicalization of age, and the tendency to assume that aging populations will "bankrupt" our publicly funded health care system (e.g., the concept of apocalyptic demography). In this chapter, we will address some issues that can arise with the health and care of older persons, but we do not want to recreate these narrow perspectives of aging.

As such, we will start by emphasizing that "declines associated with aging are neither inevitable nor universal" (Stahl & Feller, 1990, p. 25). In contrast to narrow definitions of health that focus on life expectancy or the absence of illness, most Canadians prefer broader definitions that also encompass the following: dealing well with existing illness; overall mental and physical fitness; psychological, emotional, and spiritual well-being and quality of life; and being able to continue to perform normal roles and tasks (Segall & Chappell, 2000). This broader perspective aligns with the World Health Organization's (1948) definition of health as "a state of complete physical, mental and social well-being and not merely the absence of disease or infirmity." By these definitions, many older persons tend to rate their own health quite highly (Baltes & Carstensen, 1996) and could be defined as aging successfully (Phelan, Anderson, Lacroix, & Larson, 2004; Roos & Havens, 1998; Rowe & Kahn, 1997). Although the risk of chronic conditions and activity restrictions generally increases with age, psychological well-being generally improves; further, though the risk of dementia increases with age, only an estimated 6 to 8 per cent of those over age 65 are diagnosed with this condition (Chappell et al., 2003).

Ill health is not an inevitable result of age but is related to lifestyle and the accumulation of external factors such as socio-economic status, as will be discussed in this chapter. In fact, with age, "the force of nongenetic factors [in determining health status] increases" (Rowe & Kahn, 1997, p. 436) relative to genetic factors. Lastly, as discussed in Chapter 2, apocalyptic demography persists despite the possibility that aging baby boomers might turn out to be healthier than previous cohorts and despite research demonstrating that the impact of the aging population on health care systems will be negligible compared to other factors (Evans et al., 2001; Fries, 1980).

In this chapter, we will first introduce the concept of the social determinants of health as persisting across the life course and into old age, before reviewing some contextual background information on Canada's health care system and the intersections among self-, informal, and formal care for older persons. Following this, the bulk of the chapter will focus on issues related to the delivery of formal (paid) and informal (unpaid, family and volunteer) care to older persons, with an emphasis on a sociological perspective.

The Social Determinants of Health

Contrary to popular assumptions, our diet, physical activity, and risk behaviours are not the primary determinants of our health across the life course and into old age. Neither, in fact, is the health care system. Rather, a wide range of **social determinants of health** have powerful influences on our health both directly and indirectly, and these determinants can generate inequalities in health outcomes in the Canadian population. Broadly, social determinants of health include the following examples: internal colonialism and Aboriginal status; employment and working conditions; access to and availability of healthy food; housing conditions; social inclusion and exclusion (see Chapter 6); and the distribution of income in a society (Mikkonen & Raphael, 2010). An illustrative model of how social determinants operate along with other micro-level determinants of health can be seen in Figure 4.1.

The concept of social structure helps us better understand how social determinants shape our health and can result in health inequalities. Social structure highlights how our society is organized, including our systems of statuses, meanings, roles, obligations, and rights (Chappell et al., 2003), as well as policies, practices, and political and economic foundations (Coburn & Eakin, 1998). For instance, Pinquart and Sorensen (2000) conclude that socio-economic status (especially income) is positively associated with subjective well-being among older persons. Low income and education levels are also strongly associated with older persons' likelihood of entering a residential care facility (Asakawa, Feeny, Senthilselvan, Johnson, & Rolfson, 2009; Trottier, Martel, Houle, Berthelot, & Légaré, 2000). Indeed, individuals of

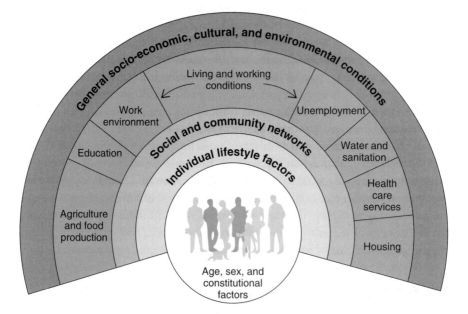

Figure 4.1 Dahlgren and Whitehead's model of health determinants
Source: Dahlgren G, Whitehead M. (1991). Policies and Strategies to Promote Social Equity in Health. Stockholm, Sweden: Institute for Futures Studies. http://www.iffs.se/wp-content/uploads/2011/01/20080109110739filmZ8UVQv2wQFShMRF6cuT.pdf

higher socio-economic status are consistently healthier than those who are less advantaged: this phenomenon is termed the **social gradient**. Though personal income levels can be viewed as an individual achievement or characteristic, a sociological perspective considers the root causes of how our society is organized politically and economically. Social structural conditions shape individuals' access to resources—such as money, power, status, and social support—in systematic ways. Social structure is thus a fundamental, underlying cause of health inequalities, as individuals are differentially exposed to both environmental and behavioural risk factors (Link & Phelan, 1996).

Specifically, **absolute material disadvantage**—the inability to meet the most basic, universal needs for survival (e.g., food, clothing, shelter, water, sanitation)—can have a direct negative effect on health by influencing our circumstances and living conditions, including access to and affordability of nutritious foods, housing and utilities, and transportation. Material disadvantage can also have an indirect negative effect on health, through shaping our lifestyle choices and behaviours (Chappell et al., 2003). For example, despite similar levels of motivation for smoking cessation, more low-income people continue to smoke: there is some indication that material deprivation is associated with increased psychological dependence to nicotine, making it more difficult to stop smoking (Jarvis & Wardle, 2002). As another example, visible minority women with diabetes tend to lack the resources needed to restructure their daily lives in a way that helps them manage their condition and integrate healthy habits: these resources include money, work flexibility and security, the ability to interact with health care providers, and access to information (Anderson, Blue, & Lau, 1998).

The social and psychological consequences of living in poverty, as a social position irrespective of access to material resources, can also have negative effects on our well-being (Shaw, Dorling, & Davey Smith, 2002). In a capitalist society, income is the primary marker of social status or relative position; research confirms that **relative material disadvantage**—that is, disadvantage in one's material circumstances relative to others in the population—has direct negative health effects (Wilkinson, 2002). In this respect, research suggests that processes of social comparison and self-evaluation shape coping, sense of control, and self-esteem, and in turn our physiological responses to stress, which are important to health and well-being (Segall & Chappell, 2000; Wilkinson, 2002). These socially influenced physiological responses can influence our overall generalized vulnerability to multiple contemporary diseases (Evans & Stoddart, 1994; Hertzman, Frank, & Evans, 1994; Link & Phelan, 1995; Wilkinson, 2002).

The association between income and health is the strongest among those in younger and middle ages, but is still evident into old age (Chappell et al., 2003; House et al., 1994). Although some researchers have argued that age "levels" or evens out differences in status and resources that are established prior to our late years, age can in fact be associated with particular disadvantages in social and economic resources (see Chapters 5 and 6). Further, the health advantages associated with power, status, and income can accumulate over the life course (Blane, 2002; Bury, 1995; Hay, 1994). This concept of cumulative advantage (or disadvantage) helps us understand how individual health outcomes are connected to broader macro contexts over time (O'Rand, 1996b).

Within this chapter, we are unable to review all of the social determinants in depth; however, you should be able to recognize that a sociological perspective considers a wide range of social determinants in shaping health across the life course and into old age. Though targeting social determinants might help prevent illnesses and promote the health of Canadians, generally in policy and practice "we pay no more than lip service" to these factors (Marshall, 1994, p. 242). Instead, most health policy initiatives target change in individual lifestyle behaviours or in health care financing and reform (Marshall, 1994).

In the following section, we will review the Canadian health care system and its key features. While playing some role in the health of older persons, our system and its structure has important implications for how care is provided for older persons, and by whom.

The Canadian Health Care System: A Backgrounder

In order to understand formal care services in Canada today, it is necessary to understand how our health care system has developed and changed over time. When the Medical Care Act was introduced in 1966, it created a system of universal public insurance (i.e., payment) for "medically necessary" care provided by physicians in **acute care** (i.e., hospital) settings. This priority on insuring services offered in hospitals or by physicians reflected a focus on a medical, sickness-based model of health services. The institutionalization of the medicare system entrenched this model while ensuring physician dominance (Chappell et al., 2003; Mhatre & Deber, 1998; Olsen, 1998). Further, institutionalized medicare based on an acute care model made it more difficult to make future changes to the system in response to social determinants, societal change, or an aging population—for instance, older persons tend to have more chronic, incurable conditions (e.g., diabetes, arthritis, heart disease), and a curative, acute care model of services is not well-suited to helping older persons manage these conditions.

The costs of Canada's universal health insurance program were to be shared between the federal and provincial governments, and the Medical Care Act was to enable access to health services to all Canadians regardless of their ability to pay. Since the Medical Care Act was introduced, however, the federal government has reduced its portion of contributions to public insurance, leaving provinces struggling to manage the financial impact. Further, in 1984 the federal government passed the Canada Health Act, legislating five criteria for national health care principles to be upheld by the provinces: essentially, that all medically necessary services provided by hospitals and doctors must be insured, and that access to services and insurance must be universal and unimpeded by financial barriers.

Yet by diminishing its own funding contributions, the federal government reduced its own power to enforce the principles of the Canada Health Act. This has led to substantial variation between provinces in available funded services. Further, the costs of medical care continue to increase in part because of rising costs of technologies and medications, but also because, as a group, physicians determine the payment they receive for their services (Segall & Chappell, 2000; Torrance, 1998). Further, fee-for-service arrangements, together with legal concerns among physicians, can provide incentives for physicians to over-service: to provide medical interventions or procedures (or callback for additional medical consultations) that may be inappropriate or unjustified based on existing evidence (Segall & Chappell, 2000). Evans, McGrail, Morgan, Barer, and Hertzman (2001) identified the over-servicing of older persons as one driver of health care costs.

Controlling the costs of physician and hospital services is the focus of most new policies and service reforms in health care (Marmor, Barer, & Evans, 1994). As noted earlier, the emphasis on cost control in this sector is in part a response to financial pressures generated when the federal government reduced its portion of funding. In addition, in the context of globalization, health care systems are increasingly guided by market principles and political ideologies that emphasize efficiency, cost reduction, profitization, and decreased regulation (Anderson, Tang, & Blue, 2007; Bourgeault et al., 2001; Rankin, 2001).

Different options to containing costs have been explored and discussed to various degrees, including alternative modes of delivery, reducing inappropriate servicing, disease prevention strategies, more effective management, and physician incentives. In some cases, there has been increased privatization, service rationing, user fees, and means testing (Aronson, 2006; Bourgeault et al., 2001; Chappell, 1993; Grenier & Guberman, 2009; Guerriere et al., 2008). Further, one of the primary policy responses has been to shift the location of care as much as possible from institutions to communities. The costs—to governments—of care provision in institutional settings, especially hospitals, are relatively high; in home settings, individuals and families take on more costs. To reduce admissions and stays in institutional care, various initiatives have been implemented, including those designed to achieve the following: discharge patients from hospitals sooner; close or cap the number of residential care beds (or use stricter eligibility criteria); and promote and support older persons to stay at home for longer before residential care or hospital admission (e.g., "home first," "home is best," "hospital-home," or "virtual ward" strategies). Such initiatives tend to align with cultural and political discourses that emphasize independence and individual responsibility. Later in this chapter, we will discuss the implications of this increased reliance on home care services and the implications for family caregiving.

In general, health care reforms have in this way contributed to the "hollowing out" of medicare—services that used to be provided in hospitals are no longer provided under the publicly funded umbrella of medicare, as the services shift to community and home locales (Williams, Deber, Baranek, & Gildiner, 2001). Though appearing to cut costs, this shift creates greater opportunity for for-profit service providers, most notably for-profit home care companies, who are increasingly entering Canadian markets with the spread of globalizing capitalism (Chappell et al., 2003; Williams et al., 2001). Some research suggests, however, that for-profit health care firms are more likely to skimp on quality, select low-need clients, and drop coverage or reduce benefits; for-profits are also more expensive, although the increased costs are carried by individuals, creating inequities in access (Chappell et al., 2003; Williams et al., 2001).

Later in this chapter, we will examine two predominant formal care services for older adults: home care and residential care. First, however, we need to attend to the distinctions and interactions between such services and two other primary forms of care: self-care and informal (family) care.

Distinctions among Self-Care, Informal Care, and Formal Care

Self-care refers to activities and strategies that individuals use to promote their own well-being, prevent disease, manage symptoms, and seek help when needed. Self-care represents the vast majority of all care for older adults, and it can help them remain in their homes. The self-care movement can in part be traced back to Ivan Illich (1975), who argued that formal health care services were paternalistic and counterproductive to health, and represented an expanding biomedicalization of daily life. Such ideas are echoed today in self-care discourse as well as in policy initiatives promoting individual empowerment in health care decision-making and provision.

Some self-care initiatives, however, may be motivated less by altruistic concerns in promoting health and more by political and economic ideologies. In practice, the concept of self-care tends to align with ideas about individual responsibility—specifically, that making choices to care for ourselves is a moral imperative, in part because self-care lessens our reliance on formal services. A one-sided focus on self-care and individual responsibility, as opposed to a perspective in which responsibility is shared with public services, might inadvertently result in victim blaming and stigmatization of the ill; further, this limited focus might obscure the role of social and economic determinants of health (Bolaria, 1994; Labonte & Penfold, 1981; Lupton, 1993; Renaud, 1994).

What is today referred to as **informal care**—the provision of unpaid support by family, friends, or neighbours to older persons who are in need of support because their health or function has deteriorated—has not always been recognized in research or policy, although it has been another key source of care for chronically ill and disabled older persons throughout history and across countries (Chappell et al., 2003). The majority of informal caregivers are women, who tend to be socialized into carer roles, to be viewed as naturally suited for these roles, and to consider care provision as a normative and moral imperative (Aronson, 1998; Binney & Estes, 1988; Hooyman, 1990). For instance, we tend to judge women by higher standards in terms of the amount, extent, and quality of care they provide, and their emotional investment in the role (Calasanti & Slevin, 2001; Hooyman, 1990). More broadly, women's greater involvement in care results from inequities in gender relations and a related lack of structural alternatives—for instance, limited formal services or male involvement in caregiving (Aronson, 1992; Baines, Evans, & Neysmith, 1998; Hooyman, 1990). Women who are informal caregivers are also more likely to report negative consequences for their paid labour force employment and careers (Martin-Matthews & Campbell, 1995).

The discourse on informal caring emerged as late as the 1980s (Heaton, 1999), and now there is a general public awareness of caregiving as an important contribution to society. However, there is also increasing recognition that in some circumstances the responsibilities of caregiving can negatively affect the health of those who provide this care. Though some family members resist defining themselves as caregivers, preferring to position what they do as a natural part of normal family relationships and reciprocal interaction (O'Connor, 2007; Rose & Bruce, 1995), feminist gerontologists raise concerns about how these ideas tend to devalue the work involved. In contrast, viewing caregiving as work similar to that provided by paid employees directs attention to recognizing and valuing this work through supportive policies and programs.

A key distinguishing factor between informal and **formal care** is that the latter type of care is provided for payment. However, this distinction becomes blurred when non-paid (but still somewhat formalized) volunteer services are considered; in addition, some programs allow older persons to indirectly or directly pay their informal caregivers. Although it might also be argued that informal care involves more "caring about" rather than "caring for," many formal care providers can and do develop relationships and emotional attachments to care recipients (and not all family caregivers have positive, loving relationships with care recipients).

The policy recognition of informal care as unpaid work—and a tendency for some formal care providers to view family members as unpaid "co-workers" in the delivery of care to older adults—further blurs the boundaries between formal and informal care. In addition, many informal caregivers perform increasingly complex medical care tasks (Ward-Griffin & Marshall, 2003). In these situations, caregivers face increasing formalization, surveillance, and regulation of their work, such that the boundary of skilled or unskilled work that might also distinguish formal and informal care becomes blurred (Heaton, 1999; Ungerson, 1997).

Social gerontologists have examined how self-, informal, and formal care tend to combine in meeting the needs of older persons. There is a tendency to assume a linear continuum or progression of care as the health of an older person declines: from self-care to informal care and then to formal care services. Further, many people tend to assume there is a substitution effect, whereby the provision of formal services would result in both family and individuals doing less (Penning, 2002). However, these three types of care should be viewed more accurately as hierarchical, for instance with each type adding to and building on the others. Further, formal services generally do not reduce the extent of informal care provision (Penning, 2002; Penning & Keating, 1999); rather, informal and self-care tend to occur simultaneously even with the receipt of formal services. Keeping this in mind, in the rest of this chapter we will focus on two particular (but not the only) kinds of formal services relevant to the care of older persons: home care and residential care. In particular, we will examine how these two care services are experienced by older adults and by their family members and paid care providers, as situated within a broader social context.

Home Care in Canada

Home care in Canada, as it was initially envisioned, encompasses both social and more traditional medical services provided in the home to help older persons (a) recover and rehabilitate at home from acute conditions; (b) stay in their home for longer with support instead of entering residential care facilities; and (c) prevent injury and disease, and maintain their health (Chappell, 1993). However, given the increasing reliance and demand on home care services resulting from the health care reforms outlined earlier in this chapter, there have been increasing constraints on home care funding. As a result, over the last several decades there has been curtailment or a lack of expansion of home-based care services (Aronson, 2002a, 2002b, 2006; Brackley & Penning, 2009; Chappell, 1993). For instance, during health care reforms in British Columbia in the 1990s, trends in home and community care services were overall more reflective of reduction and reallocation (e.g., cost reduction) rather than expansion (McGrail et al., 2008; Penning, Brackley,

& Allan, 2006). Likewise, in Alberta during a similar period, the number of home care clients doubled but the duration of care provision for each client declined (Wilson et al., 2004).

Because home care is not considered medically necessary under the Canada Health Act, there has been wide variation in the types and levels of publicly funded services available in different provinces and geographic areas. In 2004, all of the provincial governments agreed to provide publicly funded home care in the following situations: end of life; acute care follow-up for two weeks after hospital discharge; and where necessary, two weeks of mental health home care in crisis situations.

Because of the health care reform initiatives implemented over the last several decades, publicly funded home care services are increasingly dealing with a "sicker" and more complex client population. This is, in part, an organizationally created situation. For instance, if clients with more complex care needs are discharged from hospitals sooner, and if it is more difficult to gain entry into residential care, older persons will indeed spend more time at home but with higher levels of need. As these higher-need clients may require more focused, medically oriented care, home care services are less able to devote resources to long-term social care that promotes well-being and that can save health care dollars over the long-term through prevention. In other words, home care has become a new medical support system rather than a strategy to promote the health of older persons (Chappell, 1993).

Today, most provincial home and community care mandates tend to be defined as promoting **aging in place**—that is, helping older persons remain in their homes for as long as possible—yet they are also increasingly focused on meeting primarily short-term and emergency needs rather than providing long-term support. These mandates also emphasize the primary role and responsibility of older persons and their family members to meet care needs. However, when publicly funded home care services are less accessible, greater burdens fall to older persons and their family members, most often women, to manage their health conditions—or to pay for private services, if they can afford to do so. The implications for older adults and their families, as well as for paid home care workers, will be discussed in the following section.

Home Care Experiences

Older Recipients of Home Care

When quality home care is accessible, coordinated, consistent, and appropriate, it can help older persons remain in their own homes and communities—as a result, it can help older adults maintain social integration as well as individual identity, autonomy, and well-being. In this respect, home care support can result in positive outcomes. Home care clients generally value services that run smoothly and that are consistent, coordinated, and convenient, with knowledgeable and dependable workers who support trusting relationships.

Conversely, some of the challenges faced by older persons with respect to receiving home care stem from situations where the quality, coordination, and consistency of care is less than ideal. In addition, older persons may experience difficult relationships with paid workers. For instance, differing ethnic and cultural backgrounds and beliefs affect relationships between workers and clients, particularly when complicated by language and communication barriers (Bourgeault, Atanackovic, Rashid, & Parpia, 2010). Home care clients may also find it difficult to manage the lack of privacy involved when receiving home care services and sharing the physical space of the home.

The experiences of older home care clients can also be affected by changes to health care services and policies. Home care clients in various provinces have faced reduced service choices, limitations on and increased disparities in access to services, as well as inconsistencies with care providers (e.g., Aronson, 2002a, 2002b, 2006; Cloutier-Fisher & Skinner, 2006). Distress, insecurity, lack of control, isolation, and exclusion can also be experienced due to particular home care policies or situations, as will be discussed in Chapter 6 (Aronson, 2006; Grenier & Guberman, 2009). Canadian researcher Jane Aronson (2002a, 2002b, 2006) studied the experiences of older female clients receiving home support in Ontario during a time of considerable change in the provision of these services. While some of the women actively asserted their needs, others stoically accepted their situations and muted potential complaints about their experiences in part because of fear, hopelessness, a desire to avoid being seen as a "complainer," reluctance to express need, sympathy for the care providers, and low expectations (Aronson 2002a, 2002b, 2006).

Relationships between older home care clients and paid care staff are also affected by the context of home care services. One recent study (Bourgeault, Atanackovic, Rashid, & Parpia, 2010) documented how staff shortages and high workloads affected these relationships, such as when formal providers must rush through care tasks and cannot take the time to talk with clients.

Family Providers of Home Care

When older adults are cared for in the home for as long as possible, as encouraged in contemporary health care reforms, this tends to involve a heavier reliance on family members to provide care, in contrast to paid providers (Chappell & Penning, 2005). Though many family members welcome the opportunity to provide care, they can be at risk for experiencing **caregiver burden** and strain. As discussed in Chapter 7, broad-level social changes occurring in Canada—including increases in single parents, women in the paid labour force, and geographic mobility—may make the provision of care more challenging for some families. Caregiver burden can be exacerbated when existing health and social care systems and bureaucracies are too complex or provide too little information for family members to navigate easily (Brookman, Holyoke, Toscan, Bender, & Tapping, 2011; Colombo, Nozal-Llena, Mercier, & Tjadens, 2011).

There is a strong base of evidence documenting the effects of family caregiving on multiple dimensions of caregiver well-being, including physical, mental, social, and psychological factors (e.g., Cochrane, Goering, & Rogers, 1997; Kiecolt-Glaser et al., 2003; Lee, Colditz, Berkman, & Kawachi, 2003a; O'Rourke, Cappeliez, & Guindon, 2003). Indeed, caregiving has been identified as a public health issue (Talley & Crews, 2007). Families can also face substantial financial costs such as out-of-pocket expenses, income loss, and career opportunity costs, which can negatively affect their long-term economic security.

The need to support caregivers is increasingly recognized at both the policy and clinical levels. Both Australia and the United Kingdom have national caregiver strategies. Manitoba recently developed the first Caregiver Recognition Act in Canada. Among other principles, Manitoba's Act states that family caregivers should be supported to achieve greater health, social and economic well-being, as well as participation in employment and educational opportunities. These principles align with an increasing concern for family caregiving as a broader human rights issue (British Columbia Law Institute & Canadian Centre for Elder Law, 2010; Ontario Human Rights Commission, 2007).

The focus of family caregiving research has been on interventions to enhance individual coping (e.g., psychoeducational training, support groups). While these interventions are vitally important for caregiver well-being, we also need to direct attention to the broader macro-level of systems and organizations. Change at this level could yield broader, though perhaps more moderate, impacts on larger numbers of caregivers. For instance, preventing caregiver stress and burden might require providing financial compensation for caregivers or employment legislation to protect the paid employment rights of unpaid family caregivers (Keefe, 2011).

The **Caregiver Policy Lens** (CGPL) is an evidence-based "framework for examining policies, programs and services from the perspective of caregivers of older adults" (MacCourt & Krawczyk, 2012, p. 6). A series of questions are designed to help policy-makers and program managers assess how policies, programs, and services may affect caregivers. For instance, these questions include the following: "Are the contributions of caregivers formally acknowledged and valued?" (MacCourt & Krawczyk, 2012, p. 11); "Is the right of family members to decline, limit or end caregiving explicitly acknowledged?" (p. 13); and "Is the policy/program based on the identified needs of caregivers (separate from those of the senior)?" (p. 14). The CGPL represents another strategy to help promote the development of policies that do not inadvertently enhance the burdens experienced by family caregivers.

Paid Providers of Home Care

Paid providers of home care include professionally trained nurses, case managers, physiotherapists and occupational therapists, social workers, and those providing non-professional assistance with daily activities and personal care—primarily home support workers (also known as personal support workers, health care aides, or direct service workers). Home support workers provide as much as 70 to 80 per cent of all paid home care work (Lilly, 2008), representing the majority of front-line, "hands-on" care for older persons.

Health care restructuring has implications for the work of paid providers of care in the home. For instance, as access to and amounts of care are limited and rationed, Bourgeault et al. (2004) illustrate how paid providers face increasing difficulties negotiating access to care for clients. Organizational change, heavier workloads, an emphasis on faster and intensified work, and job insecurity are also documented (Aronson & Neysmith, 1996; M. Denton, Zeytinoglu, Davies, & Lian, 2002; Sharman, McLaren, Cohen, & Ostry, 2008) and can contribute to increased job stress and dissatisfaction, and poorer health (M. Denton, Zeytinoglu, & Davies, 2002; M. Denton, Zeytinoglu, Kusch, & Davies, 2007). Though many home support workers value the autonomy they can have in their daily work, they tend to have low pay, unpredictable hours, and difficult working conditions; they also tend to be marginalized relative to other providers and to suffer physical and emotional strain (M. Denton, Zeytinoglu, Davies, & Lian, 2002; M. Denton, Zeytinoglu, & Davies, 2002).

As workloads increase, home care providers are less able to deliver personalized care (Aronson & Neysmith, 1996), as well as emotional and interpersonal support (M. Denton, Zeytinoglu, Davies, & Lian, 2002)—features that enhance the quality of care as well as client satisfaction. Much of the skill and responsibility of home care work is unrecognized and devalued. For instance, workers in both home and residential settings perform **emotional labour** (Hochschild, 1983) in which they align their visible displays of emotions with organizational requirements to promote positive emotions in care recipients or families (Sass, 2000). When family members approach staff with anger about the level, quality, or type of care being provided, home care workers must deal with and diffuse these situations, as well as hide any of their personal reactions within the conflict. This and other kinds of emotional labour involve considerable skill and effort yet are often unrecognized (Dyer, McDowell, & Batnitzky, 2008; Ibarra, 2002).

As well as having less time for emotional and relational aspects of their work, home care employees may experience **moral distress**—feelings of powerlessness, helplessness, or frustration. This can occur when caregivers feel unable to fulfill their responsibility to residents and families, respond to suffering, or provide the standard of care they wish to but are unable to because of organizational constraints such as workloads and time challenges (Austin, Lemermeyer, Goldberg, Bergum, & Johnson, 2005; Ceci, 2006; Kälvemark, Höglund, Hansson, Westerholm, & Arnetz, 2004). Moral distress can generate frustration, anxiety, guilt, stress, and burnout (e.g., Austin et al., 2005; Billeter-Koponen & Ereden, 2005).

Many home care workers are economic migrants who face additional challenges (Bourgeault, Parpia, & Atanackovic, 2010). They might be immigrants, permanent residents, or temporary workers hired through Canada's Live-in Caregiver Program—situations that raise concerns about their vulnerability to isolation and exploitation (Bourgeault et al., 2009). More broadly, because the boundary between informal and formal care work is often unclear, and because home care workers themselves often enjoy the more informal relational aspects of their work, they can be inadvertently exploited. Home care workers may feel responsible for and want to help clients but face constraints in their ability to have their work recognized and appropriately compensated (Aronson & Neysmith, 1996; Stacey, 2005).

In the next section, we turn to another predominant type of formal care for older adults: residential care. Many of the same kinds of issues and concerns discussed for home care resonate with residential care. You may want to try to identify some of these similarities, as well as potential differences, as you read through the next section.

Residential Care in Canada

When thinking about residential care, you might recall your own personal experiences visiting with older relatives living in residential care facilities, or even volunteering or working with older adults in these settings. What were your impressions of these environments? Specifically, consider the following questions:

- What is the typical layout or design?
- What are the rooms like? Can residents bring their own belongings or furniture?
- What kinds of activities are offered? Who attends?
- Is there a resident/family council? What does the council do?
- What kinds of choices can residents make? What choices are made for them?
- How can and do clients and families voice concerns about their care?
- How are family members involved in the care provided in the facility?
- How do residents interact with staff? With each other?

A **residential care facility** (also known as a personal care home, nursing home, or long-term care facility) is a regulated institution providing lodging and 24-hour care and supervision for persons with chronic illnesses, physical disabilities, and/or mental impairment. About 12 per cent of older Canadians aged 75 and older currently live in residential care (Canadian Institute for Health Information, 2011). Residential care tends to be partially or entirely funded through public sources, although the care homes may use either for-profit or non-profit models of delivery. Most residents are expected to pay a means-tested fee (McGregor & Ronald, 2011).

A recent report indicates wide variation in the quality of care between Canadian residential facilities (Canadian Institute for Health Information, 2013). For instance, even when accounting for differences in resident and facility characteristics, the proportion of residents on antipsychotic medications without an appropriate diagnosis ranged from 18 to 50 per cent; those exhibiting increasing levels of depression ranged from 3 to 40 per cent; those experiencing worsening pain ranged from 3 to 32 per cent; and the proportion of residents who fell ranged from 5 to 24 per cent (Canadian Institute for Health Information, 2013).

In Canada, residential care facilities are not included as medically necessary care under the Canada Health Act, leading to variation in both funding and delivery in this sector, although the overall trend appears to be towards privately owned for-profit facilities (McGregor & Ronald, 2011). However, research evidence suggests that better care outcomes, including lower risk of death, for residents in not-for-profit facilities is in part associated with higher staffing levels in contrast to for-profit facilities (Comondore et al., 2009; Devereaux et al., 2002; McGrail, McGregor, Cohen, Tate, & Ronald, 2007). This finding led McGregor and Ronald (2011) to conclude the following:

> The policy direction in many provinces . . . seems to run counter to the research findings, with the apparent growth in publicly funded, for-profit residential care. One reason for this is governments' reluctance to finance the construction of new facilities by incurring debt, and turning instead to public-private partnerships (P3s) to build residential long-term care facilities. Since the private partner often assumes responsibility for service delivery once a P3 facility is built, the financing of new residential care beds through P3 arrangements is intimately linked to the expansion of for-profit delivery, which is inconsistent with the evidence on ownership and quality. (p. 34)

From a sociological perspective, it is important to recognize the broader context shaping the delivery and receipt of long-term residential care in Canada. This includes considering not only the aging population (demographic) but also current political (neoliberal) and economic (capitalist) systems, and a dominant culture that tends to be individualistic and ageist, viewing dependency and ill health as a failure.

A recent report from the Canadian Institute for Health Information (2011) states that rates of admission into residential care have declined in recent decades—a phenomenon that in part reflects increasing emphases on home care and a tendency to limit eligibility for facility care to those with the most intense needs. As such, over the last several decades Canada's residential care client populations are becoming more complex—residents now tend to enter care facilities only when they are in greatest need, often frailer and with higher levels of cognitive impairment than historical norms. Older adults entering residential care also tend to be closer to death, resulting in higher turnover in facilities—in some respects, care facilities increasingly serve a **hospice** function, though they often lack the resources or specialized training to fulfill this role.

Increasing levels of need in residential care populations, combined with budget pressures and staffing shortages, result in heavy workloads and time constraints in delivery of care in residential facilities (discussed further in the following sections). Facilities have responded with strategies designed to enhance efficiency and ensure quality of care. Many also rely heavily on family members, volunteers, and paid companions. Nonetheless, residential care facilities continue to frequently come under public scrutiny for the quality of care they provide, as with a recent *W5* documentary on resident-to-resident abuse (see Box 4.1).

Box 4.1   *W5* National Investigation into Resident-to-Resident Violent Incidents: "Crisis in Care"

In a documentary that aired in 2013, CTV's *W5* investigated incidences of resident-on-resident abuse in Canadian residential care facilities. The data they obtained through access to information requests in 38 health agencies indicated that in the span of one year there were over 10,000 reported events of resident-to-resident violence, which ranged in severity. The documentary also investigated personal stories of such incidents in long-term care homes in Toronto and Burnaby. The investigation led *W5* to conclude that there are insufficient systematic procedures to prevent resident-to-resident violence, which occurs most often when residents have aggressive behavioural tendencies related to dementia. Another concern raised was that low staff-to-resident ratios make it more difficult to monitor residents and prevent violence.

Source: Summary of Bandera, S. (Associate producer). (2013). Crisis in care [News report; aired in three parts in February 2013; an updated story aired in June 2013]. *W5*. Toronto, ON: CTV. Retrieved from http://www.ctvnews.ca/w5/w5-a-ground-breaking-national-nursing-home-abuse-investigation-1.1149144#.URg8x5Bke1g.blogger

Residential Care Experiences

Older Recipients of Residential Care

Entering a residential care facility is associated with a social stigma for older adults, as it symbolizes dependency, a loss of control, a lack of family care, and the inability to stay at home. Stigmatization occurs as a result of discriminatory cultural beliefs—including attitudes reflecting ageism, **ableism**, and **healthism**—that label nursing home residents as a category of "others" with undesirable characteristics. Such stigmatization can shape social interactions and lead to dehumanization, status loss, and discrimination (e.g., Dobbs et al., 2008). Dobbs et al. (2008) discuss the cultural roots of this stigma but also identify how the environments themselves further contribute: not only is the place itself considered stigmatizing, for example, but in some cases facility rules or regulations further dehumanize residents and constrain their autonomy.

As institutional environments, residential care facilities represent a new kind of culture into which older residents are required to adapt (see Box 4.2). Sociologist Erving Goffman (1961) was interested in examining how individuals become **resocialized** into new identities, norms, values, and behaviours when they enter new, highly regulated, and controlled social environments (such as asylums for the mentally ill and prisons). Goffman (1961) defined these **total institutions** as follows:

> A place of residence and work where a large number of like-situated individuals, cut off from the wider society for an appreciable period of time, together lead an enclosed, formally administered round of life. (p. xiii)

Total institutions share several characteristics, including being a hybrid mix of a formal organization and a residential place; having a strong division between staff and residents; and, upon entry, often involving a loss of personal property or other dehumanizing processes that can jeopardize individuals' sense of self (Goffman, 1961). Though there is disagreement about whether contemporary care facilities represent total institutions—generally, care facilities try to distance themselves from this idea—the concept can help in highlighting the often symbolic effects on personal identity that can result from becoming a care facility resident.

Timothy Diamond (1992) conducted extensive **participant observation** research in three nursing homes in the United States, in which he worked as a nursing aide. He concluded that a biomedical and capitalist model dominates the culture and bureaucratic organization of the for-profit nursing homes he examined, which is actually counterproductive to residents' health. For instance, a narrow focus on "chartable" medical tasks can conceal residents' social or emotional needs (Diamond, 1992).

> ### Box 4.2   "Gert's Secret"
>
> In the introduction to "Gert's Secret" from the documentary *Rage against the Darkness*, director John Kastner talks about the public's general fear of nursing homes. He then presents the story of Gert, a 102-year-old woman, as an example of the "happiest person in the home" and asks, "What is her secret?" Gert appears to be in relatively good health; she is able to come and go to horse racing events, and she has an active "zest for living." She accepts life in the facility—"I don't have a choice. . . . There's no chip on my shoulder"—yet she is assertive with the staff about her needs (for instance, she insists on staying up later than other residents). By the end of the film, however, Gert suffers from increasingly failing physical health, accompanied by depression and frustration. Her happiness and "successful aging" appear to hinge crucially on her ability to be independent.
>
> Kastner presents a rather bleak view of facility living, in which residents with cognitive impairment share aspects of daily life, and even rooms, with residents without these symptoms, resulting in conflicts—for example, wheelchair clashes and shouting as residents make their way to dinner. A sociological perspective—which is lacking in the film—might link Gert's strong desire for independence to the context of North American culture, which prizes individualism and stigmatizes dependence. It might further consider how Gert's daily life and autonomy is shaped by the particular organizational and structural context of the care facility.
>
> Source: Summary of Kastner, J. (Producer, Director, Writer). (2004). Gert's secret [Television documentary episode, Part 2]. In *Rage against the darkness*. Canada: J. S. Kastner Productions & the Canadian Broadcasting Corporation.

There has been considerable research examining how individual autonomy tends to be constrained in residential care settings; not only is independence a prized cultural value, but residents' health and well-being can be affected by their level of autonomy. Paternalistic cultures of care, and staff attitudes, are often targeted in existing research. For instance, Persson and Wästerfors (2009) report that older nursing home residents' attempts to assert their autonomy in decision-making or complaint-making tend to be trivialized or ignored by staff who view them as having diminished competence; the authors suggest this may be especially so in cases where resident autonomy conflicts with "the efficient running of the institution as a whole" (p. 1).

Restricted autonomy can also be connected to resource constraints that make it difficult to provide individualized care and flexible options, risk management concerns about safety, and features of group living such as scheduled routine activities, a lack of privacy, and general restrictions on daily activities (Kane, Freeman, Caplan, Aroskar, & Urv-Wong, 1990).

What does a lack of autonomy look like? In my own research, I surveyed 100 older residential facility residents who did not have significant cognitive impairment, and I asked them how involved they wanted to be in care decisions (Funk, 2002; Funk, 2004). Often, residents said things that did not answer my survey questions, but they still provided important insight into a loss of autonomy. For example, some residents expressed that their involvement tended to require initiative on their part—as one participant stated, "You are responsible for speaking up" (Funk, 2002, p. 118). Some residents were particularly disillusioned, as reflected in sentiments such as, "Nobody listens, it wouldn't make a difference" or "I keep my mouth shut. . . . [I]t only causes trouble and probably wouldn't change things anyways" (Funk, 2002, p. 121).

I also asked one older male resident how involved he wanted to be in decisions about his care. He responded: "Now that I'm here, what I want doesn't matter" (Funk, 2002, p. 135). In other words, because he was now dependent on their care, he deferred to the administration. This phenomenon can be viewed from the perspective of social exchange theory (see Chapter 1). In other words, older residents may find they have few ways to reciprocate for the care they receive, and so they may feel compelled to offer their compliance and give up their independence in exchange. This phenomenon, I would argue, has broader origins in societal ageism as well as daily interactions within, and symbolic meanings of, residential care living.

As well as having important implications for autonomy, Kane (2003) suggests that residential care facilities can influence older persons' well-being not only though their particular approaches to the practice and "culture" of care but also through their polices and physical environment. Good institutional care that enhances quality of life and autonomy should be **individualized care** (or "person-centred"), which "acknowledges elders as unique persons and is practiced through consistent caring relationships congruent with past patterns and individual preferences" (Happ, Williams, Strumpf, & Burger, 1996, pp. 7–8). This care model counters the traditional, overly task-focused approach, opens up opportunities for resident choice and involvement, and helps residents maintain their identity. Implementing individualized care requires staff training but can also require changes to the physical environment and organizational policies, such as those affecting workers' access to time and supplies (Caspar, Cooke, O'Rourke, & Macdonald, 2013).

Family Caregivers of Residential Care Clients

Family caregivers often face the difficult decision to seek placement for an older relative in a residential care facility when the level of need becomes too much for them to manage personally (as depicted in the 2006 film *Away from Her*, see Figure 4.2). Once the transition is made, families continue to be involved in ensuring the resident's well-being (Hertzberg, Ekman, & Axelsson, 2001);

AF archive / Alamy

Figure 4.2 The 2006 film *Away from Her*, directed by Sarah Polley and based on an Alice Munro story, details the heartbreaking experiences of an older man (Gordon Pinsent) whose wife (Julie Christie) has Alzheimer's disease and needs to be cared for in an institutional setting.

they worry about their family member and seek reassurance that appropriate care is being provided.

Though family members may provide less personal and hands-on care, they often take on roles in overseeing and monitoring care, and advocating for their family member; further, they provide social and emotional support, and can help the resident maintain a sense of continuity in his or her identity (Davies & Nolan, 2006; Hertzberg et al., 2001; Keefe & Fancey, 2000; Williams, Zimmerman, & Williams, 2012). Some family members also provide considerable assistance with finances, transportation, and in some cases (such as towards the end of life) with personal care (Gaugler, 2005; Williams et al., 2012). There are potential positive and negative effects of heavier types of involvement, and it is important to ascertain the particular ways that family members want to be involved in care. Given the resource constraints within these settings, paid staff may increasingly view family members as a kind of co-worker or resource for care. Though some family members may welcome contributing to care, others may feel relied upon in a way that enhances a sense of burden or role strain.

Well-resourced families with an institutionalized older relative[1] may privately pay for the supplementary services of **paid companions**: private, external, unlicensed providers of (primarily) friendship and socio-emotional support. Research on paid companions tends to be lacking in

Canada, although a recent study was conducted by Linda Outcalt (2013). Given existing time and workload constraints that challenge workers' ability to meet residents' needs for social and emotional support and interaction, Outcalt concluded that paid companions are being used to fill gaps in residential care, especially care for residents with dementia. Though some of the activities provided by paid companions were limited due to union regulations, some companions described helping with feeding (Outcalt, 2013).

The bulk of the literature on families and residential care for older adults focuses on relationships between family members and paid care staff, which can be problematic and antagonistic. Conflict can be related to differing expectations about roles and responsibilities, perceptions of care quality, or difficult emotions (such as guilt or helplessness) experienced by family members in regards to facility placement. A sociological perspective also directs attention to how these relationships are shaped by organizational contexts. For instance, Ward-Griffin, Bol, Hay, and Dashnay (2003) analyzed interview data with families and nurses in one residential care setting and noted that when workers faced greater time constraints, relationships with families tended to be more conflictual.

Paid Providers of Residential Care

Paid care providers working in residential care settings include but are not limited to nurses, social workers, physiotherapists, recreation workers, and resident care aides (also known as health care aides). Though many care providers find meaning in the work they do in residential settings, workloads can be considerable, and physical and emotional demands may exceed that of home care staff (Hasson & Arnetz, 2008). Job dissatisfaction is a concern (Andersen, 2009), and workers can experience moral distress much like home care workers. For instance, resident care aides who do not have the time to spend with dying residents describe a sense of helplessness, sadness, and frustration (Funk, Waskiewich, & Stajduhar, 2013–2014; Waskiewich, Funk, & Stajduhar, 2012).

Residential care workers also risk physical violence from some residents who exhibit symptoms of dementia-related illness. In one Canadian study (Banerjee et al., 2012), 43 per cent of front-line care workers report daily physical violence, yet they tend to "normalize" this as an inevitable part of their job. However, the level or extent of violence may have structural origins: for instance, resident-to-staff violence is six times higher in Canada compared to Sweden, where working conditions are generally less demanding (Daly & Szebehely, 2012). Banerjee et al. (2012) also documented how workload and time pressures can result in workers rushing through personal care, which can exacerbate agitation in residents with dementia, potentially triggering violent behaviour.

Some types of jobs in particular, such as resident care aides, are relatively low status and low pay. In his classic study on nursing homes, Diamond

(1983) argued that the culture and organization of nursing homes (i.e., bio-medical, capitalist) creates "troubles" for nursing aides (who are primarily women), whose work tends to be devalued and underpaid. The challenges experienced by nursing aides can be compounded by potential stigmas associated with working with older persons and performing the "dirty work" of personal care (Stacey, 2005).

Those who work in stigmatized occupations often display a form of agency through which they can interpret their work as having positive meaning. For instance, many residential care workers draw significant personal meaning and value in their work from relationships they develop with residents and families (Ball, Lepore, Perkins, Hollingsworth, & Sweatman, 2009; Moss, Moss, Rubenstein, & Black, 2003; Ryan, Nolan, Enderby, & Reid, 2004). Some care workers even view residents as **fictive kin**. However, this process of developing emotional attachment may inadvertently exploit workers at the same time that it enhances the quality care of residents and helps care aides manage stigma (Dodson & Zincavage, 2007; Pfefferle & Weinberg, 2008). For example, as Provis and Stack (2004) emphasize, emotional bonds with care recipients can generate feelings of responsibility for their well-being, which can motivate care staff to go "above and beyond" for some residents, such as working through their lunch break.

Relationships between residents and workers in residential care, as in home care, are influenced by the organizational and resource context. Most obviously, this is evident in the reduced time available for staff members to develop relationships with residents, limiting their ability to get to know each other over time. Further, care facilities often have formal and informal guidelines regarding personal emotions, such as the principle of **personal–professional boundaries**, and guidelines about appropriate expressions of grief after a resident dies.

In the preceding sections, we have emphasized the ways in which the experiences of older persons, their family members, and paid care providers are shaped by organizational and broader social forces. The final section of this chapter will examine another type of care provider that is often overlooked but plays an important role: volunteers.

Voluntary Providers of Care for Older Persons

Budgetary restraints that limit formally provided home and residential care services have meant that not-for-profit voluntary organizations are often left to fill in the gaps where publicly funded services are unable to meet needs (Cloutier-Fisher & Skinner, 2006; Hanlon, Rosenberg, & Clasby, 2007). Many of these non-profit organizations, as well as publicly funded community services and for-profit residential care facilities, rely heavily on the contributions of volunteers. Volunteerism can be viewed positively as reflecting civic engagement, altruism, and social participation (see Chapter 6). Yet because volunteers facilitate the delivery of quality care to older adults, a reliance on volunteers in the context of fiscal constraint can inadvertently treat volunteers as free, unpaid labour to substitute rather than supplement government services (Gagnon & Sévigny, 2000; Ilcan & Basok, 2004; Lamoureux, 2002).

Generally, care from volunteers is relatively free from strong feelings of obligation or commitment (Fischer, Rogne, & Eustis, 1990). It is therefore not surprising that existing research tends to focus on how volunteers can be successfully motivated and retained by care organizations. Yet some volunteers may find it difficult to become more involved due to a lack of time (Lasby & Embuldeniya, 2002); their sense of belonging and motivation may also be adversely affected when they feel relied upon to provide care (Field & Johnson, 1993). In one recent Canadian study (Rozanova, Keating, & Eales, 2012), researchers suggested that the volunteer contributions of older persons living in rural communities had, in the context of cuts to community services, become a kind of **compulsory altruism**.

In residential settings, volunteer involvement in care tasks such as feeding or personal care may be limited due to concerns about union grievances or safety (Mellow, 2011). Instead, volunteers tend to assist with social and recreational group-based activities, such as singalongs or bingo. In home settings, volunteers might be involved in friendly visitor or meal delivery programs. Further research should explore how volunteers are engaged as resources in differing care settings, and the extent to which volunteer roles are formalized and regulated within health and social care systems.

Conclusion

In this chapter, we built on earlier discussions in Chapters 2 and 3 by emphasizing that declines in health that can accompany aging are not inevitable or universal, and we should avoid equating age with illness. Social gerontologists have long tended to focus on research in aspects of health and aging, which has contributed to reproducing these beliefs. Further, much of this research tends to focus on individual-level factors affecting health in later life. In contrast, a sociological perspective directs attention to how our health and needs for care are shaped by broader structural or social determinants, and to the importance of macro-level change for influencing health across the life course.

Policy and health system reform in Canada, however, has generally not reflected a sociological perspective and continues to operate under the assumption that the health care system is the primary determinant of health. In response to demographic, political, and economic changes, health systems have changed in many ways—including targeted attention to promoting home-based forms of care. In part, this approach reflects a concern that providing formal services reduces self-care and family care; however, most evidence does not support this assumption.

As a result of these various changes to the Canadian health care system, which have tended to restrict eligibility to those with the most narrowly defined medical needs, the population of older adults receiving formal care services in residential and home-based settings has particularly high needs for assistance. This changing policy context thus has implications for the abilities of these services to meet complex care needs. More broadly, we have discussed how the individual experiences and well-being of older recipients of home and residential care, their family members, and paid and unpaid care workers are closely connected to broader policies, practices, and contexts. Though we have focused on home and residential care, many governments are developing more sophisticated continuums of care options for older adults that include assisted and supportive living, transitional care, and other alternatives.

There is a wide range of other sociological research examining the intersection of aging and health care that we have been unable to review within this chapter—this includes work on processes of surveillance and professionalization in care for older persons; inequities in access to health care services for particular groups (see Chapter 6); older persons' experiences with more traditional acute-care systems (such as doctor–patient interactions) and with alternative health care and self-care; and health system reform, such as research on the importance of integrated care structures for providing health care for older persons.

As a final point, though in this chapter we have focused on how older persons are cared for in Canadian society, care and support do not only flow in one direction to older persons. Much of the care discourse tends to neglect care recipients, who are assumed to be dependent, passive, and lacking in agency (Henderson & Forbat, 2002). In fact, many care providers to older persons are themselves older (e.g., spousal caregivers, older volunteers); further, older persons continue to provide significant support to their own communities and families, as noted in Chapter 7.

Questions for Critical Thought

1. Considering the social determinants of health listed in this chapter, what kinds of structural-level change would target these non-medical determinants of health?

2. What similarities or differences exist between the experiences of older persons receiving home care services and those living in residential care?

3. What similarities or differences exist between experiences of family members providing support to an older person in home and residential settings?

4. What similarities or differences exist between the experiences of workers caring for older home care clients and those caring for long-term care facility residents?

Suggested Readings

Banerjee, A., Daly, T., Armstrong, P., Szebehely, M., Armstrong, H., & Lafrance, S. (2012). Structural violence in long-term, residential care for older people: Comparing Canada and Scandinavia. *Social Science and Medicine, 74*(3), 390–398. In this study, the authors report on a survey of workers in residential care in three Canadian provinces, compared with four Scandinavian countries. Canadian workers were six times more likely to experience physical violence, and the authors suggest links to poorer working conditions.

Ceci, C. (2006). Impoverishment of practice: Analysis of effects of economic discourses in home care case management practice. *Nursing Leadership, 19*(1), 56–68. Ceci examines how economic discourses and organizational "budget realities" infuse the daily practice of home care case managers, who determine the formal responses to the needs of clients, and she considers the effects of these factors on their work experiences.

Dannefer, D. (2003). Cumulative advantage/disadvantage and the life course: Cross-fertilizing age and social science theory. *Journals of Gerontology, 58B*(6), S327–S337. Dannefer outlines how cumulative advantage/disadvantage theory is connected to current thinking about age and the life course and suggests additional directions for its use in sociology and social gerontology.

Relevant Websites

Alzheimer Society of Canada, "Living with Dementia"
http://www.alzheimer.ca/en/Living-with-dementia/I-have-dementia/Shared-experiences
> This website provides information and resources for those diagnosed with Alzheimer's disease. It includes stories of experiences shared by persons in the early stages of the illness.

Canadian Alliance for Long-Term Care
http://www.caltc.ca
> This organization represents publicly funded long-term care providers. The site also provides a library of official reports and statistics relevant to long-term care.

Canadian Home Care Association
http://www.cdnhomecare.ca
> This association of over 200 home care organizations provides information about and advocates for quality home care services, taking positions on issues including family caregiving, person-centred care, and information technology.

Public Health Agency of Canada, Canadian Best Practices Portal, "Social Determinants of Health"
http://cbpp-pcpe.phac-aspc.gc.ca/public-health-topics/social-determinants-of-health/
> This website provides a number of resources, including data and research reviews, regarding the social determinants of health, as well as strategies and potential interventions to address them.

5 The Economic Security of Older Persons in a Changing World

Learning Objectives

In this chapter, you will learn that:

◉ in Canada, a system of public and private sources of income helps ensure the financial security of many older persons, although there is increasing reliance on private sources.

◉ increases in precarious and non-standard work over time may lead to more unstable financial situations for future cohorts of older persons.

◉ despite recent trends towards a later average retirement age, the process of retirement is becoming increasingly "destandardized."

◉ policy is shifting towards encouraging older workers to remain in paid employment for longer, raising concerns that this policy trend may exacerbate socio-economic inequalities.

◉ Canada's retirement income system has helped promote economic security in old age and retirement, but some groups of older persons—such as unattached women and recent immigrants—are especially at risk of poverty.

◉ reforms to Canada's retirement income system will have implications for the economic security of future generations and for income inequality between older persons.

Introduction

Have you given much thought to when you hope to retire from the paid labour force? Do you expect that you will be able to retire with a comfortable income at that age? Why or why not? In this chapter, we will introduce you to some of the components of Canada's retirement income system. We will explore how and why this system is changing over time, and we will discuss how changes to this system affect the incomes of older cohorts.

In gerontology, a psychological perspective on retirement has traditionally focused on how to promote individual "adjustment" to retirement—for instance, through encouraging individuals to adapt to new roles and replace work with new activities (see activity theory in Chapter 1). In contrast, a sociological perspective on work and retirement turns greater attention to the phenomenon of retirement itself and to the wide variety of ever-changing social, political, and economic factors that shape both paid work and retirement across the life course. These macro-level factors have implications for financial security in older cohorts. Rather than focus on how individuals adapt to or cope with work and retirement at older ages, a sociological approach identifies experiences of work and retirement in later life as **public issues** (rather than **private troubles**: see Chapter 1) that are shaped and reshaped by collective and macro-level action. In this chapter, we will explore how our choices about work and retirement in later life, as well as our economic well-being, are fundamentally shaped by features of social structure.

Canada's Retirement Income System

Understanding the economic security of older Canadians requires understanding the elements of Canada's **retirement income system**—the mix of public and private sources of income (often referred to as the "three pillars") potentially available to retired cohorts. The combination of different retirement income options helps to strengthen Canada's system and protect many older persons from experiencing a drastic drop in their income. As we will see, however, the retirement income system is not always sufficient for some groups of older persons, who are still at risk of economic insecurity in their later years.

The first pillar of Canada's retirement income system includes **Old Age Security** (**OAS**), which is a federally funded program introduced (in its current form) in 1952 to provide a guaranteed minimum income to all except the most wealthy Canadians. OAS is based on the principle of universal public benefits to help protect older persons from a large drop in their living standards. Payment amounts are updated quarterly, and as of June 2015, the maximum monthly benefit that can be received is $563.74. Initially, benefits were provided at 70 years of age; the age of eligibility was lowered to age 65 a decade later, but recent policy changes have scheduled a gradual increase to age 67. Benefits are generally increased as the average cost of living (prices of goods and services) rises. Some very low-income older adults (e.g., an individual income of $17,088 or less in 2015) also receive a means-tested supplement to OAS: this **Guaranteed Income Supplement** (**GIS**) was introduced in 1967 to provide additional financial support for low-income Canadians. About one-third of Canadians receive this supplement (Brown, 2011), which in 2015 provides a maximum monthly benefit of $764.40. Lower-income Canadians tend to rely significantly on both OAS and GIS for their retirement income. Nonetheless, receiving both benefits does not necessarily protect older persons from living in poverty. For instance, a single, unattached older person receiving both OAS and GIS would have a yearly income of about $15,938, and the **low-income cut-off** after tax for those living in large urban areas (as of 2011) is $19,307.

Despite limitations of these income benefits, OAS and GIS still play a crucial role for many low-income older adults; the lower their income, the greater the share of that income is derived from OAS/GIS (Employment and Social Development Canada, 2012). Though there is public concern about the sustainability of Old Age Security in the context of an aging population, research and analysis has confirmed that OAS is sustainable. For instance, Brown (2011) notes that "in a normal economy, wages rise faster than prices so that the tax rate needed to fund OAS/GIS does not rise as quickly as the rate of benefits growth" (p. 397). Further, Employment and Social Development Canada (2012) indicates that the OAS program itself entails reasonable administration costs and has become more cost effective over time. However, the federal government drew on different arguments when considering the decision to increase the age of eligibility (see Box 5.1).

When Old Age Security was introduced, the benefits were insufficient for older workers to retire without a drastic drop in income (Chappell et al., 2003). Public activism thus facilitated the 1966 introduction of the federally

Box 5.1   The Sustainability of Old Age Security: An Issue in the News

In January of 2012, prior to introducing a two-year increase in the age of eligibility for future Old Age Security benefits, Prime Minister Harper was quoted as stating that demographic realities in Canada threaten the viability of the OAS program, which is funded through general tax revenues (Gollom, 2012). Although the number of OAS recipients is expected to rise with Canada's aging population, Harper's statement conflicted with a federal assessment of fiscal sustainability and elderly benefits completed on behalf of Canada's Parliamentary Budget Officer Kevin Page (Fitzpatrick, 2012; Matier, 2012). The fiscal report claimed that Canada's elderly benefits program, including OAS, is sustainable in the long term, considering predicted government revenues and economic growth (Matier, 2012). In fact, the findings suggested that the program could even affordably be enhanced (Fitzpatrick, 2012; Matier, 2012). In contrast, Human Resources Minister Diane Finley was quoted as stating, "We know there's a coming crisis, that's in Old Age Security, that's why we're taking steps now before it's too late because we do not want to burden future generations with massive, massive tax increases to support OAS" (Fitzpatrick, 2012). House leader Peter van Loan also implied that if changes were not made, Canada could follow Greece into economic ruin (Gollom, 2012).

In your own time, try to delve deeper into the issue of the sustainability of Old Age Security. Why do you think the government employs the rhetoric of apocalyptic demography (see Chapter 2) in relation to this issue? What goals is the government trying to achieve?

administered **Canada Pension Plan** (CPP) and the corresponding provincially administered **Quebec Pension Plan** (QPP), collectively referred to as the C/QPP. Representing the second pillar of Canada's retirement income system, the C/QPP requires compulsory payments from both employers and employees. These payments constitute a pooled pension fund collected and invested through the government, and benefits are returned to retired workers. The exact size of benefits received by individuals depends on the number of years they worked and the size of their contributions—the higher the income earned, the larger the contributions. Importantly, C/QPP is unavailable for unpaid family caregivers (most often women) who do not work in the paid labour force. Further, since women tend to earn less than men throughout their life course—working in different sectors and having more intermittent and part-time work involvement—women often earn lower C/QPP earnings in retirement (Gaszo, 2005).

Since the C/QPP was first established, it took some time for the fund to grow to a point where retirees could collect the full amount of benefits. The first cohort to receive the full amount of C/QPP benefits turned 65 in 1976; this point has been called the **maturation of C/QPP**, and it helps in part to explain gains in older persons' average incomes during this period. As Chappell, Gee, McDonald, and Stones (2003) note, this maturation is part of the planned operation of the program and will not improve in the future. The average amount of C/QPP retirement pension claimed by new recipients (as of 2015) is $639.44.

Canada currently spends 4.5 per cent of its gross domestic product on public pensions, compared to an average of 7.8 per cent among all member countries of the Organisation for Economic Co-operation and Development (OECD) (OECD, 2013). The C/QPP program underwent reforms in the 1990s to promote its long-term fiscal sustainability, including increased contribution rates. The sustainability of the program for the next 75 years has been repeatedly confirmed by the Office of the Chief Actuary of Canada (Brown, 2011).

The common assumption is that C/QPP benefits rely directly on what is paid into the program by those currently in the labour force, thus generating fears that as the population ages and more Canadians draw benefits, the plan will become bankrupt (see Chapter 2). However, during times when more Canadians draw benefits rather than pay into the program, the plan can start drawing on its investment income. Currently, the provinces and territories actually support increased expansion of CPP, but this has been opposed by Canada's finance minister (see Box 5.2).

Income from the C/QPP and OAS/GIS accounted for 41 per cent of the total income for Canadians aged 65 years and over in 2011 (Statistics Canada, 2011a; see also Figure 5.1). However, older people in the lower half of income distribution tend to rely to a much larger extent on income from these sources (Baldwin, 2009). Wealthier Canadians, in contrast, rely

---

Box
5.2   Expanding the Canada Pension Plan: An Issue in the News

---

Expansions to the Canada Pension Plan—focused on increasing the size of contributions now in order to increase future benefits—have been advocated by all of the provinces and territories. However, the federal government has resisted expanding the C/QPP, claiming that such an expansion will hurt the economy, through increasing payroll tax and thereby financial pressures on the business sector (Canadian Press, 2013; Hall, 2013). The federal government prefers to encourage Canadians to contribute to voluntary individual savings plans. In particular, a proposal to boost C/QPP premiums was rejected in December 2013 by then federal finance minister Jim Flaherty (CBC News, 2014; Hall, 2013). Ironically, however, a recent federal report suggested that in the long term, enhanced pension benefits for older Canadians would actually help the economy—for example, by increasing opportunities for the consumption of goods and services (CBC News, 2014). Moreover, the future economic security of older Canadians may be at risk if the program is not enhanced (CBC News, 2014). Wes Sheridan, the former finance minister of Prince Edward Island, was quoted as saying the following:

> We're talking about a generation of young people in their twenties, thirties and forties, going into the workplace with part-time jobs, no benefits and limited savings ability. If we don't act we'll have a generation of Canadians who will not be able to retire in dignity. (Hall, 2013)

Further, since provinces are responsible for delivering social services, Sheridan added that "we're going to pay either way if the next generation of retirees doesn't have enough to live on" (Hall, 2013).

---

more heavily on private retirement savings, which represent the third pillar of Canada's retirement income system: including **private employer-sponsored pension plans**—sometimes called Retirement Savings Plans (RSPs)—and individual **Registered Retirement Savings Plans** (**RRSPs**). Employer-sponsored pension plans are based on employer and employee contributions. These plans were established through the 1950s to 1970s to discourage employee strikes and enhance company loyalty (Chappell et al., 2003). Few workers initially had access to employer-sponsored plans, which as of 2012 provide coverage to approximately 38 per cent of Canadian employees (Office of the Chief Actuary, 2014). Access to these plans tends to be associated with higher income levels, unionized workplaces, and larger employers (Baldwin, 2009).

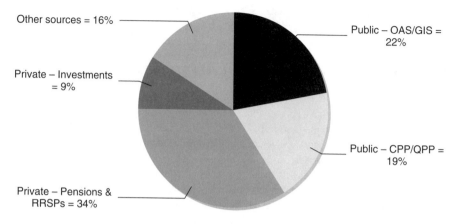

Other sources = 16%

Public – OAS/GIS = 22%

Private – Investments = 9%

Public – CPP/QPP = 19%

Private – Pensions & RRSPs = 34%

Figure 5.1 Sources of retirement income in Canada, 2011
Source: Employment and Social Development Canada. (2015). Indicators of well-being in Canada: Financial Security—Retirement Income. Retrieved from http://www4.hrsdc.gc.ca/.3ndic.1t.4r@-eng.jsp?iid=27

However, in Canada and around the world, workplace pension coverage appears to be declining, and its adequacy has been questioned (Ambachtsheer, 2008; Béland & Shinkawa, 2007; Brown, 2011). In particular, there has been a movement away from **defined benefit** to **defined contribution** plans in private sector employer pensions, in Canada and other countries (Béland & Shinkawa, 2007; Brown, 2011; Marshall & Taylor, 2005; McDonald & Donahue, 2011). This change in plan structure means that retiree benefits are more dependent on the economic return on investment that is generated by plan contributions. As such, these plans are more affected by economic fluctuation and introduce a greater element of personal risk into retirement income; this risk is now managed by individual workers and/or their financial investor, requiring higher skills in financial literacy (McDonald & Donahue, 2011). Such changes align with international shifts towards marketization and personal responsibility in pension policy (Bode, 2007).

Despite the trends in declining pension coverage among current employees, the retirement income system overall relies heavily on this source of income (as well as other private sources). The proportion of retirement income represented by employer pensions, for example, increased from 12.5 per cent in 1980 to 32.0 per cent in 2002 (Mo, Légaré, & Stone, 2006). The Conference Board of Canada (2013) indicates that Canada is actively encouraging the growth of and reliance on private sector sources of retirement income, in order to minimize reliance on public sources of income in old age. This same trend has been observed internationally by Pedersen (2004), who cautions that "private pensions are everywhere a very strong source of inequality in the income package of retired households" (p. 21).

Participation in RRSPs is growing but is lower than participation in employer pension plans; participation also depends heavily on personal level of income—the greater the income, the more likely a person is to contribute to an RRSP (Baldwin, 2009). Though RRSPs are heavily promoted by government, only about 24 per cent of tax filers made an RRSP contribution in 2012, according to Statistics Canada.

Older persons may also have other sources of income, savings, or assets (potential income) peripheral to the three pillars of the retirement income system, such as investments. They may also be eligible for certain federal subsidy programs and discounts (see Box 5.3). Though many older persons may also own a home, which influences their standard of living (Baldwin, 2009), a minority (6.5 per cent) are still repaying a mortgage (OECD, 2013). Further, some older persons may face new challenges to their economic security in late life, including out-of-pocket expenses for health care and medical equipment.

Some older persons also work past the traditional age of retirement (age 65), whether due to need or choice. The trend towards delayed retirement will be addressed later in this chapter, after a brief overview of broad socio-economic forces shaping the experiences of older workers in Canada and other countries.

Box 5.3   Do We Need "The Seniors' Discount"?

In a 2013 article in *Maclean's* magazine, Peter Shawn Taylor challenges the need for seniors' discounts. He claims that "seniors today are among the richest, most comfortable people in the country" and that both the business and public sectors are overly generous with providing discounts and tax breaks to older persons. He also suggests some businesses are now re-evaluating their policies given the dramatic declines in poverty and increases in average incomes among older persons since the 1970s, as well as the increasing labour force participation of older workers. Taylor's own writing appears to reflect a sense of intergenerational inequity (see Chapter 2). Though acknowledging business discounts are ultimately only a marketing strategy, he appears resentful: "No one ever said the marketplace had to be fair to the young. Boomers still rule, even in retirement." He then redirects his frustration to what he calls "publicly funded seniors' discounts" such as property tax discounts, free tuition, or discount bus passes. He concludes the following: "Any money forgone via such discounts is money that must be extracted from other—working—taxpayers. Plus, given their financial wherewithal, most seniors don't even need the price break."

Consider what your own response to Taylor's argument might be, after reading the material presented in this chapter. What kind of rebuttal might you propose?

Source: Summary of Taylor, P. S. (2013, November 25). Pay up, grandma. *Maclean's, 126*(46), 18–21.

Older Workers

In 2011, approximately 19 per cent of Canada's workforce was 55 years of age or older (Statistics Canada, 2011b). As you might recall from your introductory sociology courses, the nature of work in Canada is changing over time. A post-industrial society is marked by a decline in traditional industrial sector work (i.e., resources and manufacturing) and growth in the service sector and information and communication work. Not only are older workers more likely to hold traditional jobs that are in decline (Cooke, 2006), but many new jobs require skills and abilities that older cohorts may not have received during their formative years in the public education system. New work also tends to be **non-standard work**, also known as **precarious employment** (McDonald & Donahue, 2011). These jobs tend to be part-time, temporary, seasonal, and often based on contract or self-employment; workers in these jobs typically face greater job insecurity and reduced access to private employer pensions or employment benefits such as C/QPP. The aging and retirement situations of future cohorts of older persons will be particularly affected by the growth in precarious employment, which may lead to precarious economic situations in later life.

Additionally, the current labour market is also affected by significant trends towards economic globalization and privatization that can lead companies to reduce the sizes of their workforces (e.g., downsizing or outsourcing). Marshall and Taylor (2005) suggest "these changes have had a disproportionate impact on older workers" (p. 575). Using five Canadian companies as case studies, Marshall and Marshall (2003) illustrate how company policies related to downsizing—including layoffs and retirement incentive programs—have differential effects on older workers. Similarly, in the United States, Ekerdt (2009) noted that "the recent recession has seen older workers less sheltered by their seniority against displacement, downsizing, and layoffs" (p. 74).

When older workers do lose their jobs, they typically face longer periods of unemployment and greater barriers to re-employment than younger workers. Unemployment among older workers is therefore an increasingly important concern among policy-makers seeking to encourage older persons to remain in the workforce. The stigma of being unemployed may influence retirement statistics because older unemployed persons may identify themselves as early retirees, when in fact they may have become discouraged from trying to re-enter the job market (McDonald, Donahue, & Marshall, 2000).

Unemployed older job seekers may face issues related to retraining, especially when new jobs are knowledge-based and involve rapid changes and new technology. In order to help unemployed older adults, the Canadian government introduced the "Targeted Initiative for Older Workers." This initiative provides employment assistant services, including skills retraining, to unemployed workers aged 55 to 64 in eligible communities affected by significant downsizing, closures, and/or high unemployment.

Negative stereotypes of older workers may also be a barrier to re-employment, as well as an issue for employed workers. As we saw in Chapter 2, older persons can be perceived by others as slow learners, unproductive, unfamiliar with new technologies, resistant to change, and "worn out." Ageism among managers and employers, as well as a lack of accommodations for older persons in the labour market, is a concern (Ekerdt, 2009), and Canada has directed attention to reducing workplace age discrimination, including prohibiting mandatory retirement (this will be discussed further in the next section).

However, other research has suggested that in practice, ageism may be less of an active force behind corporate behaviours that have discriminatory effects. In particular, McMullin and Duerden Comeau (2011) studied age discrimination in information technology (IT) firms, through quantitative and qualitative inquiry with employees in this industry. They documented ageist attitudes regarding whether IT workers could learn and adapt to new technologies with age, yet participants downplayed the structural constraints facing workers who seek to retrain and keep up-to-date. The authors concluded the following:

> Employers operate their firms under considerable financial constraints, so hiring younger employees assumed to know new technologies saves on training and theoretically on wages. Yet these structural actions reinforce and legitimate existing ageism, linking younger workers with technically adept skills. . . . [S]olutions targeted to finances in the form of funded training and other incentives may find more success than ameliorating attitudes alone. (McMullin & Duerden Comeau, 2011, p. 155)

Likewise, in Chapter 2, we reviewed a study of garment industry workers, in which McMullin and her colleague Victor Marshall (2001) documented how older workers in that sector internalized ageist stereotypes and believed they were the target of age discrimination, when in fact employer actions were often motivated less by age and more by economic considerations.

Older workers are also going to be increasingly more common in Canadian society; a trend towards later average retirement ages is occurring in Western societies (and in Japan), as discussed later in this chapter. First, in order to understand more about how individual decisions to retire or remain in the labour force are influenced by broader social structural conditions and policies, we must understand how retirement, as a social institution, operates.

Retirement as a Social Institution: Changes over Time

Retirement first became a common occurrence during industrialization, due to the introduction and spread of both the public (C/QPP) and private (employer-sponsored) pension plans, which stipulated a fixed age of retirement, most often at age 65 (Marshall & Taylor, 2005). The structured generation of retirement through pension policies meant that retirement became an institutionalized and expected part of the life course—first for men, and then for women as they moved into the paid labour force in greater numbers. In other words, retirement became an important age-graded transition (see Chapter 1).

Modernization theory (see Chapter 1) generally takes an uncritical view of the emergence of retirement. Specifically, it highlights the role of industrialization, population growth, and social change, which increased competition for jobs and the need for new skills possessed by younger workers—demands that facilitated the introduction of retirement. Political economists (and conflict theorists), however, would focus more on the active role of corporations in this process and the struggles between business and worker groups (such as unions) to secure employment benefits. In contrast, modernization theory utilizes a structural-functionalist approach, which tends to represent society as characterized by consensus or agreement. Another structural-functionalist perspective on retirement is disengagement theory (also addressed in Chapter 1), which suggests that retirement emerged as a functional response of society to industrialization. From this perspective, retirement helps move older workers out of the labour force and creates opportunities for young workers. This idea persists today in public opinion and public policy, fuelled by an ongoing sense of intergenerational inequity (see Chapter 2).

Though worker activism was a considerable factor in helping to establish public pensions in Canada, a political economy perspective on retirement would also draw attention to the roles of the business sector—and to how government policies generally align with and support these economic interests. As McMullin and Marshall (2001) observe, retirement ultimately helped companies hire younger employees at lower wages—for example, seniority being associated with higher pay over time—and drew on and further reinforced ageist beliefs that viewed older workers as "washed up." From this perspective, older workers became pushed out of the labour force into a marginalized status with reduced income (McMullin & Marshall, 2001).

Until recently in Canada, **mandatory retirement** was also legal for employers. Now, it is prohibited in provincial and federal human rights legislation and labour codes unless it is a "bona fide" (i.e., necessary) requirement of the occupation. Currently, however, various forms of compulsory retirement (or part-time retirement) persist in negotiated collective agreements

(Cooke, 2006; Ibbott, Kerr, & Beaujot, 2006) and pension contracts that include disincentives to work beyond age 65. As Cooke (2006) observes, mandatory retirement ages are "often set unilaterally by the employer and serves the firm's interest in flexibility" (p. 392).

Although prohibiting mandatory retirement aligns with human rights principles (e.g., against age discrimination), organized labour in Canada has voiced concerns that the real motivation for governments is political and economic. In other words, prohibiting mandatory retirement paves the way for increasing the age of eligibility for pensions and public benefits—such as the recent increase in the age of eligibility for OAS. Thus, "the elimination of mandatory retirement threatens many important worker gains in economic security" (Ibbott et al., 2006, p. 173) in late life, such as OAS and C/QPP; employers may also underfund private pensions.

Once retirement became an institutionalized part of the life course in Canada, older workers' participation in paid labour generally declined through the 1970s to 1990s. Ibbott, Kerr, and Beaujot (2006) attribute this decline to a weak labour market, strong capital market, improving pension entitlements due to the maturation of the C/QPP, and an economy that generated wealth surpluses for some pensions. More recently, however, P. Taylor (2013) documents a recent upwards climb in labour force participation among men aged 55 to 64 in Canada and other industrialized countries. Whereas employment rates for older men in Western developed countries were relatively high in the 1970s and then had dropped by the 1990s, these rates started increasing again until about 2007 to 2008 (P. Taylor, 2013). Upward trends in employment rates for older adults have also been identified in Canada by the National Seniors Council (2011), which notes that 36.5 per cent of Canadians over age 55 are in the paid labour force, and this number is expected to increase. Further, Carrière and Galarneau (2012) indicated that in 2009, workers continued in paid employment for an average of two additional years before retiring, in comparison to workers in 1998. McDonald and Donahue (2011) also identify a slight upward trend in women's retirement ages. Philip Taylor (2013) adds the following:

> The situation for women is somewhat different, with a broad upward trend in employment rates, although that is not to say that some older women were not subject to the same forces that were affecting men during this period. (p. 2)

These shifts in employment trends are in part due to uncertain economic situations: for instance, people who feel less secure about their financial situation in old age may postpone retirement for longer (McDonald & Donahue, 2011; P. Taylor, 2013). The National Seniors Council (2011) refers to the role of higher education and better health in the Canadian population as extending working lives, though noting that "inadequate retirement income, higher levels of debt, and the effects of economic downturn may also be preventing seniors from retiring as early as they wish" (p. 5). Ibbott et al. (2006) also note that public pension entitlements will no longer improve as they had historically (e.g., as with the maturation of the C/QPP). Further, as noted earlier, recent trends in employer pension plans towards defined contribution plans may also have the effect of delaying retirement, through increasing the insecurity of post-retirement incomes (Cooke, 2006; McDonald & Donahue, 2011).

The trend towards delayed retirement also aligns with recent policy shifts internationally and in Canada to promote extended (paid) working lives through policy reform (Curl & Hokenstad, 2006; Marshall & Taylor, 2005; P. Taylor, 2013; see also Figure 5.2). Governments in particular are motivated in this regard because of concerns about the sustainability of public pensions (Cooke, 2006). McDonald and Donahue (2011) for instance, note the presence of a crisis mentality about pensions (see Chapter 2; see also Boxes 5.1 and 5.2). However, such reforms also align with neoliberal political-economic goals that seek to justify the erosion of social safety nets by increasing individual responsibility for economic security in later life.

Cooke (2006) provides an overview of government policies to promote delayed retirement in different countries. Though prohibiting mandatory retirement through age discrimination legislation is one option—and this has been done in Canada—it is likely to have little effect on retirement ages

Rick Madonik / GetStock.com

Figure 5.2 Policy shifts in Canada encourage older workers to remain in the workforce for longer before retiring

(Cooke, 2006; Ibbott et al., 2006). Other options include increasing the age of eligibility for public pensions or changing contributions, benefits, or funding structures. Canada has, for instance, increased the age of eligibility for Old Age Security and is currently making changes to the CPP to promote delayed retirement (Cooke, 2006; Laurin, Milligan, & Schirle, 2012). The effect of these changes on retirement timing decisions will be disproportionate for those older workers who rely primarily on these sources of income, whereas older workers who have other sources of income in retirement—such as RRSPs and employer pensions—are less likely to be strongly affected (Cooke, 2006). Overall, however, research by Baker, Gruber, and Milligan (2003) confirms that C/QPP retirement disincentives may contribute to delayed retirement decisions.

Another option Canada has pursued to curb early retirement is to develop policies and programs to address unemployment among older workers (as noted earlier). However, these active labour market policies, such as skills training and employment support programs, may be limited when they focus only on older workers: "attempting to retrain workers only near the end of their working careers, without helping them upgrade skills and knowledge throughout adulthood, may be ineffective and does not constitute lifelong learning" (Cooke, 2006, p. 395). Cooke (2006) also notes that these programs may inadvertently promote a sense of intergenerational inequity among younger workers (see Chapter 2).

Lastly, various countries have sought to promote flexible, partial, and part-time retirement through policy change (Curl & Hokenstad, 2006). Although this aligns with worker preferences (Foot & Venne, 2011), government policies may ultimately have limited influence on how work is organized by employers (Cooke, 2006). Indeed, whether any specific policy changes will influence retirement ages is uncertain—particularly if the actual drivers behind delayed retirement are general economic conditions, which create greater uncertainty for post-retirement incomes (Cooke, 2006). Further, there are still some counteracting forces motivating early retirement, such as corporate economic restructuring in response to global market conditions and (potentially) public opinion about ideal retirement ages (Cooke, 2006). Lastly, as Cooke (2006) notes, most of these policies address only the last stage of the life course—the transition from work to retirement—without recognizing that this stage is shaped by earlier transitions between paid and unpaid work and education over the entire life course.

Further, some of these policy changes also have the potential to increase income inequality in late life (Cooke, 2006). For instance, as McDonald and Donahue (2011) note, policy change promoting delayed retirement can have negative effects on those who need to retire early for reasons of ill-health, unemployment, or family care responsibilities. These situations will be addressed in the next section.

Retirement Timing Decisions

We have discussed how retirement trends are influenced by changes in the economy, the nature of work and corporate interests, population health and longevity, and government policy. These changes shape individual choices and economic security in late life. Individual-level reasons for retiring from paid work vary widely. The ideal scenario is one in which our own desire for more leisure time motivates the transition to retirement; however, this option tends to be available only for those expected to have sufficient wealth in retirement. As noted in the previous section, decisions to retire also involve being "pulled" by incentives, such as the perceived adequacy of public or employer pensions (e.g., Schirle, 2010).

Other reasons for retiring may be viewed as less voluntary. Two of the most common reasons cited by retirees are poor health and family responsibilities (McDonald, Donahue, & Marshall, 2000; Schirle, 2010; Wannell, 2007); these are often described as factors that "push" people, often involuntarily, into retirement. If the health of the Canadian population continues to improve, people may be less likely to retire due to poor health; however, if current patterns of health care reform continue, more people—women in particular—may retire to provide care for an older parent or spouse (see Chapter 4).

The role of family considerations and obligations tends to be relatively neglected in research on retirement decisions. Ekerdt (2009) identifies family as an important example of how social structure influences retirement behaviour. An individual might retire to provide care for a spouse or parent, or even for a grandchild (see Chapter 7). In one US study that considered influences of family obligations and relationships on retirement decisions, researchers found that individuals providing financial support to their children are less likely to retire (Szinovacz, DeViney, & Davey, 2001). The authors of this study also emphasize the diverse ways in which family considerations shape retirement decisions. Decisions to retire are also often influenced by a desire (or pressure) to retire at the same time as a spouse (Henkens & van Solinge, 2002); since women tend to partner with older men, this can promote early retirement for women.

As noted earlier in this chapter, some workers may be pushed into retirement when working in a sector that involves considerable threats of layoffs due to economic restructuring. These workers may also be offered an **early retirement package** from their employer to facilitate their departure. Other workers lose their job and cannot find work (Ibbott et al., 2006). For the most part, these types of retirements—as well as retiring for health or caregiving reasons—are more involuntary. McDonald, Donahue, and Marshall (2000) suggest these factors may increase as reasons for retirement in the current social context of globalization, health care reform, and economic instability.

They also found that involuntary retirees—especially those who retire due to unemployment or poor health—are more likely to have lower retirement incomes (McDonald et al., 2000; see also Alan, Atalay, & Crossley, 2008). For these involuntary early retirees, changes to public elements of the retirement income system designed to promote delayed retirement may have detrimental effects.

Whether we retire for involuntary or voluntary reasons (or both), and whether we retire before or after age 65, the retirement transition process and our financial security in retirement are shaped in important ways by social structure, including government and business policies and regulations related to pensions, the labour market and financial savings, and health care (Ekerdt, 2009; Marshall & Taylor, 2005). Ekerdt (2009) notes how, in turn, the changing social institution of retirement—and associated behaviours of retirees—reshape social structures, including the workforce, the economy and consumer markets, family life, and migration patterns.

Diversity and Flexibility in Retirement: Destandardization of the Life Course

Social conditions at a historical point in time shape the decisions made by individuals about work and retirement, but research has suggested that these decisions may be less rigidly structured than in the past. Although there is a current trend towards delayed average retirement ages, retirement transitions are overall more heterogeneous and variable than when retirement first became an institutionalized part of the life course (Ekerdt, 2009).

This "new retirement" is not always rigidly normative for the fixed age of 65, nor is retirement always a clean transition—rather, it can be gradual, partial, early, or delayed, or it can involve multiple exits and re-entries from the labour force (Ibbott et al., 2006; McDonald & Donahue, 2011; Wannell, 2007). Increasing opportunities for retirement transitions result in part from a loosening of age norms (see age stratification theory in Chapter 1); these opportunities also reflect the increasing individualization of life course transitions in postmodern society (see the life course perspective in Chapter 1). For example, retirement is less tightly regulated by the state, as with the recent prohibition of mandatory retirement. There are also more educational opportunities for people across the life course, and career changes are becoming more normative. Policy-makers are also generally seeking to lift any disincentives to work at later ages, yet it is still possible for some to retire early. These changes in late-life work and retirement can be viewed as illustrative of the destandardization or deinstitutionalization of the life course in Western societies (Marshall & Taylor, 2005), or the age integration of society (see Chapter 1). However, these changes may also reflect the move away from traditional forms of work and the rise of non-standard, precarious work that is more characteristic of globalizing economies.

Regardless, the differentiation in retirement pathways makes the very concept of retirement much more difficult to precisely define and measure in research (Ekerdt & Deviney, 1990). Further, whether or not all older workers, and not just wealthier workers, actually have more agency in their retirement decisions (Cooke, 2006) is a point for debate. In the following sections, we will explore trends in older persons' incomes, including the risk of poverty for particular groups of older Canadians.

Financial Security in Old Age and Retirement

Since the introduction and expansion of Canada's retirement income system—including the maturation of the C/QPP, and expansions of employer pensions in the 1950s and 1960s—incomes and poverty rates among older Canadians have improved considerably, and poverty rates among older persons are quite low compared to other industrialized countries (Baldwin, 2009; Brown, 2011; Milligan, 2008; Myles, 2000; Osberg, 2001). Figure 5.3 demonstrates improvements in the poverty rate for older persons after the year 1976, when the first cohort of Canadians to receive full C/QPP benefits turned 65 years of age. Increasing participation of women in the paid labour force has also contributed to this improvement—for example, as more women have become eligible for C/QPP. For instance, in 2003, only 7 per cent of older persons lived below Statistics Canada's low-income cut-off (National Advisory Council on Aging, 2005a). Income inequality in older cohorts has also improved (Chappell et al., 2003; Myles, 2000).

However, since the mid-1990s, there has been either "stability or mild deterioration" (Baldwin, 2009, p. v) in the average incomes of older adults

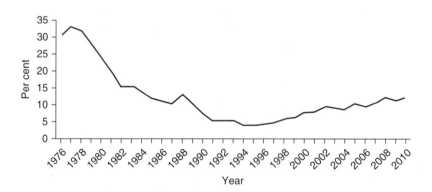

Figure 5.3 The elderly poverty rate in Canada after 1976
Source: Conference Board of Canada. (2013). Elderly poverty. Retrieved from http://www.conferenceboard.ca/hcp/details/society/elderly-poverty.aspx

(see also Milligan, 2008). There may also be a recent increase in low-income rates, though there is some variation in estimates depending on the particular measure used (Murphy, Zhang, & Dionne, 2012). The Conference Board of Canada (2013) indicated that poverty rates in older persons rose from 3.9 per cent in 1995 to 12.3 per cent in 2010. Old age poverty rates in Canada have historically been very low in comparison to other industrialized countries; however, the OECD (2013) noted that "while old-age poverty fell in 20 OECD countries between 2007 and 2010, old-age poverty in Canada increased by about 2 percentage points over the same period" (p. 1).

The future economic security of older persons is uncertain, but several forces may create challenges. These include declines in access to and changes within employer pensions, such as the shift to defined contribution plans (Baldwin, 2009; Brown, 2011; McDonald & Donahue, 2011). People are also spending longer periods of time in retirement due to extended life expectancies, requiring their private savings to stretch further. More Canadians may find it difficult to maintain their expected standard of living in retirement. For instance, about one-half of Canadians currently aged 45 to 64 are expected to face a 25 per cent decrease in their living standards in retirement; about one-third may experience inadequate incomes (Baldwin, 2009; Moore, Robson, & Laurin, 2010; Wolfson, 2011).

A tumultuous economy creates greater risk for private assets and investments. Further, inequalities in retirement income within older cohorts may increase (National Advisory Council on Aging, 2005a), for instance because of the maturation of RRSPs and the increasing importance of private savings for retirement income. As Chappell et al. (2003) note, any future gains in average income in older cohorts are likely to be generated by private sources of income (the third pillar); these sources of income are more common among wealthier Canadians (and men). The Conference Board of Canada (2013) confirms the risk of reliance on private sources of retirement income: "the most vulnerable among the elderly are being put at greater risk of poverty." This sentiment is also echoed in a recent report by the OECD (2013), which notes that public transfers (e.g., OAS, C/QPP) currently account for less than 39 per cent of gross incomes of older Canadians, in contrast to an average of 59 per cent in all OECD countries.

Economic Insecurity: Older Groups at Risk

Many retired older adults are on fixed incomes and have relatively low ability to adjust to sudden shocks to their income; for instance, they may no longer be able to take on paid work to supplement their incomes (Baldwin, 2009). Their incomes tend to be more sensitive to economic fluctuations, especially since many older persons' incomes are just above the low-income threshold (National Seniors Council, 2009). In part, this sensitivity may help explain increases in low-income rates between 2007 and 2009: "a small change in their income or the threshold may result in a large change in the incidence" of low income in older cohorts (Murphy, Zhang, & Dionne, 2012, p. 30).

Some groups of people face greater risk of inadequate economic security and poverty in their old age. In particular, the following groups of older persons face higher rates of low-income status: unattached (non-partnered) older persons, especially unattached women; older persons who are recent immigrants; older persons with fewer than 10 years in the paid labour force; urban-dwelling seniors; Aboriginal seniors; and those who retire early due to poor health and family responsibilities (Baldwin, 2009; Employment and Social Development Canada, 2012; Gazso, 2005; McDonald & Donahue, 2011; National Seniors Council, 2009). We will focus in greater detail on unattached older women and older persons who recently immigrated to Canada.

Because of a trend towards increased labour force participation among younger cohorts of Canadian women, these women may be in a stronger financial position in their retirement—for example, by having more access to and participation in RRSPs as well as employer pensions. However, this may change if the retirement income system is restructured in significant ways (Rosenthal, Denton, Martin-Matthews, & French, 2000). Marital status remains a key determinant of the economic security of older women. Being separated, divorced, or widowed in old age is associated with increased risk of poverty—especially for women, who are more likely to draw on GIS (Davies & Denton, 2002; Marier & Skinner, 2008; McDonald & Robb, 2004). McDonald, Donahue, and Moore (2000) explain that "a history of intermittent work outside of the home does not afford much protection for income in retirement" (p. 343). Both OAS/GIS and C/QPP are not always sufficient to keep these women from poverty, and few have access to occupational pensions and RRSPs. Smith, Magee, Robb, and Burbidge (2000), in examining the income of women ages 51 to 75 who live alone, conclude the following: "if future governments decide to cut real transfers to older women, and the trends in other income sources continue, the poverty problem among older women will quickly re-emerge" (p. 293).

The structural roots of the problem lie in the Canadian retirement income system's reliance on earnings-related public and private pensions—a system that disadvantages those who have more intermittent histories in the paid labour force (Marier & Skinner, 2008). Likewise, Gazso (2005) emphasizes that explaining the increased poverty of unattached older women requires knowledge of why women tend to contribute less to the C/QPP and to either private employer pensions or RRSPs. In particular, the gender gap in wages and the tendency for women to work in low-paid occupations—a reflection of **occupational segregation**—results in low earnings and limited access to private pension plans; women also tend to work in non-standard jobs (e.g., part-time, seasonal, contract, self-employed). Further, women's greater involvement in unpaid work throughout their life course—such as housework and caring for children, parents, and spouses—means they are more likely to face opportunity costs for their paid employment (e.g., fewer chances to advance in their careers) and generally less likely to have sustained involvement in the paid labour force. Yet women continue to have primary responsibility for tasks in the family domain (see Chapter 7); indeed, the gendering of both the private (family) and public (work) spheres of life restricts women's ability to develop assets and savings over time (Denton & Boos, 2007).

As Gazso (2005) notes, solutions to address poverty in women's later life should address structural constraints across their entire life course, such as access to public child and elder care services, pay equity, and equal opportunity workplace policies. Davies and Denton (2002) also highlight the challenges that divorced women face in navigating the Canadian legal system to secure the splitting of pensions and assets.

We might also consider financially compensating women who leave paid work to provide care for family members. Keefe and Rajnovich (2007) explore this concept further:

> While other countries have embraced financial compensation as an approach to support caregivers, this has not been a popular policy approach in Canada. What financial support does exist comes largely through the tax system or for a limited number of eligible employees whose family member is near death—the Employment Insurance program. Federal forays into financial support for caregivers is complicated by jurisdictional issues, since home and continuing care programs are under provincial/territorial jurisdiction, not federal. (p. 86)

Financial support and/or compensation for family caregivers is advocated within a proposed National Caregiver Strategy (Carstairs & Keon, 2009) and by the Mental Health Commission of Canada (2012). Nearly half of OECD countries have some form of direct payments for family caregivers (Colombo et al., 2011).

Another group that faces a high risk of economic insecurity and low income in later life are older immigrants to Canada, particularly those who immigrated later in their lives and thus have more limited opportunities to gain pensionable earnings in Canada (Elgersma, 2010). These immigrants are more likely to rely on GIS for their income (Marier & Skinner, 2008) and to live in poverty (Baker, Benjamin, & Fan, 2009). Further, some immigrants cannot apply for full pension or OAS/GIS benefits due to residency requirements (Kaida & Boyd, 2011; Marier & Skinner, 2008). Visible minority immigrants are also less likely overall to have employer pension coverage than other Canadians, in part due to differences in the types and sector of paid work (Morissette, 2002). Though Kaida and Boyd (2011) and Elgersma (2010) observe that poverty among older immigrants can be somewhat mitigated through financial support from their families (and co-residence with family), this can create a risk of dependency and social isolation (the sponsorship program is discussed further in Chapter 7). Kaida and Boyd (2011) recommend reducing the length of residence requirement for OAS; ironically, however, the federal government recently extended the length of residence requirement for older sponsored immigrants—specifically, sponsored parents and grandparents under the family sponsorship program—from 10 to 20 years; the residence requirement for non-sponsored immigrants to apply for OAS remains at 10 years, although some immigrants can receive partial benefits. Further, if they reside in a country that has an international agreement with Canada, some older immigrants may use pensions from their country of origin.

In sum, certain groups remain at high risk for economic insecurity in their old age, and there is concern that future changes to the retirement income system might widen the gap between these groups and wealthier older Canadians. In the final section of this chapter, we will examine some of the ways in which income inequality among older cohorts has been approached in social gerontological research.

Economic Security across the Life Course: Examining Income Inequality in Older Cohorts

How do work and retirement patterns and policies shape the distribution of resources among individuals in a society? Sociologists have been exploring this issue using the concept of cumulative advantage/disadvantage (Dannefer, 2003; O'Rand, 1996a, 1996b), a concept influenced to some extent by life course theory (see Chapter 1). The concept of cumulative advantage/disadvantage proposes a stable pattern whereby advantages in income and other resources (such as health or education) that manifest at early ages have accumulative or amplified effects over time, resulting in widening disparities at older ages. It is similar to but extends beyond the sociological concept of **social reproduction**, which focuses on the transmission of inequalities over time and between generations. Likewise, the **status maintenance** hypothesis proposes that post-retirement privilege, and resource inequality, reflect pre-retirement privilege and inequality, and that inequality remains fairly stable as cohorts age. For instance, having higher levels of resources such as income and education in earlier life affects post-retirement access to private pensions and RRSPs; in this way, high-income younger persons become high-income older persons. In contrast, cumulative advantage/disadvantage proponents maintain that disparities amplify over time. For example, having the financial means to purchase a home in young adulthood can generate increases in the value of this asset over time. The processes involved in cumulative advantage, however, are considerably complex, and they can be mitigated or changed, for instance, through factors ranging from macro-level public pension structures to individual-level job mobility (Dannefer, 2003; Ferraro & Shippee, 2009; O'Rand, 1996b).

In the United States, income inequality appears higher in post-retirement age groups than pre-retirement age groups, resulting in an evident pattern of cumulative advantage (Crystal & Shea, 2002). In Canada, however, a greater degree of **status levelling** occurs: specifically, public supports provided to older persons—such as federal pensions and Old Age Security—to some extent level out any large economic gaps that exist among working-age cohorts. This is especially the case when such supports are distributed universally, such as with Old Age Security. The result, in Canada, is a more level income distribution in older cohorts in comparison to pre-retirement cohorts (Prus, 2002). Income inequality in a cohort declines in retirement, because the lowest-income individuals experience less change due to income maintenance effects of OAS/GIS, and the highest-income individuals experience more substantial income drops (Brown, 2011). Canada also has more equal income distributions in old age compared to other countries (Prus, 2000).

Ultimately, explanations focused on age levelling, status maintenance, and cumulative advantage "each have elements of truth" (Crystal & Shea, 2002, p. 272) in describing the extraordinarily complex processes behind economic outcomes in late life and the distribution of these outcomes. Further, even though Canada's system currently supports a pattern of levelling of inequalities in old age, economic and policy changes that promote greater reliance on private sources of income in old age, including employer pensions, may exacerbate inequalities, resulting in a pattern more reflective of cumulative advantage.

Conclusion

As Baldwin (2009) notes, the significant improvements in the incomes of older Canadians reflect more than the success of our retirement income system—these improvements reflect the way this system "interacted with a particular set of financial and economic circumstances. The existing [retirement income system] will produce different outcomes under different circumstances" (p. v). Attention should be directed in particular to exploring the potential impacts of globalization on future changes to Canada's retirement income system, such as changes to eligibility requirements for public sources of retirement income and shifts in the types of employer pension coverage, as well as access to these sources of income. Globalization will also continue to shape work across the life course, with implications for income and income distributions in later life.

Canada's retirement income system has been quite successful in improving the economic security of older persons, but it operates in a shifting social, political, demographic, and economic context. Further, some groups remain at considerable risk of poverty in old age. In addition, though future cohorts of older women will have spent more time in the paid labour force, their unpaid work in the home across their life course continues to be undervalued, with implications for their income security in later life.

As Denton and Spencer (2009) note, one of the problems with the concept of retirement, which is often reinforced in research on the topic in social gerontology, is that the concept represents the following:

> It is an essentially negative notion, a notion of what people are *not* doing— namely, that they are *not working*. A more positive approach would be to focus, instead, on what people *are* doing, including especially their involvement in non-market activities that are socially productive, even if those activities do not contribute to national income as conventionally measured. (p. 63)

Indeed, it is this focus on paid labour as the ideal form of social participation that can contribute to ageism and social exclusion. In the next chapter, we will address the ways in which older persons continue to contribute to their families, communities, and societies.

Questions for Critical Thought

1. At what age would you like to retire? Does this ideal age align with when you think you might reasonably be able to retire? Draw on the concept of "social clocks" from Chapter 1.

2. In your own words, how are individual decisions to retire shaped by broader social structural influences? How did this chapter improve your understanding of the meaning of "social structure"?

3. Do you agree or disagree that retirement is becoming "destandardized"? What evidence supports your opinion?

4. Do you believe that policy efforts to promote delayed retirement will be successful in Canada? What evidence supports your opinion?

5. Can you think of any occupations in which retirement at a certain age would constitute a reasonable, "bona fide" job requirement? Check whether you can confirm your guesses (e.g., by doing an Internet search of recent court cases on the topic of mandatory retirement).

Suggested Readings

Cooke, M. (2006). Policy changes and the labour force participation of older workers: Evidence from six countries. *Canadian Journal on Aging, 25* (4), 387–400. Cooke reviews five types of policy changes that countries have pursued to encourage the labour force involvement of older workers and to delay retirement. He also reviews the potential of policy changes to make a difference, and he concludes by emphasizing that there is a greater need to consider policies that take a life course perspective.

Dannefer, D. (2003). Cumulative advantage/disadvantage and the life course: Cross-fertilizing age and social science theory. *Journals of Gerontology, 58B* (6), S327–S337. Dannefer defines cumulative advantage/disadvantage as "the systematic tendency for interindividual divergence in a given characteristic (e.g., money, health, or status) with the passage of time" (p. 327). He provides an overview of the concept and its connection to existing social gerontological areas of inquiry, including poverty and inequality in old age.

Gazso, A. (2005). The poverty of unattached senior women and the Canadian retirement income system: A matter of blame or contradiction? *Journal of Sociology and Social Welfare, 32* (2), 41–62. Gazso provides a sociological explanation for the poverty risk among unattached older women in Canada. She argues that although OAS/GIS are often insufficient, the roots of the problem lie in broad social-structural barriers operating across women's life course that serve to limit their contributions to the C/QPP and RRSPs, and their access to occupational pensions.

Relevant Websites

Conference Board of Canada, "Elderly Poverty"
http://www.conferenceboard.ca/hcp/details/society/elderly-poverty.aspx
> The Conference Board of Canada is an independent, not-for-profit applied research organization. This web page summarizes 2013 evidence regarding poverty among older persons in Canada, comparing elderly poverty rates in Canada to rates in other countries.

National Seniors Council, "Report of the National Seniors Council on Low Income among Seniors"
http://www.seniorscouncil.gc.ca/eng/research_publications/low_income/2009/hs1_9/page04.shtml
> This report provides an overview of older Canadians' financial conditions, including a focus on those with low or modest incomes. It develops recommendations for the federal government stemming in part from round-table discussions hosted in 2008.

Organisation for Economic Co-operation and Development, "Pensions at a Glance 2013: Retirement-Income Systems in OECD and G20 countries"
http://www.oecd.org/pensions/pensionsataglance.htm
> The OECD is an intergovernmental organization that advises policy-makers on how to enhance economic and social well-being. You can download the fifth edition of this report examining pension policies and outcomes for economic security across different countries. See Canada's specific "country profile" for additional information.

6

Beyond Participation: The Social Inclusion of Older Adults

Learning Objectives

In this chapter, you will learn that:

◎ sociologists have long been interested in how modernization and industrialization might generate social isolation; more recently, gerontologists have focused on the extent to which older adults actively participate in their communities.

◎ there is a strong established association between participation in social activities and health—however, just as social participation can enhance health, poor health can limit social participation.

◎ though older adults' social participation benefits society, critical gerontologists direct attention to the alignment between social participation initiatives and politically and economically motivated interests that seek to reduce the public provision of formal services for older adults.

◎ declines in social integration later in life are connected in part to age-related health challenges; life course transitions and loss; and socio-economic, transportation, and community-level barriers.

◎ a social exclusion framework directs our attention to older adults' access to material resources, social and health care services, and supportive physical environments; it also considers the exclusion of older adults in terms of cultural representations, political representation, and civic empowerment.

◎ various programs and interventions can offer and promote opportunities for the social participation of older adults, but changes at broader levels can promote social inclusion.

Introduction

Sociologists have long been interested in the social change that has occurred as a result of modernization and industrialization—in fact, the emergence of sociology as a discipline was in part a reaction to new social problems that stemmed from modernization and industrialization. One characteristic of this social change is the weakening of small, cohesive, and trusting communities rooted in family and tradition—communities that typically exhibit strong social control—relative to a proliferation of social ties that may be more impersonal and based on self-interest. A variety of factors lie behind this change, including urbanization, new technologies, mass media, geographic mobility, increasing prosperity, specialization of labour, changes in social norms, and the development of large bureaucracies. Sociologists such as Ferdinand Tönnies and Émile Durkheim were interested in the potential effects of this "mass society"[1]—particularly the risk of weakened social connections and increasing isolation in contemporary societies (Macionis & Gerber, 2011).

Social integration and inclusion among older persons is the focus of this chapter; we will try to maintain a sociological focus by integrating consideration of broader, contextual-level factors in the social environment that shape the integration of older adults into the social fabric. Existing gerontological research in this regard is dominated by a focus on individual-level **social participation** in social, leisure, civic, or voluntary activities or groups (both formal and informal), and by a focus on health as an outcome of participation. This emphasis may stem in part from the tendency of much research to draw implicitly on activity theory—the idea that promoting the ongoing engagement of all older adults will enhance their well-being and successful aging (see Chapter 1).

Indeed, the informal and formal participation of older adults in a community not only provides opportunities for them to give and receive support, but can enhance their feelings of belonging, trust, and security, as they get to know and interact with others. These feelings are commonly encompassed within the broader concept of **social capital**. In other words, social capital considers not only behavioural aspects of participation, such as group membership and number of interactions, but also related attitudinal aspects, such as sense of cohesion and trust in others. From this perspective, the behavioural and attitudinal dimensions are seen as mutually reinforcing each other (Chappell & Funk, 2010; Paxton, 1999; Petersen, 2002; Veenstra, 2000). Other researchers adopt a broader conceptualization of social capital—where social capital is seen not as a characteristic of individuals who participate, but as a characteristic of the entire neighbourhood or community. From this perspective, the extent to which neighbours and community residents are connected to and trust each other may benefit all members of the area, regardless of their own level of participation. Other sociological approaches to participation will be explored throughout this chapter, with a focus on how broader structural forces shape older persons' interests in and opportunities for participation, as well as their experiences of inclusion or exclusion.

First, some distinctions are needed between several similar concepts often used interchangeably in gerontological research. A **social network**[2] refers to the structure (e.g., density, homogeneity, size) of the entire web or set of social connections and interactions between individuals. Networks indicate the potential (but not necessarily actual) support or function of these connections for individuals. **Social integration** usually refers to the degree to which individuals are embedded within social networks, relying on objective measures such as the number of ties and connections to others. On the other hand, **social isolation** refers to a lack of connections, relationships, and interactions with others, and is based on subjective perceptions such as loneliness, a sense of emotional connection to others, and whether people believe they can rely on their neighbours for help.

Finally, **social support** refers to the functional content of our social networks and encompasses various kinds of assistance and resources exchanged between network members. Though social support normally refers to unpaid help, one might also consider the role of community services, non-profit agencies, and publicly funded government services—collectively referred to as the "**social safety net.**" Social support is crucial for older persons' well-being, and it includes the more intensive forms of caregiving in families and communities discussed in Chapters 4 and 7. In this chapter, our focus is less on social support and more on participation, integration, and inclusion—in other words, the broader ways in which older persons are engaged within networks, communities, and society.

Social Participation and Well-Being

Lack of social engagement and participation in older adults has been identified as a public health concern in Canada (Chief Public Health Officer, 2010). In addition, lack of opportunities for social participation—in education, paid work, and social activities—among family members caring for older relatives is also a health and human rights concern (see Chapter 8), as some caregivers are also at risk of isolation.

Most gerontological research on social integration tends to focus on individual participation in formal and informal groups and activities, and the associated health outcomes. Fairly robust evidence supports an association between various types of social participation and physical health, function, and delayed mortality (Avlund et al., 2004; Everard, Lach, Fisher, & Baum, 2000; Mendes de Leon, Glass, & Berkman, 2003; Menec, 2003). Attitudinal aspects related to participation, such as trust and sense of belonging, may also enhance physical health and prevent long-term illness (Andrew, 2005; Hyyppä, Mäki, Impivaara, & Aromaa, 2007; Veenstra, 2005; Young, Russell, & Powers, 2004).

Research also suggests fairly strong associations between participation and health outcomes such as cognitive function, psychological health, life satisfaction, and quality of life (Andrew, 2005; Bowling, Banister, Sutton, Evans, & Windsor, 2002; Ellaway & Macintyre, 2007; Glass, Mendes de Leon, Bassuk, & Berkman, 2006; Pilkington, Windsor, & Crisp, 2012). Similarly, trust in others and sense of belonging have positive associations with outcomes such as psychological well-being, mental health, happiness, and life satisfaction (Theurer & Wister, 2010; Yip et al., 2007; Young et al., 2004).

Social engagement therefore appears in many cases to be beneficial at the individual level, though we need a better understanding of why this is so. As we previously noted, participation may generate positive feelings of trust and belonging. Participation also expands older persons' range of available social networks and opportunities to give and receive various forms of support. However, one of the drawbacks in much research on participation and health is that many studies are cross-sectional—that is, all of the data were collected at the same point in time. Researchers tend to assume that an association between participation and health means that participation enhances health; less often do they consider that poor health might reduce levels of participation.

In other words, though participation is often viewed as a causal predictor of health outcomes, poor health—both physical and psychological—can restrict people's ability to participate and interact with others. Conditions such as strokes, heart attacks, bone fractures, vision or hearing impairments, functional limitations, and depression can constrain participation (e.g., Crews & Campbell, 2004; Ekström, Ivanoff, & Elmståhl, 2008; Ostir, Ottenbacher, Fred, & Guralnik, 2007; Strain, Grabusic, Searle, & Dunn, 2002). Indeed, age-related declines in overall social participation and network size (discussed in the next section) are often attributed to physical, cognitive, and/or psychological decline.

Age, Social Participation, and Integration

What happens to our social participation and embeddedness in social networks as we age? There is wide variation and complexity in age-related change overall in social integration and networks, and older people are diverse in terms of their social connectedness (Guiaux, van Tilburg, & Broese van Groenou, 2007; van Tilburg, 1998). A similar point is made by Cloutier-Fisher, Kobayashi, and Smith (2011), who emphasize the ways in which older persons subjectively interpret their own level of social contact. For instance, in interviews with older adults identified as being at risk of isolation, some older adults reported that they did not feel isolated or lonely, because they preferred limited social networks, or because losses they experienced were buffered by other community social ties or contacts with family members (Cloutier-Fisher et al., 2011). Keeping these important points in mind, we will overview some of the general patterns in gerontological research in terms of objective levels of integration or isolation.

As a general trend, levels of social participation tend to decline with age (Nieminen et al., 2008; Richard, Gauvin, Gosselin, & Laforest, 2009). In one study (Cutler & Hendricks, 2000), group membership increased in older persons aged 55 to 59, decreased in the 60 to 64 age group, and remained stable among age groups over age 65. However, many older adults continue to be heavily involved with some forms of participation—for instance, even though more younger adults volunteer in comparison to older adults, older adult volunteers on average contribute considerably more volunteer hours (see Table 6.1).

Though there has been considerable initiative at the policy level to recognize and promote the important social contributions made by older volunteers in North America and Europe, Martinson and Minkler (2006) remind us to question the dominance of this particular form of social activity in public discourse about older adults and social engagement. Martinson and Minkler suggest that emphasizing involvement in volunteer activities represents a narrow view of social engagement and meaning in later life. They state that the current emphasis on formal volunteer work (e.g., as represented in Figure 6.1) can be explained by its alignment with the contemporary political and economic context, in which the non-profit and voluntary sector is increasingly becoming responsible for filling the gap in eroding formal services. They further add that we must be careful not to inadvertently devalue older adults who do not or cannot volunteer. For instance, declines in social participation in older age groups are often attributed to the age-related health challenges described in the previous section, as well as life course transitions (e.g., retirement, widowhood, separation, or divorce), socio-economic barriers, and transportation barriers. Data from the 2008/2009 Canadian Community Health Survey indicated that although 80 per cent of older persons frequently participated in at least one kind of social activity, between 21 and 27 per cent wished they could be more involved (Gilmour, 2012).

Although overall levels of social and group participation may decline to some extent with age, the majority of older adults tend to be well embedded

Table 6.1 Volunteer rate and average annual volunteer hours by age group, 2004–2010

	Volunteer rate			Average annual volunteer hours		
	2010	2007	2004	2010	2007	2004
	Percentage			Hours		
Total	47	46	45	156	166	168
Age Group						
15 to 24 years	58	58	55	130	138	139
25 to 34 years	46	40	42	109	133	137
35 to 44 years	54	52	51	136	158	152
45 to 54 years	45	48	47	167	170	177
55 to 64 years	41	40	42	201	205	202
65 years and over	36	36	32	223	218	245
65 to 74 years	40	40	39	235	216	250
75 years and over	31	29	23	198	222	234

Source: Adapted from Table 2 in Vézina, M., & Crompton, S. (2012). *Volunteering in Canada* (Statistics Canada Catalogue No. 11-008-X). Ottawa, ON: Minister of Industry. http://www.statcan.gc.ca/pub/11-008-x/2012001/article/11638-eng.pdf

Michael Ventura / Alamy

Figure 6.1 Older adult volunteers on average contribute considerably more volunteer hours than younger adults

in social networks. These networks, however, tend to decline somewhat in size with age, becoming more condensed and emotionally close (Ajrouch, Antonucci, & Janevic, 2001; Cornwell, Laumann, & Schumm, 2008). However, in one longitudinal study of Dutch older adults (van Tilburg, 1998), contact frequency in social networks declined with age, yet overall network size remained stable. Where declines in network size exist, this may be due to the death of age peers, retirement, or declines in health. Other factors can mitigate potential declines in the social capital inherent in one's networks—for instance, participation in religious organizations is associated with higher levels of perceived social support among older persons (Gray, 2009). Further, some age-related transitions such as widowhood may actually increase social contacts with others in one's network, at least initially (Guiaux et al., 2007; Utz, Carr, Nesse, & Wortman, 2002). For instance, this might occur when a wife has spent the last several years of her husband's life providing intensive levels of care (which reduces social contacts with others), and then after his death she has more time (and need) to engage with others for support and interaction. As further evidence of complexity, in one study (Cornwell et al., 2008), age had a "U-shaped" relationship with the frequency of older persons' social contacts even after taking into consideration life course factors that may affect this relationship, such as retirement, bereavement, and health problems (see Figure 6.2). It is possible, for

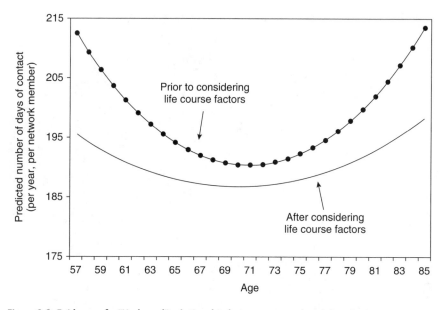

Figure 6.2 Evidence of a "U-shaped" relationship between age and social contact
Source: The Social Connectedness of Older Adults: A National Profile. Benjamin Cornwell, Edward O. Laumann, L. Philip Schumm. *American Sociological Review*. Reprinted with permission from SAGE Publications.

instance, that older persons receive more contact with others as they begin to require and receive various forms of care and support. Cornwell, Laumann, and Schumm (2008) conclude that "old age does not have a universal negative influence on social connectedness" (p. 185).

Some older persons are at particular risk for social isolation. Those most at risk include individuals of advanced old age, those in poorer health, those with fewer economic resources, those with lower levels of formal education, those living in rural or remote areas, widows, and men. Further, when older adults become family caregivers to their spouses or partners, they can be at increased risk of experiencing isolation and decreased social activity and participation, especially for caregivers of persons with cognitive impairments and for caregivers who perceive significant time and task demands (Haley et al., 1995; Seltzer & Li, 2000; Miller & Montgomery, 1990). Lack of social interaction may in turn exacerbate caregiver burden (Thompson, Futterman, Gallagher-Thompson, Rose, & Lovett, 1993). In fact, the commonly used Zarit Burden Interview—a measure of caregiver burden—includes a dimension addressing social burden, with questions about whether caregivers feel their social life has suffered and whether they feel uncomfortable having friends over to visit (Ankri, Andrieu, Beaufils, Grand, & Henrard, 2005; Zarit, Reever, & Bach-Peterson, 1980).

So far in this chapter, we have focused on objective levels of individual participation in social activity and connections to others; as mentioned, this focus tends to dominate in gerontological research. Rarely, however, are these individual levels and experiences of participation connected back to the broader, macro-level context. In the next section, we move to focus on societal-level barriers to a wider range of aspects of full participation (inclusion) in society—through this perspective, we examine how some groups of older adults become more vulnerable to social exclusion.

Barriers to Participation: A Focus on Social Inclusion and Exclusion

Bernard is 78 years old; he is retired, widowed, low income, and lives in a rural area. He can no longer drive and cannot walk far. He is socially isolated, depressed, and pessimistic. We might assume that Bernard simply needs to be encouraged to "get out more" and socialize with others in his community; we might suggest that he start volunteering. These recommendations would align with the principles of activity theory, as noted at the beginning of this chapter. However, it is problematic to assume that Bernard has full ability to control his social circumstances. In fact, it may be important to address his lack of financial, physical, and social resources in order to help him develop new social connections. The latter kind of thinking is more distinctly sociological.

Whereas research on social participation often tends to imply that individuals themselves are responsible for remaining active in their communities through various social, recreational, and volunteer activities, the concept of **social inclusion** highlights the power—and thus responsibility—of others in a society, through attitudes, policies, and practices, to influence a fuller range of aspects of individual engagement within that society. That is, social inclusion extends beyond social participation to individuals' full integration into society, including civic representation and access to formal services and economic resources; it highlights issues of power, rights, and integration within entire communities and societal organizations (Room, 1995). By extension, two definitions of **social exclusion** are provided below:

> The societal processes that systematically lead to groups being denied the opportunity to participate in commonly accepted activities of societal membership. It is an integrative concept that provides insights into how and why these groups experience material deprivation and how political, economic, and social conditions contribute to these conditions. (Raphael, 2009, p. 251)

The inability of certain subgroups to participate fully in Canadian life due to structural inequalities in access to social, economic, political, and cultural resources arising out of the often intersecting experiences of oppression related to race, class, gender, disability, sexual orientation, immigrant status, and the like. (Galabuzi, 2009, p. 254)

Old age can be considered as contributing to social exclusion—for instance, Podnieks (2006) notes how structural inequity and older persons' "lack of power and status makes it difficult for older people to access services; find out and negotiate what is due to them; respond to abuse and neglect; seek accessible information; and protest against age and gender-related discrimination" (p. 58). Social inclusion has been identified as a social determinant of health (Raphael, 2009), as referred to in Chapter 4, although it is difficult to measure and thus to trace its specific effects. However, social inclusion also tends to be valued independent of these effects on well-being, as a broader human right.

In the next section, we draw on and extend the multiple dimensions of social exclusion articulated by Scharf, Phillipson, and Smith (2005) that have particular relevance to older adults, drawing on empirical research findings to illustrate these different forms of exclusion.

Exclusion from Meaningful Social Relations

As one dimension of social exclusion, exclusion from meaningful social relations could encompass much of the current research on the extent to which older adults are embedded in informal social networks and engage in social interactions. Exclusion in this sense is similar to isolation. However, attention must be directed to how individuals become excluded from social relations. For instance, research by Bruce (2004) and Forbes et al. (2011) illustrates how negative perceptions of older persons who exhibit challenging symptoms of dementia (such as incontinence or aggression) can generate exclusion of these individuals by friends, family, acquaintances, and health care providers in interpersonal interactions. Grenier and Guberman (2009) also explain how older home care clients experience more limited opportunities for social interaction as their daily lives become increasingly structured around their medical needs and the health care system. Likewise, when health care providers do not address the socio-emotional, interpersonal, or relational needs of older clients—indeed, when care providers do not have time for this work and instead focus solely on the physical tasks—older recipients of care are denied opportunities for quality relationships and interactions (Aronson & Neysmith, 2001; Forbes et al., 2011; Grenier & Guberman, 2009).

Exclusion from Material Resources

Exclusion from material resources, such as income, is related to the distribution and redistribution of resources more broadly in a society (Galabuzi,

2009). Economic deprivation is an important concern in its own right and reflects this dimension of exclusion. Though material resources are often connected to paid employment, many older adults are retired and on fixed incomes, so it is particularly difficult for retired older adults to move out of poverty (Moffatt & Glasgow, 2009). Issues of income security for older Canadians were discussed in more detail in Chapter 5.

Poverty can limit older individuals' range of opportunities for social participation (Scharf et al., 2005; Rozanova, Keating, & Eales, 2012). For instance, Rozanova, Keating, and Eales (2012) describe how some rural Canadian seniors who lack personal resources are less able to join friends in certain activities, such as shopping, golfing, eating out, or travel. Grenier and Guberman (2009) further describe how the erosion of available publicly funded home care services tends to disadvantage those families who are unable to pay for private services, or find it difficult to do so, thereby generating exclusion.

Exclusion from Civic Activities or Civil Society

Exclusion from civic activities or civil society—including political engagement—expands beyond the traditional focus on social participation to consider whether individuals are empowered to and can participate in important political and organizational decisions (Scharf et al., 2005). **Civil society** refers to how citizens operating outside of the government can influence political decisions, for example through political parties, lobby and interest groups, the mass media, and social movements (Brym, 2014). With respect to micro-level decision-making at the institutional level, several researchers suggest that older persons—and their families—are excluded and lack power in home care assessment and eligibility decisions (Grenier & Guberman, 2009), care planning (Forbes et al., 2011), and organizational complaint mechanisms (Aronson & Neysmith, 2001). More broadly, many marginalized older persons tend to have little power in or opportunities for civic engagement, political decision-making, or collective action (Aronson & Neysmith, 2001; Grenier & Guberman, 2009; McBride, 2006). Discrimination related to age (such as an assumption of incapacity) and other marginalized social statuses (such as new immigrants) also play a role in limiting this kind of participation.

Exclusion from Basic Services

Exclusion from basic services needed to manage day-to-day life is another important dimension of social exclusion (Galabuzi, 2009; Scharf et al., 2005). The origins of this form of exclusion vary widely but are linked to cutbacks in publicly funded services in the context of globalization. Aronson and Neysmith (2001) highlight how unmet needs are generated in home care clients as a result of increasing service rationing and heavier workloads in this sector. City planning and changes associated with urbanization can also contribute to this form of exclusion, when shops and services move out of disadvantaged areas, leaving seniors without easy access to basic services and resources (Scharf, Phillipson, Kingston, & Smith, 2001). Lastly, Bruce (2004) identifies cultural and institutional origins of service exclusion in residential care providers' tendency to provide less care to residents with dementia. This may be related to both inadequate staff training and the stigma of dementia (Bruce, 2004). For example, in the study by Bruce (2004), residential care staff tended to believe that residents with the most advanced dementia no longer needed emotional and social support and contact.

Access to services and resources can shape social participation: for instance, Richard, Gauvin, Gosselin, and Laforest (2009) report an association between Montreal seniors' perceptions of their accessibility to key neighbourhood resources and their rates of social participation in that neighbourhood. In the absence of sufficient community-based supports and resources for older persons, such as affordable housing, older persons may have to relocate to other areas. In contrast, having access to these supports and resources facilitates the maintenance of social connections (Bell & Menec, 2013). Further, Rozanova et al. (2012) note that in rural areas with poor access to formal services, some older adults feel increasingly responsible to engage in care provision and service work for family, friends, and neighbours who rely on them for help. As a result, these caregivers and volunteers face limited opportunities to engage in other forms of social participation.

A lack of access to basic services for older persons can also stem from and further reinforce ageism, through a kind of symbolic exclusion: "the widespread limited public investment in care, the lack of a broad policy vision addressing elderly people's services, and the public statements made about them sustain the dominant public image of elderly people as marginal or without value" (Grenier & Guberman, 2009, p. 118).

Geographic or Spatial Exclusion

Geographic or spatial exclusion documents the effects of geographic, neighbourhood, and community environments on social engagement (Scharf et al., 2005), as well as more circumscribed ways in which a person's home can generate and intersect with other forms of exclusion. This dimension is particularly salient for older adults, who, in contrast to younger adults, tend to reside longer in the same neighbourhood, spend more time in that neighbourhood, express a greater sense of attachment to the local area, and have more localized social networks (Buffel et al., 2012). Ideally, helping older adults to remain within their own homes and communities should promote inclusion, through helping them maintain existing social ties (Hale, Barrett, & Gauld, 2010). However, the experience of disability, restrictive home care policies, lack of transportation, poorly accessible neighbourhood environments and buildings, and deteriorating social environments can mean that some older persons (and their family caregivers) become increasingly confined to their homes, while these homes themselves become transformed due to a lack of privacy and the infusion of medical equipment and tasks (Aronson & Neysmith, 2001; Bell & Menec, 2013; Grenier & Guberman, 2009; Hale et al., 2010; Scharf et al., 2001). For example, Aronson and Neysmith (2001) explain that due to home care service cutbacks over time, formal home care providers are no longer able to take older clients out for short trips in their neighbourhoods, which contributes to isolation. Grenier and Guberman (2009) further document how home care policies that directly link eligibility to clients' inability to leave their homes can enhance social isolation.

Older persons' perceptions of decline in their urban neighbourhoods can also contribute to their fear of crime and reluctance to leave their homes and participate in the community (Hand, Law, Hanna, Elliott, & McColl, 2012; Scharf et al., 2001). Though the loss of amenities and services is also a concern in deteriorating urban neighbourhoods, processes of gentrification can equally contribute to disconnection for older persons, who may find that services and spaces in newly developing neighbourhoods are designed for younger and middle-aged community residents (Burns, Lavoie, & Rose, 2012). Phillipson (2007) emphasizes the connection between various changes to urban neighbourhood environments and broader processes of globalization. He further suggests that globalization has widened the gap between older persons who are able to choose where they live and shape their environment, and older persons who are excluded from their local area, who are negatively affected by neighbourhood change, and who have less control over their physical and social environment (Phillipson, 2007).

To address these forms of geographic isolation in homes and neighbourhoods, attention needs to be paid to changes in physical and social environments, as well as to home care services that promote the inclusion of older adults. Further, we need to consider how rural older adults may be at particular risk of social isolation, because these areas tend to have high levels of poverty and unemployment, fewer (and declining) available services to facilitate participation and integration (such as transportation) or to help older persons' remain in their homes, and more out-migration of younger members of the community, including family members (Keating et al., 2011; Moffatt & Glasgow, 2009; Scharf & Bartlam, 2008). Though many rural seniors tend to be well embedded in social networks, this may change as some rural communities face increasing economic deprivation (Keating, Swindle, & Fletcher, 2011).

Cultural Exclusion

Cultural exclusion directs attention to how ageist discourses and ideas about older persons manifest at the individual level in narrow views about their needs, strengths, and experiences. This can happen within interactions, such as when home care professionals overlook the individual needs and diversity among their clients, focusing instead on narrow, medicalized stereotypes (Grenier & Guberman, 2009). This can also happen when potential employers do not hire older workers because of age-based assumptions (Rozanova et al., 2012), or when resident care aides label older residents with dementia as "difficult" and as less likely to benefit from or need care or attention (Bruce, 2004). Cultural exclusion through ageism is connected to other forms of exclusion, as noted by Podnieks (2006):

> The social exclusion of poor older people is closely allied to negative social and personal attitudes that construe ageing as a state of diminished capacities. Age-based prejudice isolates older people from consultation and decision-making processes at family, community, and national levels and can lead to denial of services and support on grounds of age. (p. 59)

As we discussed in Chapter 2, a variety of ageist discourses and ideas that have origins in the broader culture and society can also become institutionalized in common practices and policies that are age-discriminatory, as well as internalized within older persons themselves. Regarding the latter, some researchers have described how a fear of being viewed as old contributes to self-exclusion, when, for example, there is a reluctance to participate in services or activities that are specifically stated as being for "old people" (Bell & Menec, 2013). The stigma of dementia is a related concern; for instance, Forbes et al. (2011) noted that rural older adults with dementia were worried about how they would be viewed by community members.

Dowd (1975), in his development of social exchange theory (discussed in Chapter 1), suggested that because of older persons' reduced social position and lack of power or resources in an ageist society, their social relationships are more unequal, because they have reduced ability to reciprocate by offering something in return to the other person. This, Dowd believed, may explain why some older persons may be more likely to withdraw themselves from social relationships and interactions. Dowd's theory thus aligns well with the idea that social isolation has broader roots in an ageist society that reduces the power of older persons.

In addition to examining negative ageist assumptions and discourses, researchers (e.g., Bassett, 2012; Ranzijn, 2010) have directed attention to broader-level discourses that may appear to be positive (e.g., representing active or successful aging), but which can in fact serve to marginalize and exclude groups of older persons that are not able to live up to these ideals (as discussed in Chapter 2).

In examining the different dimensions of exclusion discussed in this chapter, we can trace the impact of a variety of structural (e.g., health care reform, governmental policies and practices), environmental (e.g., community development, urban planning, transportation), and cultural factors (e.g., ageism) on the social inclusion or exclusion of older adults. As you may be able to recognize, social inclusion approaches could be said to be more sociological than current approaches to social participation or integration that focus on the individual, because social inclusion directs attention to the systemic, root causes of isolation among older adults (i.e., beyond their choice to join social groups). This approach is also distinctly less biomedical in emphasis, because although social inclusion is a determinant of health, it is also viewed as a positive outcome in and of itself (i.e., as an aspect of social justice or human rights).

Some older persons experience heightened risk of social exclusion because of the intersection of age with other sources of marginalization—next, we will discuss two examples in more depth: gay and lesbian older adults, and immigrant older adults.

The Social Exclusion of Gay and Lesbian Older Adults

In recent years, some limited research attention has been directed to the exclusion experienced by lesbian, gay, bisexual, and transgendered (LGBT) older persons. Most of this research focuses on their experiences within the health and social care systems. For instance, Johnson, Jackson, Arnette, and Koffman (2005) highlight the potential for discrimination against LGBT within retirement facilities, by staff and residents, as well as through administrative policies and practices. Likewise, Phillips and Marks (2008) document how administrative discourses within aged care facilities in Australia, as evident within public brochures and facility policies, fail to represent non-heterosexual identities or address the needs of older lesbians. Lastly, a Canadian study (Brotman, Ryan, & Cormier, 2003) reports that older gay men and lesbians often fear the possibility of receiving care from existing eldercare systems, due to a mistrust created by historical, lifelong, and ongoing experiences of stigma, discrimination, and victimization. For these reasons, some gay and lesbian older adults even avoid contact with health care services or are afraid to disclose their identity to service providers. Further, even within existing gay and lesbian community services, the needs of older persons are often not well addressed, and older LGBT persons may experience ageism from within their communities (Brotman et al., 2003).

The Social Exclusion of Older Immigrants

Older immigrants can also face two intersecting processes of marginalization that can increase their risk of experiencing exclusion. In the context of increasing international migration as part of globalization, it is important to consider the needs of immigrants who either move to new countries at older ages or who immigrate young and then age within the host country. Migration can generate exclusion when it involves language barriers, cultural and family disruption, discrimination and barriers to full citizenship, or dis-advantage in material circumstances and employment (Heikennen, 2011; Torres, 2012). However, considerable variation in immigrant characteristics and backgrounds means "the risks of social exclusion in old age for people with a migrant background are, in fact, rather difficult to assess" (Torres, 2012, p. 43). One qualitative Canadian study suggests that immigrant older adults and their family caregivers may face greater risk of social isolation as well as challenges accessing formal services, in part due to a lack of culturally appropriate services (Stewart et al., 2006). Social isolation may also make older racial minority immigrants more vulnerable to abuse within their families (Tam & Neysmith, 2006).

Interventions and Broader Solutions

Different ideas about the nature of the "problem" of integration have led researchers to develop different conclusions about the most appropriate interventions and potential solutions to address issues of social isolation, integration, and inclusion in older adults. For instance, if you believe that the biggest problem of social integration is that older adults lack motivation to participate in formal and informal interactions, you would promote approaches that encourage and provide more opportunities for these activities. Many isolation interventions focus on identifying those older persons who are most at risk and then offering and promoting some form of support. There are a range of examples of interventions for older adults, which include the following: a community-based participatory arts project for disadvantaged urban older persons (Murray & Crummett, 2010), support groups for widowed older women (Stewart, Craig, MacPherson, & Alexander, 2001), a telephone support group for older spousal caregivers (Hartke & King, 2003), and a volunteer home visitor program (Andrews, Gavin, Begley, & Brodie, 2003).

However, the majority of intervention programs either lack evaluations or the quality of program evaluations are poor (e.g., they might lack a control group, pre- and post-tests, specification or rigorous measurement of expected outcomes, or sufficient sample size). As a result, it is difficult to draw overall conclusions about these programs; indeed, Findlay (2003) concludes that for this reason, "there is a belief that interventions can counteract social isolation and its adverse effects on older people, but the research evidence in support of this belief is almost non-existent" (p. 655). Tentatively, three reviews of interventions for social isolation specifically in older adults suggest combinations of social and educational or physical activities in group format, such as support groups, are promising, though programs may be more successful with women, when they involve older persons' active input into the program, and when they are implemented for at least five months (Cattan, White, Bond, & Learmouth, 2005; Dickens, Richards, Greaves, & Campbell, 2011; Findlay, 2003).

Much of the material presented in this chapter also highlights the importance of addressing barriers to older adults' social participation. Approaches could include developing and planning **age-friendly communities** with adequate physical accessibility and transportation services for older persons, or ensuring adequate income supports for low-income seniors. Other approaches could involve developing policies to encourage aging in place, but with sufficient supports for both older persons and their family caregivers. The interventions one might suggest are usually not discrete or bounded, as with a particular service or program—for instance, they might be policy-level changes. The challenge is that it is far more difficult to evaluate the effects of these broader structural changes on individual engagement or social integration.

Further, if issues of social participation or integration are viewed as part of a broader problem of social exclusion, one might consider a wide variety of types of changes. For instance, one potential way to address the problem of exclusion for LGBT older persons is through developing specialized residential care facilities, as discussed in Box 6.1.

Box 6.1   Social Exclusion among LGBT Older Adults

In his article entitled "For Gays, Entering Seniors Home Can Mean Going Back in Closet," Jeremy Nuttall raises public awareness of the need for personal care and retirement homes to develop a more inclusive approach towards older persons from the lesbian, gay, bisexual, two-spirit, and transgender community. As Nuttall states, "checking into a retirement home can be like taking a time machine back to the days when homosexuals were underground and didn't risk letting people know about their sexuality." In other words, some older persons may keep their sexual orientation a secret to avoid bigotry, isolation, or being bullied by other residents or staff persons.

Nuttall profiles the recent work of Alex Sangha, a social work graduate student and resident of Delta, BC, who is seeking to develop a retirement facility—called "Dignity House"—that specifically fosters an environment that is welcoming towards the LGBT community. Although facing criticisms from those who believe this approach further segregates different groups within the community, Sangha's idea garners the support of Brian O'Neill, a University of British Columbia social work professor, who is openly gay himself. O'Neill states that "these institutions have been basically and still are largely organized on the assumption that everybody is heterosexual." This can result in an unwelcoming atmosphere and sense of difference, contributing to depression.

Continued

Nuttall concludes by citing Sangha's response to the idea that Dignity House would create segregation: "gay and lesbian people are one of the most discriminated groups in society. If anyone ever needed a special place for them so they can live and be safe and live in dignity, it is gays and lesbians."

Source: Summary of Nuttall, J. J. (2012, December 31). For gays, entering seniors home can mean going back in closet. *The Tyee*. Retrieved from http://thetyee.ca/News/2012/12/31/Dignity-House/

As another example, potential solutions to address some of the barriers to the inclusion of older immigrants are discussed in Box 6.2. What is interesting about the article summarized in Box 6.2 is that the authors claim that promoting inclusion would boost the Canadian economy and help more efficiently "allocate human capital." This statement seems to reflect a phenomena critiqued by Lui, Warburton, Winterton, and Bartlett (2011): specifically, they point to narrow applications of the concept of inclusion that imply that everyone in society should "fit into" the existing social arrangements and functioning of dominant society. When older people become portrayed

---

Box 6.2   Social Exclusion of Older Immigrants to Canada

In a 2011 article in *The Globe and Mail*, Ghazy Mujahid (research associate, York University's Centre for Asian Research) and Thomas Klassen (political science professor, York University) identify how seniors who immigrate to Canada through the family sponsorship program can be socially excluded due to language and employment barriers. Language barriers can inhibit paid employment, and residency requirements mean that many immigrant seniors are unlikely to receive public supports such as Old Age Security. To prevent this form of exclusion among immigrant seniors, Mujahid and Klassen recommend that the federal government allocate more immediate and substantial assistance for immigrant seniors to learn either English or French. They also emphasize that the federal government should further help immigrant seniors by recognizing foreign educational credentials (or facilitating services to upgrade credentials) or previous employment experience in other countries. The authors claim that this approach would not only reduce exclusion but also help to more efficiently manage human capital and boost the productivity of the Canadian economy.

Source: Ghazy, M. & Klassen, T. (2011, June 27). Canada's neglected (immigrant) seniors. *The Globe and Mail*. Retrieved from http://www.theglobeandmail.com/globe-debate/canadas-neglected-immigrant-seniors/article584849/

primarily as "opportunities" for enhancing the economic functioning of society, other aspects of social inclusion—for instance, income security, political activism, or access to basic services—may be left unaddressed.

It is no surprise that research examining older adults' exclusion within health and social care systems recommends more effective training and support for individual service providers, in order to develop inclusive and culturally sensitive services (Forbes et al., 2011; Stewart et al., 2011). For instance, Bruce (2004) recommends that residential care staff be supported to provide person-centred care and develop positive attitudes towards residents with dementia and their behaviours. Beyond the attitudes of particular providers, Grenier and Guberman (2009) suggest that we consider how health care reforms in Canada more broadly can generate social exclusion in older adults. There have also been calls for more effective inclusion of older persons within health and social care organizations, including providing input into program planning and decision-making within organizations (Whitfield & Wismer, 2006) as well as at the individual level in terms of personal care planning.

Generally, the concept of social exclusion also highlights the role of broad, macro-level structural factors, such as policies, that can generate exclusion for older adults—not only in terms of their integration into social activities and health and social care services, but also in terms of their income security and citizenship needs. From this perspective, it is necessary to examine larger social processes and structures. For example, Ogg (2005) draws on European survey data to conclude that countries that provide more extensive formal social services generally also have higher levels of social inclusion among older adults. Podnieks (2006) recommends that policy-makers utilize an **inclusion lens** (see Shookner, 2002): essentially, this is like a tool or checklist that government organizations would use to systematically consider whether a given policy or program might, even inadvertently, have an impact on the inclusion or exclusion of older adults.

Research regarding structural barriers to participation, access to services, and income distribution highlights the importance of broader political and economic contexts for social inclusion. In addition, you can review the introductory paragraph of this chapter to remind yourself that sociologists are also interested in other ways in which the social context may shape isolation more specifically.

Conclusion

In this chapter, we have briefly reviewed a body of research common in social gerontology that focuses on the participation of older adults in their neighbourhoods and communities, in voluntary organizations, and with friends and family. The academic and policy interest in this area stems from a desire to promote older persons' well-being, a belief in the universal benefits of social engagement, and concerns about age-related declines in participation and network size among many older adults.

A sociological perspective on social participation requires that we also seek to understand how individual rates of participation among older adults are related to broader historical and social contexts. For instance, this could involve attention to how social changes related to modernization and industrialization affect social isolation and the bonds between individuals in contemporary society. From a critical perspective, one might consider how the social participation of older persons (as a societal resource) indirectly serves to fill the gap in community need left by the politically and economically motivated erosion of health and social services over the last several decades in Canada. Further, a sociological perspective directs attention to how older persons' individual experiences of social isolation may be explained by understanding their intersecting social positions (e.g., age, income, immigrant status, sexual orientation) as well as broader, structurally generated barriers to participation and connection (e.g., ageism, transportation and community-accessibility, the demands of caregiving, income distribution in a society, health and social care policies and practices).

The broader conceptual framework of social inclusion/exclusion holds considerable promise for advancing a sociological perspective on the participation and engagement of older adults in Canada and other countries. However, researchers need to reach agreement on the dimensions of social exclusion. For instance, some researchers continue to focus primarily on the dimension of social participation and connectedness, and they view other dimensions, such as income, as influencing social connectedness. Other researchers, in contrast, work with an expanded understanding of exclusion as including not only participation but also access to material resources, basic social and health care services, and supportive physical environments, as well as opportunities for more positive cultural representation, political engagement, and civic empowerment.

Ultimately, the findings in this chapter do not suggest that we abandon efforts to enhance social engagement among older persons, but that we simultaneously (a) recognize that some older adults do not wish to or cannot be engaged—and that this is not their personal failure; (b) critically reflect on why we are promoting social engagement and what immediate and broader long-term goals this explicitly (or even inadvertently) serves; and (c) pursue changes at broader levels that can promote inclusion, including developing age-friendly communities, stronger income supports, more appropriate and inclusive health care and social services, and policies and practices that support these changes.

Questions for Critical Thought

1. Looking back at the macro-level factors identified in this chapter as contributing to social isolation and exclusion among older adults, can you think of an innovative way to evaluate or assess the effects of a macro-level intervention?

2. In Box 6.1, it is noted that some people feel that a separate care facility for LGBT older adults amounts to segregation. What do you think is meant by this? What evidence supports the potential effects of a separate care facility like Dignity House?

3. Because many older persons are retired from paid labour, it is sometimes argued that participation in paid employment, as a dimension of inclusion, is less relevant for older persons. What changes might we see in the future that could change this?

4. Early sociologists spoke of the possibility that individuals in modern societies would face increasing social isolation. Do you believe these claims are accurate? What evidence supports your position?

Suggested Readings

Bruce, E. (2004). Social exclusion (and inclusion) in care homes. In A. Innes, C. Archibald, & C. Murphy (Eds.), *Dementia and social inclusion: Marginalised groups and marginalised areas of dementia research, care and practice* (pp. 123–136). London, UK: Jessica Kingsley Publishers. In this article, the author draws on research on residential care facilities for older persons with dementia to examine the risks of social exclusion and to highlight how a person-centred, individualized approach may help mitigate the risks of exclusion. Research found that residential care staff members tended to develop collective mental pictures of residents with dementia that influenced their responses to the residents in practice, resulting in exclusion. The findings underscore the importance of educating staff and addressing their common-sense assumptions about and reactions to persons with dementia.

Grenier, A. M., & Guberman, N. (2009). Creating and sustaining disadvantage: The relevance of a social exclusion framework. *Health and Social Care in the Community, 17*(2), 116–124. The authors apply a social exclusion framework to an analysis of home care services in Quebec, outlining examples of seven different ways that these services, in the context of increased rationing and restriction, can generate exclusion in older clients.

Martinson, M., & Minkler, M. (2006). Civic engagement and older adults: A critical perspective. *The Gerontologist, 46*(3), 318–324. The authors use a critical gerontological approach to reflect on the ways in which the civic engagement of older adults is framed in public and policy discourse. They suggest that a narrow emphasis on a volunteer role, although beneficial for many older adults' well-being, also aligns with American policy directions. In other words, as public, formal services are increasingly eroded, older Americans can be viewed as being asked to fill in the gaps through contributing their time to supporting others; in contrast, other forms of engagement, such as political or activist engagement, are not emphasized.

Scharf, T., Phillipson, C., Kingston, P., & Smith, A. E. (2001). Social exclusion and older people: Exploring the connections. *Education and Ageing, 16*(3), 303–320. This article, drawing on research from three disadvantaged urban areas in the United Kingdom, provides several good examples of different dimensions of social exclusion in this context. In particular, the findings highlight the ways that social participation is connected to neighbourhood change.

Relevant Websites

National Seniors Council, "Overview of Volunteering among Canadian Seniors"
http://www.seniorscouncil.gc.ca/eng/research_publications/volunteering/page07.shtml
This web page provides an overview of Statistics Canada data (from the 2007 Canada Survey of Giving, Volunteering, and Participating) regarding the contributions of older persons as volunteers, including the characteristics of older volunteers, the types of work they do, the motivations behind their contributions, and the reported benefits and barriers.

Public Health Agency of Canada, "Age-Friendly Communities"
http://www.phac-aspc.gc.ca/seniors-aines/afc-caa-eng.php
This website outlines the Public Health Agency of Canada's approach to developing age-friendly communities, and it includes links to relevant work in various Canadian provinces. Click on the link to the "Checklist of Age-Friendly Features," and pay attention to the features that seem to overlap with concerns about the participation and inclusion of older adults within their communities.

Volunteer Canada, "Engaging Volunteers: Older Adults"
http://volunteer.ca/older-adults
This website illustrates Volunteer Canada's interest in promoting volunteer activities among baby boomers and older adults, and it includes links to additional resources on the topic.

7   The Family Lives of Older Persons: Implications of Change

Learning Objectives

In this chapter, you will learn that:

◎ a variety of social forces are shaping the forms of and diversity in families of older persons over time, though these forces have less effect on the functions of family in society.

◎ late-life stepfamilies can expand the latent kin matrix, yet normative expectations for support may be unclear.

◎ "living apart together" relationships can occur when older persons, especially women, repartner and choose to retain more independence in their intimate relationships.

◎ globalization may be contributing to a rise in transnational families who exchange considerable support across geographic distances yet face unique challenges.

◎ though the contributions of older persons to family life are often neglected in research, many older persons provide important support to their families, particularly care for their grandchildren.

◎ future research should explore how increased needs for family care, alongside reduced capacities to provide this care, affect the well-being of older persons, their families, and family relationships.

Introduction

Marshall, Matthews, and Rosenthal (1993) note that the study of aging families is primarily dominated by research on family caregiving and elder abuse, largely from a structural-functional or family systems approach: "family life has been reduced, in most of the gerontological literature, to caregiving and its associated stress and burden, or to its dangers as illustrated by elder abuse" (p. 46). They argue that, as such, existing research often fails to convey the richness and complexity of family life, as well as the social contexts that shape our experiences of family life—for example, power relations, state policies and practices, culture, and patterned behaviour. In this chapter, we identify some of the broader social forces that shape family life in Canada and other industrialized countries, and we trace the implications of family changes for older persons and late-life families.

Sources and Types of Family Change

In Chapter 2, we explained how population aging is a demographic change driven not only by increasing life expectancies but also by decreasing fertility rates. Families are generally having fewer children and delaying the onset of their first child. Trends in fertility and child-bearing are shaped by social factors such as increasing societal affluence and women's empowerment (McDaniel, 1987). These family-level decisions have direct consequences for the relative proportions of older persons and younger persons in the population (Beaujot, 1990).

In turn, the aging population has implications for families. First, at a statistical level, an increasing proportion of couples report not having children living at home—44.5 per cent in 2011, compared with 39.2 per cent of couples with children at home (Statistics Canada, 2012). Although these statistics might appear to reflect a trend towards childless couples in society, to a large extent it more accurately reflects the greater proportions of older persons in the population whose children have left the parental home.

More directly, longer life expectancies and lower fertility rates may create greater potential for extended families with a beanpole structure (see Figure 7.1), in which there are multiple generations in a family alive simultaneously, yet relatively small numbers of family members within each generation (Bengtson, Lowenstein, Putney, & Gans, 2003).

At a broad level, the coexistence of multiple family generations may enhance the contributions of family to Canadian society,[1] such as promoting

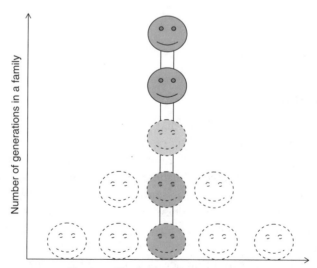

Figure 7.1 Predicted beanpole family structure (grey) compared to pyramid family structure of the past (dotted lines)

continuity, socialization, and the exchange of support among family members (Bengtson et al., 2003). However, younger generations may face a greater number of years providing care for older family members, and generations with poor-quality relationships would endure these challenges for a longer period of time (Bengtson et al., 2003). Some caution is needed, however, in predicting the likelihood of beanpole family structures—for example, drawing on a comparison of national surveys and databases in Europe, Dykstra (2010) concludes the following:

> Contrary to popular belief, vertically extended families with four or five generations alive at the same time are not the norm. . . . The majority of adults are members of three-generation families. Increased longevity and postponed childbearing have opposing effects on the generational structure of families. (p. 3)

In addition to longer life expectancies and declines in fertility rates, other social, cultural, and technological changes are also altering Canadian families and intimate relationships. In this chapter, we focus on the implications of these changes for older persons and late-life families. For instance, social and cultural patterns characteristic of post-industrial North America mean that individuals generally have more life opportunities and greater freedom to construct their life trajectories and identities (Brym, 2014). As such, our life journeys and transitions are becoming less structured or predictable—and less strongly tied to age-related, normative expectations—with a greater range of options. This phenomenon has been referred to as a deinstitutionalized or destandardized life course, in contrast to earlier decades with stronger normative expectations of age-appropriateness for particular life transitions, such as retirement (Cooney & Dunne, 2001; Mayer, 2004). Not only does deinstitutionalization create more diversity in individual trajectories, but, because events in our individual lives have implications for the families of which we are a part,[2] there is increasing diversity in family structures and forms (Bengtson, 2001). For example, increases in social equality for women, who are now more able to leave abusive or unhappy relationships and pursue higher education and full-time work, have generated more dual-earner families, childless families, partnership separations, and both lone-parent and step-parent families (Cooney & Dunne, 2001). Though married couples still represent 67 per cent of families in the 2011 Census of Canada, we have also seen a rise in common-law partnerships and lone-parent families (Statistics Canada, 2012). For older populations, these changes can result in more diversity in relationship choices, family forms, and living arrangements in later life.

Much of family research tends to be dominated by structural-functionalist assumptions that family change will somehow disrupt the societal equilibrium.

However, gerontological research has instead confirmed that families remain important despite changes to family forms. For example, families still provide high levels of socialization and support—indeed, the vast majority of care and support received by older persons comes from their families—and strong intergenerational ties persist (Bengtson et al., 2003; Phillipson, 2010). Despite changes in family structures, families continue to socialize younger family members: for instance, Bengtson (2001) reports that "intergenerational influences on youths' achievement orientations remain strong" (p. 11).

Along with greater diversity in family forms and types, we have seen some changes in social norms regarding families, such as increasing tolerance of non-traditional and non-nuclear family forms. The deinstitutionalized life course may be connected to cultural shifts in how we tend to interpret the meaning of family. For instance, it has been suggested that particularly in North America, we tend to *perceive* family bonds as more open, voluntary, and rooted in mutual affection and personal benefit as opposed to necessity (regardless of the actual presence of obligation), reflecting broader patterns of individualization (Beck & Beck-Gernsheim, 2001; Bellah, Madsen, Sullivan, Swidler, & Tipton, 1985; P. Smith, 1993). Indeed, "family" is increasingly difficult to define in concrete terms, due to the diversity that exists. During the industrial period, the predominant definition of family tended to focus on the traditional **nuclear family** form—a family group consisting of a heterosexual couple and their children, where the man is the primary breadwinner and the woman is responsible for child-rearing and housework. Due to various social changes, however, the nuclear family is far less common today. As such, broader, more diffuse meanings of family have emerged that incorporate extended family members and non-kin; this phenomenon has been termed the "postmodern family" (Bengtson, 2001). In fact, MacRae (1992) explains how some friends or neighbours become defined as fictive kin by older women who have no available family members.

At the same time, however, families today face many constraints related to a changing political and economic context, which can actually strengthen normative expectations of family obligations—especially for women. Critical feminist studies of aging families highlight the disproportionate contributions of women to the care of aging family members, as well as the gendered ideology of **familialism** that shapes this involvement and is used to justify the erosion of publicly provided supports (Aronson, 1992; Baines, Evans, & Neysmith, 1998; Calasanti & Slevin, 2001; Hooyman & Gonyea, 1995).

Further, Phillipson (2010) emphasizes the importance of understanding the effects of population aging within the context of **globalization**. Globalization refers to "how the world 'shrinks' as capital, ideas, corporations, commodities and workers rapidly cross vast distances" (Johnston, 2014, p. 463), and how this aligns with increasing pressure by international organizations on national governments to implement neoliberal economic reforms, such as cutbacks to publicly financed social and health care policies.[3]

For example, international organizations (e.g., the World Bank and the International Monetary Fund) now influence national-level social policies related to older persons. This has the effect of transferring more responsibility for the financial and care-related costs of old age to individuals and their families. The erosion of publicly funded services directly affects the needs of older persons for support from their families (Chappell & Penning, 2005). This, in turn, can shape family relationships and even living arrangements—for instance, more families may cohabit because of economic need or to provide care.

Emerging Trends in Late-Life Family and Intimate Relationships

In this section, we will examine some emerging family forms that are of particular interest to those studying aging, including late-life stepfamilies, living apart together relationships, and transnational families. Broad-level factors influencing these changes will be identified; we will also discuss the implications for older persons, and the giving and receiving of support in old age.

Late-Life Stepfamilies

Statistics Canada only began collecting data on stepfamilies (sometimes referred to as "blended" or "reconstituted" families) in the 2011 Census of Population. This data classifies 12.6 per cent of families with children under age 24 living at home as stepfamilies (Statistics Canada, 2012). However, we do not know how many older persons are members of non-cohabiting stepfamilies that are formed after adult children have left the parental home (or that were formed at younger ages, and the children have since grown older and left the home). Increasing rates of divorce/separation and repartnering throughout the life course—which are related to broader phenomena such as increases in life expectancy, common-law partnerships, and women's labour force involvement and financial independence—suggest that late-life, non-cohabiting stepfamilies may be on the rise. In some cases, this occurs when adult children themselves divorce or separate and then repartner; in other cases, older parents may divorce or separate and then repartner.

Research on late-life stepfamilies emphasizes the implications for the social functions of families: in particular, for the giving and receiving of support between family members. Bengtson (2001) argues that stepfamilies increase the potential for expanded family support networks, because they create families with more parents and grandparents—this is referred to as a **latent kin matrix** of multigenerational ties. However, some research suggests that family obligations between stepchildren and step-grandparents are viewed as more conditional, and that there are fewer normative guidelines for roles and responsibilities in these relationships (see Box 7.1). For instance, research conducted in the United States sought to assess levels of public support for the filial obligation of adult stepchildren to older step-parents (Coleman, Ganong, Hans, Sharp, & Rothrauff, 2005). Most respondents perceived adult stepchildren to have fewer responsibilities to their step-parents than to their biological parents, and stepchildren were

---

Box 7.1   Stepsiblings and Care for Older Parents: A Literary Perspective

In an article written for the *Canadian Journal on Aging*, Lashewicz, Manning, Hall, and Keating (2007) direct attention to how siblings within families negotiate caregiving for older parents, drawing on a social exchange perspective and the idea of "genealogical equivalence"—the norm that parent care should be balanced between siblings in the same generation. Lashewicz and colleagues present a literary analysis of the 2002 novel *Family Matters* by Rohinton Mistry. They explain how the novel brings the moral issue of genealogical equity to the fore and demonstrates the challenges and benefits of filial care work. In the novel, the responsibility for parent care is placed solely on the biological daughter, Roxana, by the elderly gentleman's two stepchildren, Coomy and Jal:

> Comparably vivid are the fairness implications in the contrast between Roxana's selfless willingness to care for her father under strained conditions and Coomy's self-preserving avoidance of caregiving despite living in more comfortable surroundings, having received the greater part of the care recipient's assets. (Lashewicz et al., 2007, p. 95)

The stepchildren not only hold resentment towards their stepfather, but also do not view themselves as "owing" their stepfather. As the authors of the article note, the novel "leaves the reader fully aware of the ironies and contradictions in these difficult matters of care" (Lashewicz et al., p. 95). It is also noteworthy that the novel draws on some dominant assumptions within the wider culture about the attitudes of stepchildren towards caring for step-parents—and it presents a rather narrow view in this regard. Ultimately, however, we should think about the potential ways that sibling relationships in families may be influenced by difficult negotiations regarding the realities of parent care in a context in which it will be increasingly difficult for siblings to meet these needs.

Source: Summary of Lashewicz, B., Manning, G., Hall, M., & Keating, N. (2007). Equity matters: Doing fairness in the context of family caregiving. *Canadian Journal on Aging, 26*(Suppl. S1), 91–102.

not believed to be obligated to perform physical care tasks; indeed, step-parents tended not to be viewed as family members (Coleman et al., 2005; Ganong & Coleman, 2006).

Recent Canadian research by Morris (2012) further indicates how commitments to a step-parent are in some cases generated as a kind of side effect of love and concern for one's biological parent—specifically, children may feel committed to help the step-parent based on gratitude that the step-parent had been kind to the biological parent. In other cases, the primary commitment is to the biological parent who has since become a primary caregiver for the step-parent, and the adult child seeks to assist in a secondary role to help their biological parent.

Family commitments in late-life stepfamilies are also contingent upon the extent of co-residence (if this occurs), relationship closeness, shared interaction, and mutual support (Ganong, Coleman, McDaniel, & Killian, 1998; Schmeekle, Giarrusso, Feng, & Bengtson, 2006). However, as Finch and Mason (1993) note, this is in fact how commitments between any family members develop—there are simply more opportunities for these commitments to develop within cohabiting families that remain intact over time.

Living Apart Together Relationships

Despite ageist assumptions that older persons do not have sexual relationships, there has been some attention in academic research devoted to intimate relationships in late life. Much of this research focuses on the effects of late-life transitions such as widowhood and divorce on subsequent intimate relationships. For example, Canadian research by Deborah van den Hoonaard (2002) indicates that most widows do not wish to remarry, viewing this as a risk; widows also describe uncertainty regarding their new interactions with men and how to communicate their marital and sexual intentions. Similar findings have been reported in the United Kingdom (Davidson, 2001): widowers (men) tend to want to repartner, whereas widows (women) are more reluctant to give up their relatively recent freedom from care responsibilities.

When older persons who are separated or divorced decide to repartner, they are more likely to engage in common-law cohabiting partnerships than are younger adults (Brown, Lee, & Bulanda, 2006; de Jong Gierveld & Peeters, 2003). This reflects the socio-historical context of intimate relationships in late life: specifically, more options are available than in the past (Cooney & Dunne, 2001), especially to older women.

Another option for older persons is a **living apart together** (LAT) relationship. In this type of relationship, two romantically involved individuals continue to reside in separate homes, rather than cohabit (Levin, 2004). There is limited Canadian research on LAT arrangements. Analyses of 2001 and 2011 Canadian General Social Survey data suggested that 7.4 to 8.4 per cent of Canadians "live apart together" (Milan & Peters, 2003;

Turcotte, 2013). We need to distinguish, however, between more transitory dating relationships and those in which living apart is a long-term lifestyle choice between committed individuals. The latter relationships are more common among older adults (see Figure 7.2), particularly those who have been previously partnered. In 2011, almost 60 per cent of persons aged 60 or older who were in a LAT partnership did not intend to cohabit; 37 per cent stated they made the choice to retain independence (Turcotte, 2013). In contrast, LAT arrangements in younger adults, though more common, may reflect increasingly delayed home-leaving patterns among young adults in Canadian society.

Existing research (primarily from Europe) suggests LAT relationships are a relatively new (or more visible) and small but increasing non-traditional family form, reflecting demographic, social, economic, and normative change. Historical growth in economic prosperity and social welfare, the women's rights movement and increasing female labour force participation, decreasing fertility, increasing life expectancy (and a greater chance of being widowed), increasing proportions of divorces and repartnerships, and cultural changes related to individualism may all contribute to change in the meanings and forms of intimate relationships, such as reflected in LAT arrangements (Beck & Beck-Gernsheim, 2001; Davidson, 2002; Karlsson & Borell, 2005; Levin, 2004; Strohm, Seltzer, Cochran, & Mays, 2009). For instance, individual decisions to avoid cohabitation may reflect a desire to preserve independence, privacy, and time alone, as well as freedom from gendered duties experienced in previous, more traditional relationships—this may be especially salient for older repartnered women (Karlsson & Borell, 2002; Haskey & Lewis, 2006).

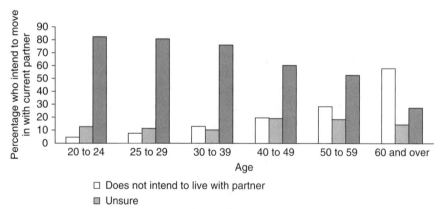

Figure 7.2 Age and attitude towards future cohabitation with current "living apart together" partner
Source: Turcotte, M. (2013). Living apart together. *Insights on Canadian society* (Catalogue No. 75-006-X). Ottawa, ON: Statistics Canada, Minister of Industry.

In my own research with Karen Kobayashi (Funk & Kobayashi, 2014), we interviewed 28 LAT couples in Vancouver and Victoria, British Columbia, who had explicitly chosen to live separately: their average age was 59 years. Participants emphasized the value of preserving their independence, protecting themselves should the relationship be unsuccessful, and minimizing the risks to their relationship posed by cohabiting (e.g., tensions). They emphasized how living apart strengthened their relationship—for example, they always looked forward to seeing each other, because of the time spent apart. It did seem that women in particular desired the emotional and practical independence that a LAT relationship provided. The findings may suggest that LAT relationships represent the empowering potential of what Anthony Giddens terms a **pure relationship**, in which gender roles are more egalitarian and relationships are based primarily on affection rather than obligation. However, LAT relationships can also represent individual-level solutions to broader, gendered inequities in cohabiting relationships, rather than addressing these inequities at a structural level (Funk & Kobayashi, 2014).

Long-Distance and Transnational Older Families

From older couples who decide to live apart, we can springboard to the related issue of whole families living across vast geographic distances, even within different countries. Drawing on data from Canada's General Social Survey, Vezina and Turcotte (2010) noted that approximately 22 per cent of caregivers aged 45 and older who provided care to a parent or parent-in-law lived more than one hour away from that parent. Nonetheless, these long-distance caregivers often still completed various tasks, including visiting or temporarily staying with their parent. However, the out-of-pocket expenses of care were higher, and these caregivers were more likely to miss periods of paid employment. Further, in a recent review of research in the United States, Cagle and Munn (2012) conclude that long-distance family caregivers, particularly women, experience greater emotional stress than caregivers who live close to the care recipient, even though these long-distance caregivers provide a lot of support to care recipients as well as to other, closer primary family caregivers.

In recent decades, globalization has also fuelled international migration, which in turn has created more potential for **transnational families** in which family members live in separate countries. As Phillipson (2010) notes, this creates "considerable diversity in respect of the social networks within which growing old is shaped and managed" (p. 22). This is salient when we consider intergenerational relations between older parents and their adult children and grandchildren living in other countries. Baldassar (2007) and Baldock (2000) suggest that the caregiving contributions of adult children who live in different countries from their older parents are often underestimated and that caregiving does not necessarily require geographic closeness: extended families living across long distances often remain in contact and put considerable effort into supporting each other emotionally and financially.

Extreme geographic separation between family members has been a topic of research focusing on the following: (a) how these families maintain a sense of togetherness and intimacy (indeed, a family identity) while living across national borders; (b) the implications for support and care exchanged between family members; and (c) challenges or facilitators of family relations and support exchanges across distance. For example, Loretta Baldassar (2007, 2008) examined interactions between three cohorts of migrants from Italy to Australia, including the ways they maintained and affirmed their family relationships across distance: for instance, putting time and money into staying in touch (e.g., through letters, email, gifts) symbolically reinforced their sense of family commitment.[4]

Some factors may enhance families' abilities to provide support across distances, such as relatively affordable and accessible travel and communication technology (Baldassar, 2007; see Figure 7.3). Challenges involved in transnational caregiving, however, include the following: less access to information about what help is needed (Baldassar, 2007; Zechner, 2008); limited ability to provide certain kinds of in-person help (Zechner, 2008); financial and employment costs of travel (Lunt, 2009) and associated stresses, such as using holidays to provide care (Baldock, 2000); communication technology costs (Lunt,

Barry Lewis/Alamy

Figure 7.3 Trends in international migration generate more transnational families who provide support across geographic distance. Here, a multigenerational family meets in the arrivals area at Heathrow Airport in London, UK.

2009); lack of access to caregiver support services (Lunt, 2009; Zechner, 2008); operating within and across two cultures and societies (Zechner, 2008); and restrictive national immigration and travel policies (addressed in the following discussion). Though much of the research focuses on how adult children care for their older parents in other countries, Zhou (2012) examined older Chinese parents who take extended visits to Canada in order to provide child care to their grandchildren. These visits are important sources of support for their immigrant children who are struggling to achieve labour market success in a new country. Zhou (2012) concludes the following:

> Although these seniors' unprecedented mobility has helped alleviate the childcare deficit experienced by their children as skilled immigrants in Canada, it has also had long-term effects on aging that are in contrast with their own cultural expectations about and individual preferences for their later lives. (p. 234)

We must also recognize that state-created immigration and travel policies can affect transnational caregiving not only through creating the phenomenon in the first place but also by influencing how often family members can visit each other—it is also important to consider inequities in this regard based on socio-economic status (Lunt, 2009; Zhou, 2012). For instance, Canada's family reunification policies have helped older parents and grandparents immigrate to Canada, sponsored by their adult children who permanently reside in this country. In 2011, a moratorium was placed on this program, and families were encouraged to use the far more restricted 10-year "super visa" program, which only allows parents and grandparents to visit if they meet certain requirements (rather than to immigrate): see Box 7.2 for more details. The sponsorship program was recently reopened in January 2014 for a limited number of 5,000 applications (and under stricter criteria such as a higher minimum necessary income and a sponsorship dependency period of 20 years), and as of July 2014 new applications were no longer being accepted. Policy changes and strategies such as this will ultimately result in more transnational families.

In sum, the diversity of family and relationship forms is well demonstrated in three emerging phenomena: late-life stepfamilies, living apart together relationships, and transnational families. A sociological perspective seeks to understand the emergence and persistence of these forms within the current socio-historical context, as well as identify potential implications for older persons.

Exchanges of Support to and from Older Persons in Families

Families are a primary source of exchange of resources, support, and care for all individuals, including older persons. As such, much of the research

---

<table>
<tr><td>

Box 7.2

</td><td>

Canada's Super Visa Program: "New Super Visa Is 'Super Disappointing'"

</td></tr>
</table>

For many Canadians waiting to bring parents overseas for a visit, a government promise to speed up the process with a new "super visa" is a "super disappointment," critics say.

"There are so many, so many requirements, you're prevented from coming in. And you have to have a lot of money," said Fred DeVilla, who works in the insurance industry and is a prominent member of the Filipino community.

The federal government requires that one year of $100,000 in health coverage for those 55 and older has to be purchased up front, he said. It costs at least $1,200 a year and there's no monthly payment plan. If your parent stays for just a few months, there are no refunds, DeVilla said.

The 10-year super visa was announced last month. At the same time, Immigration Minister Jason Kenney froze for two years sponsorships for parents wanting to immigrate to Canada. The super visa was supposed to take just eight weeks to process and give the feds time to deal with a lengthy backlog of sponsorship applications.

"There was a huge amount of excitement and no one, including myself, thought we'd get blindsided," said Winnipeg North MP Kevin Lamoureux. The Liberal immigration critic later learned about the cost involved—an average $1,500 per parent, per year. . . .

"There will be hundreds, ultimately thousands, who will not be able to get it" across Canada, he said.

"Not only for Winnipeg North but for anyone who had any hope of getting a parent or both to come under the super visa, [it has] taken away their hope," Lamoureux said.

The MP said he is starting a petition demanding changes to the super visa. . . .

On top of paying for the insurance, the host family has to meet super visa income requirements. A family of four has to make $45,000 a year, whether they live in high-priced Vancouver or low-cost Winnipeg.

"It's based on a national average," Nychek [Director of Citizenship and Immigration in Winnipeg] said. The same test is applied for sponsoring people. Having different income requirements for different regions would be difficult, he said.

Lamoureux said that inflexibility is hurting homesick new Canadians. "They miss their mom, they miss their dad. . . . It can be lonely." They're scraping by in low-paying jobs and saving for their parents to come for a visit.

"We're pricing it out of their reach," Lamoureux said.

Source: Abridged from Sanders, C. (2011, December 21). New super visa is "super disappointing." *Winnipeg Free Press*, p. A4. Reprinted with permission from Carol Sanders and the Winnipeg Free Press.

---

on families and aging concentrates on these exchanges of support, including measuring the frequency, level, and form of support provided. Typically, we talk about support as multidimensional—including, for example, emotional support, companionship, advice and information, support navigating the health care system, financial aid, transportation, and in some cases, hands-on help with basic (e.g., bathing, toileting, feeding, dressing) and instrumental (e.g., using the telephone, doing laundry, shopping, preparing food, housekeeping, managing finances) **activities of daily living** (Chappell & Funk, 2011).

From a sociological perspective, we must consider broader-level factors that shape older persons' needs for support, as well as family members' abilities to provide this support. We will address these considerations in the remainder of this chapter. First, however, we must address another gap in gerontological research, which stems from a tendency to assume that care is provided solely to older persons in families, rather than by older persons to their families. To explore this topic, we will describe some of the research that exists on the contributions of older persons in the care of their grandchildren.[5]

Grandparenting

In Chapter 2, we emphasized that, from a life course perspective, most support over time flows primarily downward from older to younger generations in families (Dykstra, 2010). This is particularly salient when we examine research on intergenerational transfers of economic support, and indeed, this is one reason why Foner (2000) and Connidis (2001) argue that public supports and programs for older people also end up benefiting younger generations—reflecting the interdependence and solidarity between generations.

The grandparent role is another good example of the support provided by older generations to their families. For instance, Canadian research by Candace Kemp (2005) suggests that grandparent–grandchild relationships represent important "mutual latent reserves of unconditional support" (p. 161) and help ensure family continuity. In another study (Ploeg, Campbell, Denton, Joshi, & Davies, 2004), older adults expressed a strong desire to help their children and grandchildren manage challenging life transitions (e.g., through financial assistance) and "build or rebuild secure lives and futures" (p. 113). The grandparent role may become increasingly important as more women enter the labour force and tend to work non-standard hours, and in situations where families experience events such as divorce and separation, lone parenthood, mental health or addictions, or economic challenges (Attias-Donfut & Segalen, 2002; Bengtson, 2001).

Older persons often provide considerable assistance to their adult children through child care. Hank and Buber (2009) estimated that about 50 per cent of grandparents provide some form of child care, especially if they live close to their grandchildren or if mothers are employed. With projected increases in working mothers (and non-standard work hours), the need for grandparent child care may increase, especially in countries that lack publicly financed and accessible child care (Gray, 2005; Wheelcock & Jones, 2002). However, we also need to acknowledge potential costs and risks for these grandparents, including economic and opportunity costs (Wheelcock & Jones, 2002); some grandparents may retire early to provide child care, or they may restrict other activities. One study of American female nurses reported that providing care for grandchildren for nine or more hours per week was associated with an increased risk of coronary heart disease (Lee, Colditz, Berkman, & Kawachi, 2003b).

There is increasing gerontological interest in situations wherein grandparents—especially grandmothers—assume greater than normal roles in raising their grandchildren, in a custodial or adoptive role. This occurs most often when the adult child is no longer able to parent effectively, for instance due to mental illness, incarceration, or addictions. Antonucci, Birditt, Sherman, and Trinh (2011) observe that "disrupted families with children and fewer resources often rely on grandparents for basic care rather than the traditional honorific role" (p. 1087). Further, as Biggs and Powell (2003) note, "when extensively relied on [grandparenting] is more likely to be a response to severely eroded inclusive environments and the self-protective reactions of families living with them" (p. 114).

The effects of this atypical grandparenting role are of concern to those interested in protecting the well-being of older adults. For instance, older adults who adopt younger kin or grandchildren perceive more negative impacts on their families compared to older adults who adopt non-kin (Hinterlong & Ryan, 2008). There are risks for psychosocial well-being, physical health, isolation, and finances (Hayslip & Kaminski, 2005), and these grandparents may also have fewer economic or social resources to begin with (Hinterlong & Ryan, 2008). Further, custodial grandparents are also more likely to be caring for children with behavioural and emotional issues, which make the role more challenging; they also must negotiate difficult relationships with non-custodial parents, including their own adult child (Hayslip & Kaminski, 2005). One Canadian study (Callahan, Brown, MacKenzie, & Whittington, 2004; MacKenzie, Brown, Callahan, & Whittington, 2011) noted that many of these grandmothers are Aboriginal; they face considerable challenges in providing full-time child care in their later life, have difficulties accessing help, and tend to distrust the child welfare and formal support systems.

Older Persons' Needs for Family Support: Root Factors

Having considered some of the ways that older persons contribute to their families, we now turn to examine broad-level factors shaping older persons' own needs for support from their families. Usually, research focuses on the logistics of meeting needs for support within families and how to ensure the availability of family supports, with relatively less attention to broader

issues that shape older persons' needs for that support. As older generations live longer, they will be more likely to live to ages where they require
longer periods of "substantial and prolonged assistance" (Brothers & de
Jong Gierveld, 2011). There has also been some research seeking to project
older persons' needs for care on health status trends, as reviewed in Chapter
4. For instance, there has been uncertainty about whether we will see a
trend towards the **compression of morbidity** in older adults that might
reduce future needs for support. There has also been research seeking to
examine trends in rates of dementia and cognitive impairment, and other
health conditions.

In addition, societal trends in divorce and separation may also affect
older persons' needs for various forms of support from their families—those
who are particularly affected include older women, who tend to be disadvantaged financially after a partnership separation, and those who do not
repartner (more often women). This is a different pattern than in the past,
with a similar outcome: in the past, widowhood, rather than separation, was
a more common source of need for family support.

Health care reforms in Canada in the last several decades have pro-
foundly influenced older persons' needs for support from their families, by
reducing the supports available through publicly funded services. Since the
1990s, globalization and its associated political and economic effects have
promoted reforms towards privatization, deregulation, erosion of the welfare state, and a more pronounced shift towards private responsibility for
care (Chappell & Penning, 2005). Attempts to minimize institutional costs
have led to increasing reliance and demand on home care services: yet home
care is not covered under the Canada Health Act, and over time there has
been curtailment and/or a lack of expansion of publicly provided home and
community care services (e.g., Penning et al., 2006). From 1995 to 2005, the
percentage of seniors (over age 65) in British Columbia who received home
health services declined from 13 to 9 per cent (McGrail et al., 2008). In
other words, even if funding has increased, the proportions of older persons
receiving help are declining during a time when the health needs of community-dwelling older persons are more complex and significant, because of the
trend towards avoiding institutionalization.

Insufficient home and community care supports during a time of downsizing medical and in-patient care ultimately shifts responsibility to families.
Governments are concerned with emphasizing the importance of familial
responsibility for caregiving in order to set limits on the role of formal services
(Biggs & Powell, 2003; Binney & Estes, 1988; Bould, 1993). As Keefe, Légaré,
Charbonneau, and Décarie (2012) emphasize, this downloading of responsibility may work "in the short term and for some people with resources"
(p. 154) but is not a long-term solution. Families, especially women, are the
backbone of care for the chronically and terminally ill in Canada, yet families

face increasing expectations for their involvement in and responsibility for this care (Canadian Home Care Association, 2008; Canadian Hospice Palliative Care Association, 2004). Such changes can increase family care burdens (Chappell, 1993; Fast & Keating, 2000).

In addition to changes that are working to emphasize the provision of care in the home for older persons, we should also consider the ways in which the quality and complexity of the traditional medical and institutional care systems create more need for support from family members. In consultations with 400 family caregivers that I completed for the Manitoba government (Funk, 2012a), one of the top concerns of family caregivers involved the quality of and access to health care supports for the care recipient. Respondents suggested that when they did not trust the health care system to adequately care for their family member, they felt they needed to take on the role of "advocate." In addition, when the health care system involved time-consuming and complex navigation through bureaucratic procedures, as well as searching for a variety of pieces of information, caregivers felt they also needed to be a "navigator." The need for family members to take on both the advocate and navigator roles is a direct result of family members' concerns about the health care system.

Finally, broad-level trends in the economic situations of older persons will influence their needs for assistance (particularly financial assistance) from family members. As discussed in Chapter 5, Canada has seen overall improvements in the financial situations of older persons over the last several decades, although there is variation. Some of the improvements have in part been due to Old Age Security (OAS) and Guaranteed Income Supplement, as well as maturation of the Canada/Quebec Pension Plan. However, recent plans by the federal government to increase the age of eligibility for OAS from 65 to 67 may affect the economic well-being of future cohorts of older persons. Further, what will happen to the Canada Pension Plan in the future, and which seniors will be left vulnerable? As globalization generates increasing employment and income insecurity for Canadian citizens, what will the future hold for the economic well-being of future seniors?

Family Support for Older Persons: Myths about the Past and Present

At the same time as the needs of older persons for care and support from families is changing, there are simultaneously other factors working to shape the capacities of families to support older persons. First, however, it is important to acknowledge the ways that social gerontologists have dispelled certain myths of family support for older persons. In particular, contrary to popular assumption, families in the past did not commonly live together in multigenerational households (Connidis, 2001; Nett, 1981), in part because of the much lower life expectancies that reduced the chances of multiple generations being alive. Further, when multiple generations did live together it was largely due to economic necessity and the absence of public services, or reflected the power of older family members through their control of land (Connidis, 2001). In other words, there is no evidence to suggest that support for older persons through multigenerational living arrangements automatically reflected higher levels of affection or concern for older generations in the past.

In 2011, 2.7 per cent of all Canadian households were classified as multigenerational; about 8 per cent of persons over 80 years of age lived with relatives; and 4.8 per cent of children under 15 years of age lived in a household containing one or more grandparents (Statistics Canada, 2012). It is possible that multigenerational living will increase in the future, in part due to economic necessity and needs for care, but also because of a trend towards delayed home leaving among young adults. Canadian work by Barbara Mitchell (2003) in this area suggests that young adult children are remaining at home for longer than in the past, into their twenties and thirties, or they are returning home for periods of time after an initial departure from the parental home. Delayed home-leaving is more common among ethnocultural minority families, and, in addition to cultural norms, financial situations of the adult children are a key determinant. Implications for late-life families have been explored by these researchers, who generally find that those who do remain at home, as well as their parents, tend to be satisfied; however, parenthood itself may become more unpredictable and complex in late life.

For the most part, however, multigenerational households are still rare. Another factor working against their formation is the tendency for many older adults to wish to remain living independently from their children, even after divorce or widowhood—though generally desiring high levels of contact with their adult children, many healthy older adults prefer **intimacy at a distance** (Brothers & de Jong Gierveld, 2011).

Exchanges of support are bidirectional in multigenerational households, but most research focuses on co-resident caregiving to older persons. In a recent analysis of Canadian data, 18 per cent of family caregivers who lived with the care recipient were unemployed, compared to 10 per cent of caregivers who did not live with the care recipient; co-resident caregivers provided care for an average of 29 hours per week, compared to 9 hours per week for other caregivers (Vezina & Turcotte, 2010).

Contrary to popular assumptions, the majority of help and support for older persons today is provided by family—in other words, older people are not abandoned by their families. In fact, research indicates that adult children today express higher levels of support for norms of filial responsibility than do their older parents (e.g., Blieszner & Hamon 1992; Spitze & Gallant 2004). Further, access to formal supports in contemporary societies does not erode family support or cohesion, despite providing a buffer that allows family generations to be more independent of one another (Aboderin, 2004; Daatland, Herlofson, & Lima, 2011; Daatland & Lowenstein, 2005). Families continue to provide care, and "generous welfare states enable families to redistribute their resources and to provide the kind of care that they are best equipped to provide" (Dykstra, 2010, p. 10), such as social and emotional care. Existing research suggests that both self-care and family care tend to complement, not supplement, formal services (Penning, 2002; Penning & Keating, 1999). Further, some public supports can actually be an incentive for family responsibilities (Dykstra, 2010), such as paid or unpaid employment leave provisions.

Why does the myth of abandonment persist? In part, this could be because it aligns with contemporary neoliberal discourses circulating in the media and broader society. Further, we commonly tend to conflate "caring for" someone (as in the tasks provided) with "caring about" someone (as in love or concern) despite the fact that not all caregiving is driven only by affection, and that even when one strongly cares about someone, one cannot always "care for" them (e.g., for reasons of distance, employment, or the other person's refusal of help). In addition, public talk about abandoned elders may also reflect adult children's feelings of guilt—the sense that one can never fully repay one's parents for everything they have done (Antonucci et al., 2011). I have also suggested elsewhere (Funk, 2010) that adult children have a strong desire to view themselves as responsible (this being a normative moral imperative), and one way to do this is to contrast oneself against "unfilial others," which strengthens the boundaries of the "normal" self (Goffman, 1961, 1963).

Families' Capacities to Support Older Persons: Root Factors and Implications

It is time to put aside narrow views about family support for older persons that do not reflect existing evidence. Rather, the primary issue of concern should be that given longer life expectancies and eroding publicly funded care services, there will be an "unprecedented responsibility" on families, and on adult children in particular, to provide support for older persons (Coontz, 2000, p. 289, as cited in Brothers & de Jong Gierveld, 2011). For instance, longer life expectancies mean that older persons may face a longer period of time in advanced ages (e.g., over age 85) where they are more likely to require intensive support.

However, increases in the need for family care are occurring at a time when many family members, particularly adult children, may have a reduced capacity to provide that care. Indeed, demographic projections based on these trends suggest that "current patterns of [family] assistance cannot be assumed to continue" (Keefe et al., 2012, p. 152). Families are having fewer children than in the past due to reductions in fertility; more women are in the paid labour force; and more children are separated geographically from their parents (Keefe et al., 2012). For example, as Figure 7.4 indicates, there was a steady increase in female labour force participation since 1976 (Bushnik, 2006); over the last few decades, this increase has tended to level off. In 2014, total female labour force participation rates for women over age 15 were around 61 per cent, according to Status of Women Canada (2015), drawing on Statistics Canada labour force survey data.

Dykstra and Hagestad (2007) argue that older persons without children in particular have been "rendered invisible" in most research on aging and families. Childless older adults are an interesting population—not only because they may have higher needs for formal supports, but because of how their life trajectories deviate from normative expectations, whether voluntarily or involuntarily. In Canada, the proportion of women over age 85 with no surviving children was 22 per cent in 2001 (Carrière, Keefe, Légaré, Lin, & Rowe, 2007), but this is estimated to increase (after a brief drop) to 28 per cent in 2051. These figures differ somewhat from the projections of Gaymu et al. (2010) who suggest that the proportion of women over age 75 with no surviving children was approximately 18 per cent in 2001 and that this number will fall slightly over time until 2030. Dykstra and Hagestad (2007) observe that when childless older persons are addressed in gerontological research, "overwhelmingly, they are perceived in a negative light, as problem cases. Moreover, the childless are seen as being disadvantaged" (p. 1284) or at risk for a lack of social support or integration. In response to this problem, Dykstra and Hagestad (2007) remind us to move beyond a deficiency-based lens to examine the diversity and complexity within this population in future research.

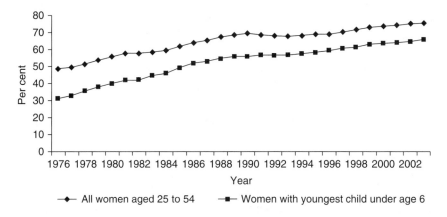

Figure 7.4 Increases in female labour force participation over time
Source: Bushnik, T. (2006). Child care in Canada. *Children and youth research paper series* (Catalogue No. 89-599-MIE—No. 003). Ottawa, ON: Statistics Canada, Minister of Industry. http://publications.gc.ca/Collection/Statcan/89-599-MIE/89-599-MIE2006003.pdf

Projections of future reductions in the capacity and availability of family caregivers are also made by Johnson, Toohey, and Wiener (2007) and by Grundy (2010). Gaymu et al. (2010) suggest that such projections indicate increased need for formal services. Further, although the extent of the **sandwich generation** is currently overstated (Dykstra, 2010), more families are delaying the age at which they have their first child, and as a result more women may find themselves faced with caring for both older parents and young dependent children. Drawing on 2002 data from the General Social Survey, Williams (2005) reported that a relatively small number (712,000) of Canadians between the ages of 45 and 64 were caring for both children and older persons simultaneously.

The geographic dispersion of kin may in part be mitigated by new technologies that facilitate long-distance caregiving, as noted earlier. Further, though adult children may be less able to provide care, Grundy (2010) suggests that trends towards improved health in the older population may increase the potential for support from spouses; other forces, such as an increase in blended families, may expand the kin matrix available for older people (Bengtson, 2001). Finally, the impact of employment on family eldercare could be mitigated through a comprehensive strategy to introduce family leave benefits and other accommodations for workers facing these competing responsibilities. Ultimately, there are many unknowns. In a context of globalization, we are also seeing erosion of workers' rights and declines in wages and economic insecurity: these forces could make it more difficult for family members to provide care (Chappell & Penning, 2005).

Given increasing demand for and potential reductions in capacities to provide family support, what might be the implications for older persons and their families? The most obvious concern is an increase in caregiver burden and stress, as more family members struggle to balance competing responsibilities of caregiving and employment and to deal with increasingly complex care tasks for older persons. In both Western and Eastern societies, increasingly the ideal of family (and filial) responsibility does not match the reality of constraints upon its enactment. Groger and Mayberry (2001) describe this as a kind of **cultural lag** in the US, where material conditions affecting the ability to provide informal care are changing faster than individual cultural beliefs about filial obligation. According to Finley, Roberts, and Banahan (1988), "structural features make it difficult for some to act consistently within [norms of filial responsibility]" (p. 73). Future research should also explore whether this kind of incongruence may increase psychological stresses. The potential effects of family caregiving more generally on the well-being of caregivers are well documented, as discussed in Chapter 4.

Connidis and McMullin (2002) refer to the struggles of family caregivers for older persons trying to balance family responsibilities with the requirements of paid employment as representing **ambivalence**. Though experienced at the individual level by those faced with competing normative role expectations, these contradictions, the authors argue, are structurally generated—for example, they represent broader tensions between societal domains, such as the labour market, health care, and families (Connidis & McMullin, 2002).

Families with more resources may hire private care to supplement public services; as such, disproportionate effects may be shouldered by those with fewer household resources (Chappell & Penning, 2005). Older family members, too, already concerned about being a "burden" on their children, may be negatively affected as they see their children struggle to provide assistance. Family relationships may also be more strained as they change under these circumstances.

Changing Expectations of Family Responsibility?

In this section, we address research regarding family members' own interpretations of the responsibility of family members to provide certain types of support and care for each other (expectations that practitioners and policy-makers have of family were discussed in Chapter 4). Kemp and Denton (2003) found that the mid- and late-life Canadians they interviewed did not believe that their family members bore primary responsibility for helping them with housing, financial help, or personal care. Other research studies have concluded that *younger* adults express higher support for and expectations of their filial responsibility in comparison to older individuals, who may be more focused on the needs of their adult children, ambivalent about depending on children, and realistic about the impact of caregiving (e.g., Stein et al., 1998; Spitze & Gallant, 2004; Whyte, 2004). These findings are all the more interesting given the general perception that attitudes of family responsibility are declining and were stronger in the past—in which case, one might expect that a cohort effect would translate into more support for these norms among older generations.

In lay circles, however, there is considerable concern that our individualistic culture in North America is changing our understandings of family relationships and responsibilities. However, such change, to the extent that it exists, may not only reflect cultural shifts, but may actually be the result of changes in the capacities of individuals to meet the needs of family members. For instance, Lan (2002) examines how immigrant Chinese families to California transform or "renegotiate" cultural norms to adapt to newly encountered conditions after immigration. In Lan's qualitative study of dual-earner Chinese immigrant families, adult children "subcontracted" filial piety through privately hiring non-family employees or utilizing public services to care for their older parents; these children maintained the ideal of filial piety by viewing this as a legitimate way to fulfill their obligations and by constructing the hired care workers as "their filial agents and fictive kin" (Lan, 2002, p. 813). Rather than viewing this as a weakening of family bonds, Lan (2002) suggests that this process helps adult children keep their aging parents living with them at home despite constrained employment circumstances; both the adult children and their aging parents maintain a sense that the cultural ideal is being fulfilled. Lan (2002) concludes the following: "the subcontracting of filial care indeed has an impact on family relations; however, the filial norms and ideals of the family do not disappear but remain elastic, taking on different social configurations" (p. 833). Further, Zhan (2004a, 2004b) reported that adult children from one-child families in China still strongly uphold the tradition of filial piety, yet express reluctance to co-reside or adjust their jobs for parent care, which reflects their awareness of the pressures of providing for their parents both financially and physically.

Indeed, the nature of how filial responsibility is expressed may be changing or shifting, rather than declining. The move towards "intimacy at a distance" documented in Western society is one example (Cantor & Brennan, 2000). Another is the ritualistic co-residence described by Wang (2004), whereby multigenerational co-residence in China is replaced by marriage in the parents' household followed by a short stay, which functions as symbolic expressions of filial piety allowing the elderly to maintain face and prestige.

Two recent studies conducted in Montreal, Quebec, with baby-boomer caregivers (Guberman, Lavoie, Blein, & Olazabal, 2012; Guberman, Lavoie, & Olazabal, 2011), concluded that there is a trend towards the **denaturalization of caregiving** in the context of North American individualization, whereby family members, though still supporting filial responsibility norms, seek to limit their caregiving contributions in order to juggle multiple social role demands, and view public supports as sharing responsibility for eldercare. In fact, that people even self-identify as family caregivers not only reflects the awareness-raising efforts of advocacy groups and policy-makers to draw attention to caregiver needs, but may also mean we are less likely to view care work as an extension of our normal family role and to identify it as an unusual circumstance (Guberman et al., 2011; Guberman et al., 2012; O'Connor, 2007). These changes do not solely reflect a changing culture, but in part may represent the adaptation of the practice of family responsibility to fit with changing structural realities.

Conclusion

In this chapter, we have focused on explicating some of the connections between older persons' micro-level experiences of family life and intimate relationships, and broader social, cultural, political, economic, demographic, and historical contexts. Not only is an aging population changing the structure of families, but cultural and structural individualization is enhancing the diversity of family and relationship forms. However, families continue to perform important social functions, such as socialization and support. In fact, in current times, older persons' roles—both in supporting and being supported by their families—are particularly salient. This is in contrast to assumptions of a historical decline in family functions or supports for older persons. For instance, grandparents represent a key form of child care as more women enter the labour market and when publicly funded child care supports are unavailable or inaccessible. Further, older persons are at the forefront of many newer family and relationship types that are emerging in the current context, such as late-life stepfamilies, living apart together relationships, and transnational families.

Older persons' needs for support from their families are linked to population-level trends in health status, life expectancy, financial security, separation and repartnership, as well as the political and economic context of health care reforms that shift the emphasis from institutional to in-home sites of care. Rather than viewing changing cultural interpretations of family and family responsibility as a weakening of values related to individualism, we should consider an alternative perspective: this may in part reflect a response to increasing constraints on families' abilities to provide care in contemporary Canada. Declines in the average number of children in a family, the delayed onset of child-bearing, migration patterns, increases in women's involvement in paid labour, and the relative absence of strong family-related employment policies are all relevant factors. Future research should also explore how increased needs for family care, alongside reduced capacities to provide this care, affect the well-being of older persons, their family members, and family relationships. Ultimately, however, though most gerontological research and health care policy tends to reproduce a narrow view of families as "resources" for care and support, we must remember that the meanings and functions of family are far more complex and diverse, and these considerations should be explicated in future sociological research on late-life families.

Questions for Critical Thought

1. Who do you count as "family"? How does your concept of family align with or differ from the discussion of family presented in this chapter?

2. What are likely outcomes of the squeeze between increasing pressures and reduced capacity for family care of older persons? What kinds of individual and collective solutions might be possible?

3. What are your expectations for your own future family life trajectory? After reading the evidence presented in this chapter, did your expectations change? Why or why not?

4. Do you agree or disagree that living apart together relationships are more empowering and egalitarian than cohabiting partnerships? Explain.

Suggested Readings

Bengtson, V. L. (2001). Beyond the nuclear family: The increasing importance of multigenerational bonds. *Journal of Marriage and Family, 63* (1), 1–16. Bengtson argues that relationships between extended generations in families will become more important (relative to nuclear family ties). This is because of the aging population, resulting in generations of family members sharing more years of their lives together, and the increasing importance of grandparents and other kin in fulfilling family functions given current trends in divorce and remarriage. Positive and negative implications are discussed, and Bengtson provides evidence to suggest that intergenerational relationships will also be more diverse in terms of their structures and cohesion, but that they will not necessarily decline in their key function of socializing younger family members.

Biggs, S., & Powell, J. L. (2003). Older people and family in social policy. In V. L. Bengtson & A. Lowenstein (Eds.), *Global aging and challenges to families* (pp. 103–119). New York, NY: Walter de Gruyter. In this book chapter, the authors draw on a discourse analysis of policy in the United Kingdom to explain how "policy both is an attempt to shape and is itself shaped by" (p. 104) the meanings of family. They provide a critique of neoliberal policies that construct families as primarily responsible for eldercare to support the erosion of formal supports; however, they also critique what they call a "social democratic" policy frame that focuses on social participation of older persons through volunteering and grandparenting—these roles are not only peripheral, but this policy direction can also support the erosion of formal supports, for which older persons are encouraged to fill the void.

Cooney, T. M., & Dunne, K. (2001). Intimate relationships in later life: Current realities, future prospects. *Journal of Family Issues, 22* (7), 838–858. This is a useful review article for those interested in relationship types and forms among older adults. It not only highlights the broader socio-historical context shaping available relationship options for older adults, but also reviews some of the research regarding the outcomes for older adults' well-being.

Marshall, V. W., Matthews, S. H., & Rosenthal, C. J. (1993). Elusiveness of family life: A challenge for the sociology of aging. *Annual Review of Gerontology and Geriatrics, 13* (1), 39–72. The authors begin with a critique of the narrow range of topics currently covered in most research on the sociology of aging and family, including its tendency to focus only on the individual rather than on broader social contexts. They call for more attention to the latter, which includes examining a wide variety of aspects of family structures, social systems and patterned behaviours of interaction, and culture within and beyond the family. They also call for more research that uncovers the complexity of the family lives of older persons as well as diverse meanings of family.

Relevant Websites

Canadian Caregiver Coalition
http://www.ccc-ccan.ca
> This national, not-for-profit coalition promotes the needs and interests of family caregivers, including distributing resources and information about community supports, and advocating for the development of a national caregiving strategy.

Public Health Agency of Canada, "Seniors Caring for Seniors"

http://www.phac-aspc.gc.ca/seniors-aines/scs-spaa-eng.php

> This archived webpage outlined the Public Health Agency of Canada's acknowledgement of family caregiving as an important health concern for Canadians. They described their efforts to identify effective interventions to promote the well-being of spousal caregivers, including helping professionals respond to caregivers' needs and address health risk. It is noteworthy that this page has since been removed by the organization, which may indicate reduced emphasis on this issue within the work of the agency.

Statistics Canada, 2011 Census Data on Families, "Portrait of Families and Living Arrangements in Canada"

http://www12.statcan.gc.ca/census-recensement/2011/as-sa/98-312-x/98-312-x2011001-eng.cfm

> This article provides detailed information about, as well as selected highlights from, the 2011 census data on Canadian families and living arrangements. Stepfamilies are measured for the first time.

8

Emerging and Salient Topics in the Sociology of Aging

Learning Objectives

In this chapter, you will learn that:

◎ social gerontology has devoted very little attention to First Nations, Inuit, and Métis older adults, despite their risk of marginalization due to processes of colonization; caution and sensitivity is needed when seeking knowledge in this regard.

◎ sociologists explore how social change influences population aging and aging experiences, and how population aging drives new social change.

◎ the sociological study of aging in contemporary societies requires knowledge of how globalization can have a disproportionate effect on older persons throughout the world.

◎ an international human rights framework is being called for to protect the well-being of older persons, in part as a response to the effects of globalization.

◎ sociological research has added much to our understanding of structural constraints in old age, but further research is needed to more fully explore and conceptualize forms of agency in later life, including whether or not these forms look the same as or different than forms of agency in earlier life.

Introduction

Gerontology has made important contributions to both policy and practice to improve the lives of older adults. The dominant focus has been on issues of health in relation to aging and on the micro level of individual biology, physiology, function, and psychology. A sociological perspective has certainly influenced the field; however, the purpose of this book is to help revitalize a sociological perspective that oftentimes becomes lost in the larger interdisciplinary field of gerontology. In particular, sociology can help enhance the use and development of theories in social gerontology that link micro- and macro-level contexts across time. Theories are crucially important even for applied fields such as gerontology that directly seek to change the lives of older persons. Current gerontological research does well at developing knowledge designed to be applied through interventions at the individual level and through changes to gerontological best practice in working with older persons. Sociological knowledge and theories can extend our understanding of how broader, population-level and policy interventions, as well as social interventions targeting marginalized groups of older persons, also play an important role. In this section, we will highlight emerging and salient areas warranting greater—or, in some cases, renewed—attention by sociologists studying aging and aging societies.

Older Aboriginal People in Canada

The aging of First Nations, Inuit, and Métis people—collectively referred to here as **Aboriginal people**[1]—in Canada has attracted very little attention in gerontology. The Aboriginal population in Canada tends to experience lower life expectancies and higher fertility rates in comparison to non-Aboriginal Canadians. As a result, only a very small proportion—about 5 to 6 per cent—of this population is over 65 years of age (Health Council of Canada, 2013; Turcotte & Schellenberg, 2007; Wilson, Rosenberg, Abonyi, & Lovelace, 2010). Because of the relatively low life expectancies among Aboriginal people in Canada, some researchers have suggested that 55 years may be a better marker of entry into old age for this population, at least for research and service-delivery purposes (Health Council of Canada, 2013). More broadly, however, it is important to note that being an **Elder** in most Aboriginal cultures is not necessarily based on age "but on demonstration of emotional well-being, community engagement, spirituality, physical health, and wisdom gained through life experiences" (Braun, Browne, Kaʻopua, Kim, & Mokuau, 2014, p. 122).

Older Aboriginal people in Canada often live in rural and remote communities, many of these being reserves, and they have strong ties to these places and communities, making the issue of aging in place even more salient. However, a lack of access to health services is of concern: "the need to travel for most health care services was identified by participants as one of the most significant issues affecting the quality of life of seniors and their families" (Health Council of Canada, 2013, p. 11). In addition, in some cases older Aboriginal people are displaced far from their communities to receive care in a residential care facility, as these facilities are often unavailable in remote areas.

As the Health Council of Canada (2013) reports, "losing Elders and seniors to distant long-term care facilities can be a cultural blow to entire communities" (p. 8). Older Aboriginal people are more likely than younger Aboriginal people to speak Aboriginal languages, and older adults represent important sources of community leadership and mentorship, transmitting language, cultural heritage and traditional knowledge, oral history, and wisdom (Braun et al., 2014; Turcotte & Schellenberg, 2007). A focus group with Elders of the Mi'kmaq community in Cape Breton also identified how

Elders passed along knowledge about herbal medicines (Auger & Tedford-Litle, 2002). As noted in Chapter 7, Aboriginal grandmothers also play a key role as full-time grandparents. However, the role of older Aboriginal people has been significantly disrupted by the process of **colonization** (Turcotte & Schellenberg, 2007); this process includes, for instance, the loss of traditional ways of living, negative environmental effects of resource extraction, and the destructive effects of the **residential school system**.

Around 14 per cent of older Aboriginal people in Canada living off reserve in 2001 attended a residential school during their lifetime (Turcotte & Schellenberg, 2007), which has effects on their overall well-being in old age, as well as effects on subsequent generations through **intergenerational trauma**. Older Aboriginal people in colonized English-speaking Western nations typically face higher social and economic disadvantage than non-Aboriginal older persons—including associated challenges with housing and access to healthy food and clean water—that can limit their quality of life and life expectancy (Braun et al., 2014; Wilson et al., 2010). For instance, 2001 Census of Canada data indicated that 22 per cent of Aboriginal seniors lived in homes requiring major repairs (see Figure 8.1); more recent statistics regarding the housing conditions of Aboriginal seniors have not been published, yet we do know that Aboriginal people of all age groups still face significant housing challenges.

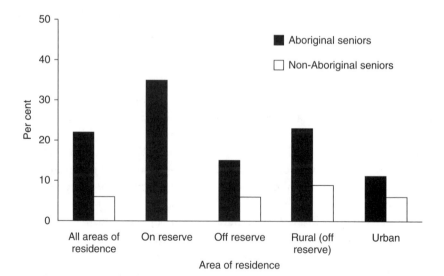

Figure 8.1 Per cent of older Aboriginal people living in homes requiring major repairs (by area of residence), Canada

Source: Turcotte, M., & Schellenberg, G. (2007). *A portrait of seniors in Canada* (Catalogue No. 89-519-XIE). Ottawa, ON: Statistics Canada, Minister of Industry. Retrieved from http://www.statcan.gc.ca/pub/89-519-x/2006001/4122091-eng.htm

Socio-economic determinants of health generate high needs for support in old age that is compounded by barriers to accessing formal services (Beatty & Berdahl, 2011; Buchignani & Armstrong-Esther, 1999; Health Council of Canada, 2013). We should be careful not to overly idealize Aboriginal cultural values of family and kin care—though interdependence tends to be highly valued in many Aboriginal traditions, this should not be used as rationale for inadequate formal services; further, we need to be cognizant of the implications for those providing care, most of whom are women who are also providing care for young children (Buchignani & Armstrong-Esther, 1999).

Though social gerontology can be criticized for ignoring the aging of Aboriginal people in Canada, caution and sensitivity is needed when considering this area of study. This is because Western science and research methods have traditionally worked to oppress and colonize Aboriginal people in Canada and around the world. As Braun and colleagues (2014) note, for instance, Western research on Aboriginal persons has been criticized for the following reasons: research has been ethnocentric, often suggesting or implying that Aboriginal societies are less developed or backwards; the focus on scientific knowledge for understanding the world dismisses Indigenous ways of knowing; and lastly, research on Aboriginal people has often used unethical research practices. As such, there have been increasing calls for different approaches to research *with* Aboriginal populations, including participatory, action-oriented research in which control of the entire research process remains with Aboriginal communities, and **decolonizing methodologies** that revalue ways of knowing other than the Western scientific method and are culturally appropriate for particular local Aboriginal groups. As Braun and colleagues (2014) emphasize, "ideally, indigenous research should be led, designed, controlled, and reported by indigenous people" (p. 125).

Social Change and Aging

As well as directing attention to issues of diversity and inequality, a sociological perspective is concerned with examining the precursors, processes, and outcomes of social change. In relation to the study of aging, social change is also an area requiring further inquiry. At a broad level, sociologists are interested in examining the social and historical changes that influence fertility rates and life expectancies (see Chapter 2) and contribute to an aging population. In turn, there is an interest in how aging populations will alter societies, not only because of changing demographics, but also because population aging may be used ideologically to justify neoliberal political and economic changes (see Chapter 2). Olshansky et al. (2011) also suggest a need to actively redesign society to adjust to population aging: to prioritize preventive, health-promoting interventions and age-friendly environments, create meaningful roles (e.g., jobs) for older persons, and provide more opportunities for lifelong learning.

The concept of social change is central to a life course perspective and in gerontological research engaging with concepts of time, cohort, and generation (see Chapter 1). Through articulating the ways that history shapes the identities and actions of members of a cohort or generation, for instance, we can better understand how social change influences individuals within successive generations, which in turn shapes their aging experiences. In addition, each generation responds to new social events and circumstances in ways that can reshape the nature of that society for future generations. For instance, generations faced with increasing family caregiving demands yet decreasing abilities to meet these demands may modify existing social norms of family responsibility. As noted within age stratification theory, however, there can be structural lag between changing social norms and societal structures.

There has been considerable attention, at least in theory, to the impact of specific social changes on older people and their social status. Modernization theory is a key example of this, but as noted in Chapter 1, disengagement and exchange theories also reflect concerns that industrialization—and the introduction of retirement—has lowered the social position of older people relative to younger people. This is believed to explain, in part, a tendency to view aging negatively and as a social problem. The expansion of biomedicalization is another social change that has affected how we view older people and the way we experience aging. There is a wide range of other ways in which social change affects aging experiences—the possibilities seem endless and include changes to family structures and social roles for women (see Chapter 7), and changes associated with the development of post-industrial or postmodern societies (e.g., see Chapter 1). With respect to the latter, for instance, there has been discussion of how social change contributes to a destandardization of the life course, resulting in potentially greater variability in experiences and outcomes in old age. As noted in Chapter 5 and elsewhere in this book, the expansion of neoliberal economic policies and globalization also has particular implications for aging; this will be discussed further in the next section.

Globalization and Social Change

Globalization has been a theme throughout this book, and it is also an increasingly important area of research in the sociology of aging. Sociologists explore the implications of globalization for aging and care in a number of different areas, such as how risk and responsibility become individualized to older persons and their families, often facilitated by a discourse of apocalyptic demography (see Chapter 2). In this way, population aging and globalization are intertwined phenomena (Neilson, 2003).

Much of the research in this area is driven by an international political economy of aging approach (Walker, 2005). Globalization is associated with decreasing power of nation-states and increasing powers of international governmental organizations and transnational corporations to influence national policies. There has been pressure—for example, from the World Bank and International Monetary Fund—on various countries including Canada to implement neoliberal economic reforms that jeopardize the sustainability of publicly financed social and health care services for older persons. In Chapter 4, we also noted the effects on health care policies. Estes and Phillipson (2002) expand on the role of international governmental organizations and free trade agreements in the marketization of elder care— specifically, the expansion of private for-profit corporate involvement in the insurance and delivery of health and social care for older persons. The rise of profit-making interests in health and social care may reduce access to these services among low-income older persons in particular, generating inequities in health outcomes.

In Chapter 7, we also noted the potential implications of health care reforms for families. More specifically, drawing on a political economy approach, Chappell and Penning (2005) explain how political and economic pressures associated with globalization facilitate the expansion of health care policies in Canada and other Western industrialized countries that reinforce health care as a private, individual, or family responsibility. They argue that the shift in policy to home- and community-based care for older persons, alongside reduced access to formal services, results in "greater demands on family caregivers at a time when unemployment is increasing and gaps between rich and poor are widening" (p. 457); the latter is associated with increasing needs for care (wealth being a key determinant of health). Further, Chappell and Penning argue that these changes will disproportionately affect women, those with low income, and marginalized ethnic/racial minorities. For older persons in these groups, the needs for care are greater, yet they possess fewer personal resources to purchase private sources of home care. Family caregivers in these vulnerable groups also face greater socio-economic and health challenges that could be exacerbated by the demands associated with caregiving responsibilities.

In Chapter 5, we examined the effects of globalization on pension policies. This is further discussed by Estes and Phillipson (2002), who highlight the active role of international governmental organizations such as the World Bank in promoting private pension provision, which will reduce income security in older persons—especially those from already marginalized groups—and generate greater income inequality in old age. In Chapter 5, we also discussed how corporate and industry restructuring and downsizing, a phenomenon tied to globalization, tends to have disproportionate effects on older workers. Further, increases in precarious and non-standard work associated with globalization may lead to more precarious financial situations for future cohorts of older persons.

In Chapter 7, we noted how globalization may be contributing to a rise in transnational families; multiple generations of family members can exchange considerable support across geographic distance, yet face unique challenges. Neilson (2003) observes how older people can be negatively affected when their children move to other countries to find work—a phenomenon that may become more common as wealth inequality throughout the world increases. Population aging and globalization may also increase the transnational migration of women to Western countries, including Canada, for employment in the long-term care sector, for instance as live-in caregivers for older persons or as health care aides (Browne & Braun, 2008). Many of these women leave their own families and can experience exploitation, discrimination, and language barriers.

One outcome of globalization is the increasing wealth disparity between countries across the globe. Further, the global population is itself aging, with some of the most rapid increases predicted for developing countries: for example, between 2006 and 2030, the number of older persons in more developed countries may increase by about 51 per cent; in less developed countries, by 140 per cent (National Institute on Aging & National Institutes of Health, 2007). Considering the world as a whole, greater numbers of older persons (61 per cent) live in poor nations, despite the fact that Western countries tend to have higher proportions of older persons within their own populations—poorer nations have larger populations across all ages (Neilson, 2003). The implications of population aging for these countries, which are disadvantaged within the global economic system, are of concern (Olshansky et al., 2011).

Estes and Phillipson (2002) suggest that because globalization has particular effects on older persons, there is a need for older people—and organizations representing them—to have a greater role and influence in the global arena. Some potential also lies with the human rights agenda, which will be addressed in the next section.

Aging and Human Rights

International **human rights** frameworks can help challenge the structured dependency of older persons in the face of threats to their well-being in the context of globalization: "use of such frameworks may become essential given the rise of care organisations operating across national borders, and the drive to deregulate and privatise hitherto public services" (Baars & Phillipson, 2013, p. 23). Mégret (2011) emphasizes that "in the right circumstances, international treaties come with a *force obligatoire* that can obviously have a significant impact on domestic policy and legal reform" (p. 64), as well as draw political attention to issues of aging, and transform the discourse of older people as passive and dependent to participatory and entitled to rights.

Currently, however, existing legal frameworks for international human rights do not contain specific references to older persons, and there is no existing international obligatory legal framework (such as a United Nations convention) protecting older persons' human rights. Further, in most countries, existing legal frameworks "are patchy and inadequate—a reality that reinforces the need for more robust international instruments" (Kalache, 2012, p. 89). The 2002 Madrid International Plan of Action on Ageing (MIPAA)—see Box 8.1 for more details—is a step forward, as is the 1991 United Nations Principles for Older Persons. However, despite their potential for advancing the global discussion of age equality and dignity, neither is legally binding nor constitutes a concrete human rights framework (Kalache, 2012; Olshansky et al., 2011). Kalache (2012) observes that there has been inconsistent implementation of the MIPAA, and HelpAge International notes that over 10 years after the adoption of the MIPAA, despite significant progress in aging policies, "the mechanisms and budgets necessary to implement them are not there. . . . There are also limited or no policy coverage in several core areas" (HelpAge International, n.d.).

There are increasing calls for a specific international human rights framework for older persons (e.g., Kalache, 2012; Olshansky et al., 2011; Tang & Lee, 2006). Some movement is indicated in this regard, with the establishment in 2010 of a United Nations working group to consider this proposal, and the appointment to that body, in 2014, of an independent expert, Rosa Kornfeld-Matte, who will provide leadership and guidance. The rationale for an international human rights framework for older persons is based on the argument that existing frameworks do not sufficiently account for the needs of older persons, that their human rights are often violated, and that they are vulnerable to distinct human rights violations because of their group membership (Mégret, 2011). As just a few examples, Mégret (2011) identifies the following considerations for the human rights of older persons:

- Older persons are at risk of poverty and rely heavily on social security systems, making them vulnerable to economic human rights violations.
- There is a human right to life, which may be violated by implicit or explicit policies of health care rationing based on age.
- Older persons with reduced physical and cognitive capacities are vulnerable to inhuman treatment such as neglect or the use of restraints in care facilities.
- Older persons' rights to family life may be violated when older couples are separated into different nursing homes.
- Older persons' rights to equality and freedom from discrimination may be violated in a number of ways due to ageist treatment.

Box 8.1   The Madrid International Plan of Action on Ageing

In 2002, representatives of 159 governments adopted 19 non-legally binding principles as part of the International Plan of Action on Ageing to promote "the development of a society for all ages" and equality for persons of all ages, through national leadership and international support and co-operation (United Nations, 2002). Selected principles are highlighted below:

> **Article 5.** . . . We commit ourselves to eliminating all forms of discrimination, including age discrimination. . . . [P]ersons, as they age, should enjoy a life of fulfilment, health, security, and active participation in the economic, social, cultural, and political life of their societies. We are determined to enhance the recognition of the dignity of older persons and to eliminate all forms of neglect, abuse, and violence.

> **Article 6.** . . . [C]oncerted action is required to transform the opportunities and the quality of life of men and women as they age and to ensure the sustainability of their support systems. . . . When ageing is embraced as an achievement, the reliance on human skills, experiences, and resources of the higher age groups is naturally recognized as an asset in the growth of . . . societies.

> **Article 7.** . . . [O]bstacles to further integration and full participation in the global economy remain for developing countries. . . . [W]e recognize the importance of placing ageing in development agendas. . . .

> **Article 8.** . . . We recognize the need to mainstream a gender perspective into all policies and programmes to take account of the needs and experiences of older women and men.

Kalache (2012) argues that existing legislation regarding the rights of older adults tends to focus on employment discrimination and "seldom extends to such vital areas as social and health care, long-term support, or provision of other goods and services. The right to adequate social security is significantly under-addressed globally, as is the right to an accessible and affordable healthcare that is appropriate to older persons' needs" (p. 89). As such, one can envision how an international human rights agreement might assist in drawing political attention to the rights of older persons as they are increasingly threatened by the processes of globalization described earlier.

Article 9. We commit ourselves to protect and assist older persons in situations of armed conflict and foreign occupation. . . .

Article 12. . . . [O]lder persons [should] be able to participate in the economic, political, social, and cultural life of their societies. . . . The empowerment of older persons and the promotion of their full participation are essential elements. . . .

Article 13. We stress the primary responsibility of Governments in promoting, providing, and ensuring access to basic social services, bearing in mind specific needs of older persons. . . .

Article 14. . . . We commit ourselves to providing older persons with universal and equal access to health care and services, including physical and mental health services, and we recognize that the growing needs of an ageing population require additional policies, in particular care and treatment, the promotion of healthy lifestyles, and supportive environments. . . .

Article 15. We recognize the important role played by families, volunteers, communities, older persons organizations, and other community-based organizations in providing support and informal care to older persons. . . .

Article 16. We recognize the need to strengthen solidarity [and mutually responsive relationships] among generations and intergenerational partnerships. . . .

Source: "Political Declaration and Madrid International Plan of Action on Ageing: Second World Assembly on Ageing." United Nations. Madrid, Spain, 8-12 April 2002. Accessed June 10, 2015.

Individual Agency and the Sociology of Aging

Another relevant theme of sociological inquiry is *individual agency*, though attention to the forms and meanings of agency in old age require further attention. In Chapter 1, for instance, we highlighted how symbolic interactionist perspectives, through focusing on diverse meaning constructions at the level of interactions, accord a greater degree of agency to all individuals, including older persons, to define and reshape the subjective meanings of their experiences. For example, older persons may reject the label of old age as irrelevant for their personal identities in late life, as Sharon

Kaufman's work in *The Ageless Self* (1986/2000) demonstrates (you may wish to refer back to Box 1.2 in Chapter 1).

As Wray (2003) notes, disengagement theory and other theories of aging, and indeed many existing gerontological perspectives, tend to ignore or minimize older persons' agency, focusing instead on the deterministic and constraining influences of social structure, especially for women. Though activity theory and concepts of successful aging highlight a kind of agency, Wray identifies limitations of this concept for relying on Western ideals of agency as maintaining a youthful body, identity, and social life, and resisting age itself. Wray's (2003) own definition of agency focuses on the "ever-present possibility of individuals to act in a way that generates feelings of power and control" (p. 514) and to "transform and resist [potentially disempowering] social and economic constraints" (p. 517) such as low income and racism.

In Chapter 3 in particular, we focused on older persons' agency using the concept of embodiment and drawing on the work of postmodern scholars. We considered, for example, how older persons demonstrate agency in redefining and challenging sexist and ageist social norms of physical appearance, or in actively managing the personal impacts of gendered and ageist stigmas by purchasing anti-aging products and services to modify their bodies (e.g., cosmetic surgery). Some researchers have suggested that when older persons transform the physical appearance of their bodies, they express individual freedom and widen the range of options for bodies and identities in old age (e.g., Garnham, 2013). Similar interpretations were suggested in research exploring the ways that older persons use assistive technologies such as wheelchairs or hearing aids, at times creatively, to maintain independence (Joyce & Loe, 2010; Long, 2012).

In Chapter 4, it was noted that health is given meaning at the individual level, in terms of how older persons subjectively interpret their symptoms. Further, Wray (2003) identified how older British women exhibited agency through maintaining a subjective sense of control over their lives despite health challenges. Agency is also demonstrated by low-paid, marginalized employees in the long-term care sector, for example by actively constructing positive meaning in their work despite the marginalization of their position. It is also important to note that although much of the research on care tends to imply that it is a unidirectional process done by an active caregiver to a passive care recipient, agency can also be demonstrated by older persons who receive care. For instance, Lewinter (2003) described how older recipients of family and formal care continue to participate in reciprocating social interactions through hospitality and gift-giving strategies, as well as in expressing gratitude and appreciation. Likewise, Fine and Glendinning (2005) draw on **relational theories of care** to emphasize the agency of both caregiver and care recipient. From this perspective, care is "the product or outcome of the relationship between two or more people" (Fine & Glendinning, 2005, p. 617); the care recipient is actively involved in the process and its outcomes.

In Chapter 7, we considered how some older persons who repartner can be seen as agents of social change in the establishment of living apart together relationships, as older women in particular choose to retain more independence in their intimate relationships. Wray (2003) noted that some older women identified freedom from family responsibilities in later life as a form of agency; however, Wray appears ambivalent in her interpretation, arguing that older women who are providing care for others (e.g., for grandchildren) nonetheless maintain a sense of fulfillment, which she argues is akin to a form of agency.

Connidis and McMullin (2002) suggest family caregivers may have agency despite the constraints of social structure, which can generate ambivalence (conflicting thoughts, feelings, or beliefs stemming from conflicting social roles or responsibilities). Ambivalence, Connidis and McMullin argue, triggers social action, which may either reproduce the existing status quo (e.g., through acceptance of family role responsibilities in the absence of formal services) or contribute to change in these arrangements (e.g., through setting boundaries, redefining roles and renegotiating traditional demands, hiring private sources of care, or cutting back work hours). Caregivers who have more resources through their position in the social structure (e.g., gender, class, ethnicity/race) may have greater agency (Connidis & McMullin, 2002).

The ways in which older persons demonstrate agency remains to be more fully explored in sociological research. As far back as 1974, Neugarten highlighted the potential role of the "young-old" (55 to 75 years) as agents of social change in American society—a group she described as increasingly empowered and politically active. Though some research emphasizes the participation of older adults in their communities, for instance through volunteering (see Chapter 6), there has been little attention to their civic participation, perhaps the most obvious example of individual and collective agency. In Chapter 6, we discussed how social exclusion among older adults can constrain empowerment and participation in civil society. There has been some research on older women's participation in collective action, and Maureen C. McHugh (2012) identifies this group as having considerable potential to contribute to social change. Charpentier, Quéniart, and Jacques (2008) spoke with older women who were active in different political parties or community groups in Quebec. The involvement of these women demonstrated considerable consistency over time as well as in both public (civic life) and private (family) spheres of their lives; in other words, their activism occurred alongside commitments to care for family members or close friends. Charpentier et al. (2008) conclude the following about these older women:

Whether influenced by their family history, incited by great indignation over a specific issue, or aroused by a personal situation that required improvement, the shape and form of their involvement has evolved consistently over the years in a way that corresponds with the main stages of their adult lives. . . . [T]heir involvement did not begin at retirement and does not result from this social state. (p. 354)

Several qualitative researchers (Caissie, 2011; Hutchinson & Wexler, 2007; Narushima, 2004; Sawchuk, 2009) have spoken with Canadian older women participating in the "Raging Grannies" (see Box 8.2). Narushima (2004) notes that "to be a Raging Granny is to engage in an on-going process of self-actualization and liberation both individually and collectively, while making their social concerns more visible to Canadians at the same time" (p. 38). Group members tend to be relatively healthy and financially secure, and their age affords them relative freedom from family responsibilities and social norms, and more freedom to engage in empowering collective political activity. Sawchuk (2009) emphasizes how the Grannies challenge stereotypes of older women—for example, through the exaggerated reproduction of these stereotypes. However, their overall focus is on social justice concerns more broadly, and they tend to dramatize ageist and sexist stereotypes through song and dress ("the granny mask") as a strategy to attract political and media attention.

In many ways, the activism of the Raging Grannies represents the ideal of empowerment through productive action, conscious choice, and claiming a voice; such forms of involvement are often dependent on some degree of health. In stark contrast, Grenier and Phillipson (2013) draw attention to differing forms of agency that may be present among older people with significant cognitive and physical impairments—they may be bed-bound, institutionalized, and unable to communicate through language. Older people in this stage are referred to as being in the "**fourth age**," which is often symbolically contrasted against the "third age" of older persons who are able to remain active and independent. Older persons with significant health impairments face considerable constraints on traditional forms of participation and active forms of agency, yet they may nonetheless express more everyday or ordinary forms of agency. For example, through touch, voice (e.g., screams, cries, or moans), or aggressive or defiant behaviours that might be viewed as problematic, persons with dementia may seek to engage with others, deal with boredom, communicate, and react to their environments (Grenier & Phillipson, 2013).

Further, Wray (2003) sought to identify examples of agency among older women from diverse cultural backgrounds, by examining interviews with 170 older British women. Wray conceptualizes agency as a subjective sense of control gained from social participation. For instance, some older

Box 8.2   The Raging Grannies

The "Raging Grannies" originated in Victoria, British Columbia, in 1987. There are now more than 60 Raging Grannies groups across Canada and more groups across the United States and beyond (Roy, n.d.). Grannies groups draw on techniques from street theatre, using humour, parody, and satire to draw attention to political and social justice issues through non-violent protest (Roy, n.d.). They dress in an exaggerated stereotype of "little old ladies," and they challenge that stereotype through their strong, empowered public action. Here, we include a sample song written by the Victoria Grannies to the tune of "Take Me Out to the Ball Game," entitled, "Take Me Out to the Clearcut":

Take me out to the clearcut

We'll picnic on a few stumps.

I want you to know I'm a tree-farming nut

Who thinks like a chainsaw that's stuck in a rut.

Weyerhauser gets a hip hooray.

They make black picnic grounds pay.

So it's one, makes you two

Dear investors, thank you.

You have spruced up our day!

Take me out to the clearcut

The timber's been tidied away.

It's been sold down the stream

In a businessman's dream.

It's swell to stand here

In a landscape so clean.

So it's off to lumbering elsewhere.

I'll lumber you and you me.

It's the buzz of the mill

That produces the thrill

Worth a million trees!

Source: "Take me out to the clearcut," Raging Grannies International. October 28, 2009. Reprinted with permission from Hubert Meeker.

women in her research gained a sense of power and resisted ageism by participating in paid employment (which also increases financial independence) and leisure activities, by participating in group-based religious activities, or by participating in community groups or organizations that challenge racism. Wray (2003) concludes the following:

> These examples of agency are present throughout the life course and are not simply a reaction to the supposed problems and disadvantages of later life. Neither are they an attempt to remain "forever young." Rather, they represent the individual and collective creative capacity, purpose and agency of women. (p. 525)

In sum, examining agency in old age requires us to re-examine what we mean by the concept. Rather than focusing solely on agency as active forms of resistance and advocacy (both individual and collective), we are challenged to consider alternative forms of agency, such as the ability to express creativity; to generate and expand one's own unique life story, emotional expression, self-awareness, and identity; to resist decline and discourses of decline; and, in the process, to challenge restricted normative narratives and identities in old age (Tulle, 2004). In expressing agency, however, Tulle (2004) reminds us that the possibilities can be constrained by the broader culture and structural context.

Spotlight on Sociological Research on Aging in Canada

Graduating with training in the sociological study of aging equips one to conduct both quantitative and qualitative research addressing social phenomena related to individual and population aging, and to analyze the complex social factors contributing to the well-being and security of diverse groups of older persons. Sociologists might pursue further training towards social work or legal careers, or they might seek work in health care or social service management and case coordination. Sociologists also apply their skills in analyzing and developing federal and provincial policies, or in conducting research and developing programs within not-for-profit agencies or for research consulting agencies. Sociologists employed within academic institutions continue to research aging issues from a sociological perspective. A search of sociological aging research funded by the Social Sciences and Humanities Research Council of Canada reveals specific examples of research on aging led by Canadian researchers employed and/or trained in sociology, social gerontology, or closely related disciplines (see Table 8.1).

In addition, many sociological researchers work with and lead interdisciplinary teams of researchers in examining health and aging issues; this research is generally funded by the Canadian Institutes of Health Research

Table 8.1 Examples of sociological aging research funded by the Social Sciences and Humanities Research Council of Canada (Insight Grants, Standard Development Grants, and Community-University Research Alliances), 1998–2014

Lead researcher	University	Award date	Title or focus
Laura Hurd Clarke	University of British Columbia	2012	Older men, ageism, and the body: Everyday embodiment in later life
Amanda Grenier	McMaster University	2012	Homelessness in late life: Growing older on the streets, in shelters and long-term care
Markus Schafer	University of Toronto	2012	Network structure and the quality of individual and partnered life among older adults
Peggy McDonough	University of Toronto	2012	Economic inequalities among women in later life: The role of structured life course processes in comparative context
Julia Rozanova	University of British Columbia	2011	Digital dating: Online romance and sexuality in later life
Susan McDaniel	University of Lethbridge	2010	Income inequality in mid-life, looking toward the later years: A Canada/US longitudinal comparison
Pat Armstrong	York University	2009	Re-imagining long-term residential care: An international study of promising practices
Normand Carpentier	Université de Montréal	2008	Monitoring a cohort of caregivers involved in caring for those with Alzheimer's disease: Empirical and theoretical exploration
Laura Hurd Clarke	University of British Columbia	2008	Body image and identity: The experience of multiple chronic conditions
Neena Chappell	University of Victoria	2007	Filial responsibility across cultures: A comparison of filial attitudes and behaviours in caregiving to older adults
Kim Shuey	University of Western Ontario	2006	Aging within the context of a changing labour market: The relationship between workplace factors, aging, and health
Debbie Laliberte Rudman	University of Western Ontario	2006	Shaping the modern retiree: A comparative discourse analysis of media texts and individuals' narratives
Barbara Mitchell	Simon Fraser University	2006	Mid and later-life parenting and the launching of children: Cultural dynamics and implications for health and well-being
Andrea Willson	University of Western Ontario	2006	Health and socioeconomic status over the life course: A comparative analysis of Canada and the United States
Peri Ballantyne	University of Toronto	2005	Exploring cultures of medicines-related health care decision-making by elderly women and men
Amanda Grenier	McMaster University	2005	Late life transitions: Understanding the "fit" between policy and personal experience
Barbara Payne	University of Manitoba	2005	A study of successful aging in Manitoba
Lynn McDonald	University of Toronto	2005	Retiring to caregive
Laura Hurd Clarke	University of British Columbia	2003	Body image, aging, and the experience of non-surgical cosmetic procedures
Deborah Stienstra	University of Winnipeg	2002	Voices at dying: End of life issues and persons with disabilities
Lynn McDonald	University of Toronto	2002	Divorce and separation in retirement

Continued

Table 8.1 *Continued*

Lead researcher	University	Award date	Title or focus
Frédéric Lesemann	Institut National de la Recherche Scientifique	2001	Older workers in different modes of production
Deborah van den Hoonaard	St. Thomas University	2001	By himself: The older man's transition to widowhood
Cheryl Cott	University of Toronto	2000	The structure of helping networks for community dwelling seniors with arthritis
Lori Campbell	McMaster University	2000	Exploring men's experience in filial care in the context of family and work
Ellen Gee	Simon Fraser University	1999	Culture and coresidence: A comparative analysis of ethnicity, living arrangements, intergenerational relations, and support in Canadian families
Janice Keefe	Mount Saint Vincent University	1998	Work and eldercare: The contribution of elderly parents to their employed children

Source: Compiled from Social Sciences and Humanities Research Council of Canada. (2013). Awards search engine [Database]. Retrieved from http://www.sshrc-crsh.gc.ca/results-resultats/award_search-recherche_attributions/index-eng.aspx

(CIHR). However, as with much social science research in the field of health, social science research in aging faces marginalization within a funding framework that tends to prioritize theoretical and research models that reflect a natural sciences approach (Albert, 2014). Further, CIHR's funding of aging-related social science research may contribute to the biomedicalization of aging, as sociologists may slowly adapt the focus of their research towards a focus on health and aging in order to access funding—leading to a growth in research addressing health and aging. Though health and aging research from a social science perspective is important and necessary, other fields of sociological inquiry into aging-related phenomena should not be left behind.

Conclusion

As should be evident by now, a sociological perspective indicates a need for broad and collective solutions to promote inclusion and well-being among older adults. The focus on macro-level considerations is a common sociological approach despite some variations evident within and between particular sociological theories of aging (see Chapter 1). Issues related to the organization of society, social responsibility, and social justice are commonly highlighted. In this section, we will conclude by drawing attention to some of these implications for policy and practice, derived from Chapters 2 through 7.

Reducing ageism and promoting positive intergenerational relations (see Chapter 2) requires public demand for a greater diversity of cultural representations of later life and support for intergenerational learning and socialization. It further requires identifying and reversing existing age discriminatory practices and incorporating older persons' needs when designing policies, services, and physical environments. Critical gerontologists would also highlight the need to recognize and critically assess the claims of apocalyptic demography in favour of more nuanced views of intergenerational interdependence alongside careful consideration of proposed changes to social institutions purporting to address population aging. From this perspective, addressing ageism may also require broad political and economic change and collective action.

To promote positive body images and experiences in old age (see Chapter 3), we need cultural images that reflect a diversity of body types and appearances in old age. Further, the tendency towards the biomedicalization of old age in policy and practice discourse, as well as in popular culture, should be countered with other, non-medicalized representations and discourses. In particular, practitioners should be aware of the ways in which, through social interaction, they can reinforce the structured dependency in the aged and those with cognitive impairments. An educational focus on media literacy across the life course could also help those of all ages to critically assess and evaluate images and discourses circulating within popular culture.

To promote health and well-being in old age (see Chapter 4), we need policies and interventions to address the social determinants of health, such as housing, employment, and inclusion. Improving the experiences of and outcomes among older persons facing physical or cognitive impairments requires the provision of adequate, accessible, and coordinated levels and types of home and residential care supports. Consistency and trusting relationships with paid providers should be encouraged, as should opportunities for autonomy and individualized care. Improving the experience of family caregivers requires attending to gendered inequities across the life course, recognizing and valuing this work, and making it easier for caregivers to navigate and access existing services for the care recipient. A national family caregiving strategy would represent an important step forward, but it needs to be accompanied by macro-level changes such as financial compensation or employment legislation, as well as ongoing attention by policy-makers to the impacts of policies on family members. Lastly, these changes should also attend to how to improve the experience of paid providers of care to older adults, particularly in the context of increasing workloads.

Promoting economic security among all older adults (see Chapter 5) requires monitoring the ways in which changes to the retirement income system affect older adults' sources and levels of income, as well as disparities in this regard. Though it will be challenging to maintain the high levels of income security experienced by current cohorts of older persons in a globalizing economy, paying close attention to employment, income security, and family care policies across the life course and in current cohorts of younger persons is crucial to this endeavour.

Promoting social inclusion among all older adults (see Chapter 6) requires policies and practices that contribute to the following, as examples: removing barriers to participation in community events and activities, strengthening community transportation, improving income supports, promoting representation and input from older adults in service design, challenging ageist stereotypes in popular culture and among practitioners, and providing adequate public services. Policy-makers may also use various policy tools to consider the impact of particular policies on the inclusion or exclusion of older adults.

Promoting the well-being of late-life families (see Chapter 7) requires recognizing and supporting a wide variety of family and relationship forms and types in policy and practice. For instance, federal immigration policies can significantly affect the experience of transnational families. In addition, we must recognize the ways in which health and social care policies and practices, as well as pension policies, shape family relationships, and we must strive for supportive policies in this regard. For example, health care reforms currently increase older persons' needs for support from their families, yet there is a tendency to assume that family caregiving is always the ideal form of care. Further, there is a need for greater attention to how policies, such as employment policies about family leave, influence the experience of family caregiving.

In sum, I hope that by reading this book and participating in independent inquiry and discussion with others, you have gained an enhanced understanding of a sociological approach and of age-related issues and concerns in Canadian society. The ability to think sociologically about aging will help anyone interested in challenging discourses that limit our understanding of aging, as well as changing practice and policy to improve the experience of aging among all Canadians.

Questions for Critical Thought

1. Does existing evidence (such as the research presented throughout this book) support the argument that older persons need a unique international human rights framework? Discuss.

2. How might your own future experience of old age be influenced by macro-level processes of globalization?

3. Drawing on your sociological knowledge, do you agree or disagree that aggressive and difficult behaviours in older persons with dementia can reflect individual agency?

Suggested Readings

Estes, C. L., & Phillipson, C. (2002). The globalization of capital, the welfare state, and old age policy. *International Journal of Health Services, 32* (2), 279–297. Using a political economy perspective, the authors critically examine the private interests that define the "problem" of population aging as one that requires a shift from social responsibility and public welfare for older persons to greater individual responsibility. The operation of global neoliberal ideology is explained, including how it expands the power of corporations and other economic interests in society, facilitated by international governmental organizations. Implications for pension and health care policy, and for older people and particular groups of older people, are addressed.

Fry, C. L. (2005). Globalization and the experiences of aging. *Gerontology and Geriatrics Education, 26* (1), 9–22. Anthropologist Christine Fry provides a detailed explanation of the historical development of globalization and its consequences. Globalization's effects for those at or near old age are particularly salient in the following areas: changing family structures and changing meanings of kinship; declining standards of living for workers, posing challenges for economic security in old age; and the restructuring of the welfare state.

Mégret, F. (2011). The human rights of older persons: A growing challenge. *Human Rights Law Review, 11* (1), 37–66. The author identifies arguments both for and against the need for a unique international human rights framework for older persons, and explains why the argument for such a framework has emerged. The article also provides an overview of the various ways in which older persons' human rights may be more easily violated, as well as the implications of human rights violations for older persons' well-being and dignity.

Relevant Websites

First Nations Information Governance Centre, "The First Nations Principles of OCAP"
http://fnigc.ca/ocap.html
This website specifies the principles of ownership, control, access, and protection that should be met by researchers working with First Nations communities in Canada to collect and analyze data.

Raging Grannies International
http://raginggrannies.org
This website provides a hub for Raging Grannies groups across the world, including a "starter kit" of suggestions for those starting their own local group (a "gaggle"). There is also a link to their Raging Grannies' Songs website, videos and photos, and a summary of their history and philosophy.

United Nations Office of the High Commissioner for Human Rights, "Human Rights of Older Persons"
http://www.ohchr.org/EN/Issues/OlderPersons/Pages/OlderPersonsIndex.aspx
This website provides a brief overview of the human rights of older persons and provides access to the *Report of the Secretary-General to the General Assembly* that focuses on this topic in detail.

Notes

Chapter 1

1. This perspective does not imply an organized conspiracy, but is a view of how society operates overall in such a way as to maintain inequality because it is set up to support a status quo that benefits the powerful.
2. Some conflict theorists study how different nations struggle over resources and power globally, and how these struggles over time have left some countries (e.g., less economically developed "third world" countries) more unequal than and vulnerable to exploitation by more powerful countries (e.g., more economically developed "first world" countries).
3. Modernization theory reflects a structural-functionalist approach, because it explains the devaluing of older persons by considering their role in the functioning of society, and because it takes a linear view of social change.
4. Commonly, gerontologists consider a 30-year period for this purpose.
5. The concept of structural lag is similar to structural functionalism's emphasis on societal balance.

Chapter 2

1. Increasing rates of immigration, especially of younger immigrants, can also help offset population aging, but only to a very limited extent.
2. This is an example of structural lag in the normative age of expected retirement.
3. Chicken Little is a folk tale about a chicken who believes "the sky is falling" after an acorn falls upon his head, and he becomes hysterical, spreading his unjustified fear of an imminent catastrophe to those he meets.
4. When samples are not randomly selected from the population, the findings may not be statistically representative. Older persons who would join the Canadian Association of Retired Persons might respond differently to questions about ageism than other older persons.
5. This is essentially a structural-functionalist approach.
6. The concept of segregation is similar to the concept of social exclusion: see Chapter 6.

Chapter 3

1. In other words the cause of the disease is real, identifiable, observable, and "out there," as opposed to socially constructed.
2. Not to be confused with the separate concept of "boundary work" mentioned earlier in this chapter.

Chapter 4

1. Paid companions might also be used by families providing home-based care.

Chapter 6

1. This is a structural-functionalist approach, because the focus is on how broad-level social changes might affect the structure and functioning of that society.

2.   The term *social network* does not refer solely to online networking applications and systems such as Facebook or MySpace. However, such web-based networks can be part of a person's entire social network, which extends beyond the online world.

Chapter 7

1.   This perspective reflects a structural-functionalist approach, which tends to focus on the ways that family is a social institution, helping to fulfill basic functions that society as a whole needs in order to keep running smoothly.
2.   This reflects the principle of "linked lives," which is commonly used within a life course perspective.
3.   The study of neoliberalism and globalization tends to be undertaken by sociologists working from a conflict theory perspective or an approach known as global political economy.
4.   This research utilized the sociological theoretical tradition of symbolic interactionism.
5.   Spousal caregiving between older persons is also another important contribution of older persons to their families.

Chapter 8

1.   A caution about generalizations about Aboriginal people: there are important distinctions in identity, history, and experiences between First Nations, Métis, and Inuit persons in Canada.

Glossary

ableism Discrimination against those with disabilities; implicit assumptions that everyone has the same physical and mental abilities. This form of discrimination is often institutionalized in policies, procedures, practices, and environmental design.

Aboriginal people In Canada and other countries, groups of people who have originated within and long occupied a geographic area prior to the arrival of invading and colonizing groups. After colonization, Aboriginal people face considerable disadvantage yet strive to retain their distinct identity and ways of life.

absolute material disadvantage The inability to meet the most basic, universal needs for survival (e.g., food, clothing, shelter, water, sanitation). Also known as *absolute poverty*.

activities of daily living A term used in health care practice often in reference to an individual's ability to complete certain everyday tasks of daily life, reflecting level of function and independence.

activity theory An often implicit theory of aging that views aging as a problem requiring individual adjustment; specifically, aging-related role loss requires that individuals replace these roles with new productive activities.

acute care Often discussed in contrast to longer-term chronic care, this type of health care involves a patient receiving short-term, often emergency, diagnosis and treatment of a severe or urgent illness or injury. Most often, acute care is provided in a hospital or similar environment.

advance directives In health care, this refers to a document that outlines the requests and wishes of an individual regarding care and treatment plans and decisions should the individual become incompetent (i.e., due to incapacity or illness) to communicate these plans and decisions at a future point in time. Also known as an *advance care plan* or a *living will*.

age-based rationing Occurs when decisions and policies about the allocation of public health care services and treatments favour younger patients and impose limits on the levels or types of services accessible to older patients.

age effect In gerontological research, this refers to a change that is explained by the individual-level process of aging.

age-friendly communities A movement promoting the development of policies, services, and structures in local communities and cities that support older people to age well by targeting the social and physical environment in which they live.

age grading Similar to the concept of **age strata**, this term refers to how society organizes on the basis of age, for instance allocating differing normative roles and responsibilities on the basis of chronological age.

age-integrated society A term from age stratification theory that refers to an ideal-type society in which there are no age-related constraints (such as social norms or institutional barriers) on the entry and exit of persons through education, work, and leisure.

age norms Commonly held ideals about behaviours and life events that are expected and appropriate at certain ages. Also known as *social clocks.*

age relations The ways in which age is a feature of how societies are organized, and how differing age groups gain or lose power in relation to other age groups.

age segregation Occurs when age groups tend to isolate in relation to each other, with limited social interaction. This can occur within social institutions, physical environments, and cultural milieu.

age strata A term from age stratification theory that refers to a characteristic of society which assigns differing expected roles, rights, and responsibilities to different age groups.

age stratification theory A theory focused on explaining how individual aging and cohort aging intersect with changing age structures in society. Also known as *aging and society paradigm.*

ageism Stereotyping of older persons that can lead to discriminatory behaviours or practices, which can become embedded into policies, procedures, and practices.

agency principle In life course theory but also sociological discourse more broadly, *agency* is often used to refer to our own role in making choices and navigating our lives and identities within the constraints of social structure; however, it can also refer to our abilities to redefine the subjective meanings of our experiences, and the various ways we might resist or reinforce stigmatization and

dependency. See also **individual agency**.

aging enterprise Within political economy theories of aging, this term refers to a wide range of groups, industries, and professionals that have vested interests in providing services to older persons, and thus contribute to the construction of age as a problem requiring treatment and commodification.

aging in place The ideal of older persons remaining in their homes and communities for as long as possible.

ambivalence Conflicting thoughts, beliefs, values, and feelings stemming from conflicting social roles or responsibilities.

anti-aging industry The commercial production, marketing, and consumption of products, technologies, and services purporting to slow, stop, or reverse the biological aging process—in particular, as reflected in physical appearance.

anti-aging movement Attempts to slow, stop, or reverse the biological aging process and to extend the human lifespan through the use of products, technologies, services, and scientific research.

apocalyptic demography A concept that describes the process of overstating the negative effects of demographic trends, particularly of population aging, for society. The concept also highlights how this process may be used to suggest that particular policy directions are unavoidable and inescapable. Also known as *demographic alarmism* or *demographic scapegoating.*

applied knowledge Knowledge that provides direct guidance about the most effective and beneficial practices and policies.

atheoretical Empirical research that does not actively use, apply, refer to, or generate theoretical (abstract, generalized) knowledge. Much of this research might, however, express some implicit theoretical assumptions and reflect particular ways of looking at the world and interpreting research data.

beauty work Work done on our physical bodies with the goal of making them more beautiful according to youthful standards or ideals. Also known as *youth work*.

biographical work Work done by individuals to interpretively assemble, sustain, and reconstruct their life story, including interpreting inconsistencies to fit within the expected pattern of the whole.

biomedical model The dominant paradigm of medicine in Western societies, which emphasizes rational control and technical, medical solutions to cure a wide range of conditions; such conditions are believed to have specific, objective, physical causes within the individual.

biomedicalization A social process whereby a particular behaviour, event, or condition becomes interpreted and labelled from a medical perspective as a medical problem requiring medical treatment (e.g., childbirth, alcoholism, obesity, dementia, aging).

boundary problem The difficulty distinguishing between life-extension efforts designed to change the very biology of aging, and health promotion efforts designed to alter certain conditions or symptoms that are associated with the passage of time in individuals.

boundary work The efforts of in-group members to define the boundaries of its membership and group identity, and to defend those boundaries against out-group intrusions.

Canada Pension Plan/Quebec Pension Plan (C/QPP) One of the three pillars of the Canadian retirement income system, C/QPP is a federally administered program requiring compulsory payments from both employers and employees. These payments constitute a pooled pension fund collected and invested through the federal government, and benefits are returned to retired workers.

caregiver burden At the individual level, this includes both objective burden (i.e., based on the level, amount, and types of care provided) and subjective burden (i.e., based on perceived distress and impact of care).

Caregiver Policy Lens (CGPL) A tool designed to be used for program and policy developers, in order to encourage them to systematically consider the intended and unintended effects of their programs and policies on caregivers for older adults.

civil society Refers to the ways in which citizens operating outside of the government can influence political decisions, for example through political parties, lobby and interest groups, mass media, and social movements.

cohort A group whose members together shared a common event (often, their birth) during a particular time period. For instance, individuals born in the same year might comprise a cohort for longitudinal research studies.

cohort effect In gerontological research, this refers to a change explained by membership in particular cohorts and the common experiences (e.g., historical events and social structures) that these cohorts face at particular times.

colonization The forced settlement and political control (colonialism) of an area of land and its Indigenous people, by settlers from another country; the dispossession of Indigenous people from this land, as well as from their rights, culture, and identity, establishes a long-term unequal power relationship between colonizer and colonized.

compression of morbidity A hypothetical public health scenario wherein the average age of onset of disease and chronic conditions continues to rise or be postponed, and as such future populations will spend fewer average years before death in ill health.

compulsory altruism When an unpaid care provider (e.g., family member, volunteer) is in a position where they become relied upon to continue to provide selfless care for the welfare of others, due to circumstances beyond their control.

conflict theory A general category of sociological theories that view social groups as in constant struggle for scarce resources and power within an overall system of stratification, resulting in marginalization and oppression of less powerful groups.

continuity theory Suggests that older persons ideally need to continue the kinds and levels of lifestyle activities that were normal for them before the loss of particular roles, and that are important for their identity and personality. A later, reconceptualized version of the theory emphasized to a greater extent the ways that social structure and personal resources shape individuals' abilities to continue in particular roles and activities.

critical gerontology A theoretical approach that problematizes the social construction of old age and aging, and highlights the ideological functions of these constructions. This approach seeks to challenge existing societal arrangements, give voices to marginalized groups of older adults, and advocate for social justice.

cultural lag When traditional cultural beliefs in a society no longer match new material circumstances.

cumulative advantage/disadvantage theory Proposes that advantages in income and other resources (such as health or education) that manifest at early ages have cumulative or amplified effects over time, resulting in widening disparities in older cohorts.

death doulas Like a "death midwife," these are paid, trained providers of social, emotional, and bereavement support to dying individuals and their families. Doulas generally support a demedicalized approach to the end of life and support family involvement in after-death care of the body.

decolonizing methodologies Approaches to the production of knowledge that challenge or disrupt Western scientific models of knowledge, and that highlight and provide space for alternative and Indigenous forms of knowing.

defined benefit A structure of pension plan in which the contributions by employee and employer are pooled with contributions of other members, and the risk of investments are managed by employers. Income received in retirement is predetermined.

defined contribution A structure of pension plan in which the contributions by employee and employer are assigned to the individual employee who manages the investments (and risk). Income received in retirement is based on how well the investments perform.

deinstitutionalization The erosion of particular social structural constraints, such as traditional social norms or state laws or regulations, and how life paths become more varied and individualized as a result. Also known as *destandardization*.

delayed reciprocity The principle that individuals will receive a reward at some future point in time, in exchange for resources or support provided today.

demographic The composition and distribution of human populations, or changes in these characteristics over time.

demographic transition As societies industrialize, they experience an aging population as they move from patterns of high fertility and mortality to low fertility and mortality.

denaturalization of caregiving A trend towards viewing the caregiver role as unexpected and abnormal, rather than as a natural part of the life course.

discrimination Behaviours, actions, or practices towards a person or group that are based on perceived group membership (e.g., rather than individual merit). These actions have negative, exclusionary effects.

disengagement theory A theory that posits that in modernized societies, the mutual withdrawal between the older individual and society is natural and functional for both the individual and society.

double-edged sword Something that can have both positive and negative aspects or effects.

early retirement package Specific offers from employers that detail incentives for employees to retire before age 65.

Elder A person identified by an Aboriginal community according to characteristics such as traditional wisdom and knowledge, respect of the community, and cultural and spiritual leadership.

emancipate To free oneself or others from oppression.

embodied habitus Cultural tastes and practices related to the body and physical appearance.

embodiment The ever-present and immediate ways in which we experience phenomena within and through the physical, tangible realities of our bodies, and demonstrate agency and transformative power through our bodies.

emotional labour The work of bringing one's feelings (or displays of feelings) into alignment with normative or organizational imperatives, often done to promote a desired emotion within another person.

ethnocentric Evaluating an ethnic or cultural group (often negatively) in contrast to the idealized standards of one's own culture.

ethnocultural minority seniors Older people whose ethnic or cultural background differ from that of the dominant ethnic majority, including those born in Canada, as well as immigrants from other countries.

exchange theory Proposes that each individual in a relationship or interaction possesses different resources or power, and that each participant strives to gain rewards that meet or exceed the costs of these relationships.

familialism A set of normative ideals that emphasize the moral imperative of family responsibility; that families should be free from outside influence; and that the nuclear, patriarchal family is the most important unit of social organization.

feminist gerontology A wide variety of approaches to the study of age and aging, but which generally seek to identify and explain gender differences and inequalities, as well as the social construction of gender.

fertility rates The average number of children born to a hypothetical female (aged 15 to 49) in a specified population.

fictive kin Subjectively interpreted family bonds that are not based on traditional measures of family affiliation such as genetic or marriage relations.

filial piety In Eastern cultures, the cultural, moral norm of filial responsibility, which includes not only an imperative to provide support for aging parents, but also the need to obey their wishes and demonstrate politeness and deference to them as well as to honour one's ancestors.

formal care The provision of paid support to persons who are in need of this support as their health or function has deteriorated. Formal care provision is often more formalized and provided

by trained care professionals. It may be delivered by private (not-for-profit or for-profit) and public agencies.

fourth age Groups of older people in a stage of cognitive and physical decline, illness, frailty, and disability, often symbolically contrasted against the "third age" of older persons who are able to remain active and independent.

gender lens A way of looking at issues, policies, and programs with the consideration of gender equality and gender relations in mind; may also refer to tools or frameworks designed to facilitate this consideration.

gender relations Taken-for-granted processes by which people align their behaviours and identities to gendered ideals, and how this reproduces between-group power relations and patterns of advantage and disadvantage relative to each other.

generation A horizontal social location based on individuals born around the same period of time (often, 30-year periods are considered definitional of generations); generations may share common experiences and collective identities.

gerontocracy A form of political command or rule in which power rests primarily with leaders who are of advanced ages (who rule in their own interest).

globalization Social change towards increased international flows of capital, culture, communications, trade, and people across national borders, as well as increased activity by international governmental and non-governmental organizations and transnational corporations. A process that results in increased global interdependence and the reduced power of nation-states.

governmentality How processes of power and social control that align with the goals of the state are internalized within the taken-for-granted beliefs and actions of individuals who ultimately govern themselves in ways that meet the best interest of the state and its policies.

Guaranteed Income Supplement (GIS) A means-tested addition to **Old Age Security** benefits in Canada, designed to assist very low-income older adults.

health A concept defined in multiple ways, ranging from the absence of disease or physical symptoms, to broader definitions focused on overall physical, mental, social, and even spiritual well-being.

healthism A concept referring to the negative evaluation of those who are ill by viewing illness as a personal failure, in the context of a strong moral imperative to remain healthy.

hospice A health care service provided (often, but not always, in a free-standing facility) for those who are diagnosed with terminal conditions, focused on the provision of quality care and comfort at the end of life for the person and their family.

human rights Rights or entitlements shared universally by all human beings, including economic, social, cultural, political, and civil rights.

identity foreclosure The loss of social interactions and mechanisms that would normally validate one's sense of self-concept and identity, particularly when describing the experience of widowhood.

ideologies Sets of cultural beliefs and values that support, explain, and legitimate particular ways of life,

practices, and actions. Often, this term is used in critical gerontology to refer to ideologies that support the vested interests of powerful groups in society as well as the existing political and economic structures of society.

inclusion lens A way of looking at issues, policies, and programs with the consideration of social inclusion in mind; may also refer to tools or frameworks designed to facilitate this consideration.

individual agency Our own role in making choices and navigating our lives and identities within the constraints of social structure; our abilities to actively redefine the subjective meanings of our experiences, and the various ways we might resist or reinforce stigmatization and dependency. See also **agency principle**.

individualization The proposition that changing social, economic, and demographic features weaken traditional structural and collective constraints on individual lives and behaviours. It is further proposed that in this context, individuals paradoxically enjoy more personal freedoms yet are increasingly constrained to be responsible for constructing their own life paths and managing risks.

individualized care Care that is tailored to the unique needs and preferences of individual patients and their particular circumstances.

informal care The provision of unpaid support by family, friends, or neighbours to persons who are in need of this support because their health or function has deteriorated.

institutionalized ageism Ageism that becomes embedded into established and taken-for-granted policies, procedures, and practices in our culture, social institutions, governments, or particular organizations.

intergenerational relations In some cases this refers to the level or quality of interactions and exchanges of support between family members of different cohorts. In other cases it refers to how age cohorts develop distinct identities in relation to one another, and the degree of conflict or segregation between cohorts at a societal level.

intergenerational trauma The negative and long-lasting emotional and psychological effects of colonization experienced by one generation within a family or community on subsequent generations.

internalized ageism A form of ageism that occurs when older persons accept and integrate ageist beliefs as part of their own self-concept and identity.

interpretive shift Refers specifically to the shift in gerontological theorizing from the dominance of positivist or normative perspectives to the greater use of interpretive or social constructionist perspectives. Interpretive ways of viewing the world emphasize that truths are multiple, subjective, and socially constructed in interactions between people, and that knowledge about aging is socially constructed.

intimacy at a distance A preference for emotionally close relationships with geographically distant relatives.

latent kin matrix A term describing a family network as the total number of family members who represent a potential resource available to provide support if needed.

life course perspective An approach to the study of aging that examines how

individual lives unfold through various patterns of changes over time and within broader social and historical contexts.

lifelong process principle Earlier experiences in our lives affect subsequent events and life chances, and therefore affect our well-being and position in later life.

linked lives principle Because humans are interconnected, an event or change in our own lives will have implications for others with whom we share relationships, and vice versa.

living apart together (LAT) Romantic relationships in which the persons involved choose to continue to reside in their separate homes, rather than cohabit.

low-income cut-off In Canada, the estimated income threshold under which an individual or family would spend 20 per cent more than the average individual or family on food, shelter, and clothing.

macro level Broad features of society, such as the political and economic system, government, legal and judiciary systems, mass media, culture, and other dominant social institutions, and the position of a society within the global system.

mandatory retirement Refers to policies through which employers can require compulsory retirement of employees.

maturation of C/QPP The point at which C/QPP funds grew such that retirees from that point onwards could collect the full amount of C/QPP benefits. See **Canada Pension Plan/ Quebec Pension Plan (C/QPP)**.

micro level Individual identities, experiences, and social processes between individuals, such as relationships and face-to-face interactions.

mild cognitive impairment A set of symptoms indicating mild abnormal problems with memory and other cognitive abilities that have been noticed by the individual and others in their social world but are not impairing their function in everyday life to the point where they require assistance.

modernization theory Proposes that because of industrialization and urbanization, the social position of older people in these societies declines.

moral distress Feelings of powerlessness, helplessness, or frustration generated when care providers feel unable to fulfill their sense of responsibility to patients, respond to suffering, or provide the standard of care they wish to but are unable to because of organizational constraints or other barriers.

mortality rate The number of deaths in a given population or time period.

neoliberalism The beliefs and associated practices and policies supporting the expansion of free trade, market competition, privatization, and restricted government involvement in both markets and social welfare. This includes, for instance, beliefs that emphasize the presence of rational, self-interested individuals who make free choices.

non-standard work Includes paid work that is temporary, part-time, seasonal, often based on contract or self-employment, and with non-standard work hours. Often these jobs have no benefits. See also **precarious employment**.

nuclear family A family group consisting of a heterosexual couple and their children, where the man is the primary income earner and the woman is responsible for parenting and housework.

occupational segregation The unequal distribution of people in particular social groups (such as gender) across types of jobs in the labour market (i.e., with high representation in some jobs and low representation in others).

old-age dependency ratio The proportion of dependent older adults compared or relative to the proportion of the working-age population. See also **total dependency ratio**.

Old Age Security (OAS) A federally funded program to provide a guaranteed minimum income to all except the most wealthy Canadians, based on the principle of universal public benefits to help protect older persons from a large drop in their living standards.

paid companions Private, unlicensed, paid providers of (primarily) friendship and socio-emotional support.

palliative care A care approach focused on supporting the dying and bereavement processes through providing comfort; maintaining dignity; and minimizing physical, emotional, and spiritual pain and suffering.

participant observation A research method in which the researcher acts both as an observer within the culture, community, or setting, and as an active participant in the activities of that setting.

participatory action research A research methodology that actively involves the researched individuals or groups as collaborative partners in aspects of the research design, data collection and analysis, interpretation, and dissemination.

period effect In gerontological research, this refers to individual change that is explained by environmental shifts in social and historical conditions, experienced by all cohorts.

personal narratives The focus of narrative gerontological research, these individual stories about oneself and one's life can take the form of autobiography, memoir, or diaries, for instance.

personal–professional boundaries Avoiding personal emotional displays or talk about personal life in the workplace; avoiding talk about the workplace, and relationships with colleagues or patients, in one's personal life.

political economy theory Examines how particular forms of capitalism, and the governmental systems that support capitalist goals, shape the ways that social phenomena such as old age are constructed, which generates inequality.

population pyramids Visual representations of the age structure in a population, including the proportion of males or females (represented on the horizontal axes) occupying each age category within a population (represented on the vertical axis).

positive ageism Overly idealized representations and beliefs about aging, which can inadvertently devalue and stigmatize older persons who cannot meet this ideal.

positivism A view of the world that reflects a belief in the ability to objectively and accurately know certain facts or truths (through scientific inquiry) that exist external to us.

post-industrial society The state of society after industrialization, emphasizing the dominance of the service industry and information work in these economies.

postmodern society A society reflecting disillusionment with the ideas of Western modernism (e.g., progress, science, traditional bases of authority) alongside rapidly changing social institutions and declines in normative consensus.

precarious employment Paid work in which the future is uncertain, with little or no job security, and in which individuals manage their own risk. See also **non-standard work**.

principle of historical time and place Our personal life course—including the opportunities and constraints we face, and our actions and decisions—is shaped by historical time, social context, and geographical place.

private employer-sponsored pension plans Retirement pension plans provided at the discretion of some employers to their employees, drawing on contributions from both employer and employee.

private troubles Concerns, problems, or issues faced by an individual.

prolongevity Lifespan extension in an individual or population.

public issues Concerns, problems, or issues that are held in common by many individuals and thus inspire collective action.

pure relationship A relationship unfettered by structural constraints such as marriage, relying solely on bonds of affection, which lasts as long as both participants continue to gain happiness.

Registered Retirement Savings Plan (RRSP) A private (individually held) savings account designed for promoting retirement savings (e.g., through tax advantages).

relational theories of care Approaches to the theory and professional practice that emphasize reciprocity, solidarity, and interdependency in the relationship between care recipient and caregiver.

relative material disadvantage Disadvantage in one's material circumstances relative to others in the population (e.g., compared to the median income of that population).

residential care facility A regulated institution designed to provide lodging and 24-hour care and supervision for persons with chronic illnesses, physical disabilities, and/or mental impairment, who are unable to manage on their own. Also referred to as a *personal care home*, *nursing home*, or *long-term care facility*.

residential school system In Canada, the federally funded and church-administered system of boarding schools for First Nations, Métis, and Inuit children, operating between about 1876 and 1996. The schools were designed to assimilate these children into settler culture and society.

resocialized A process of breaking down and then reshaping individual identities based on new values, norms, and belief systems. See also **socialization**.

retirement income system The mix of public and private sources of income potentially available to retired cohorts

of individuals, including the **Canada Pension Plan/Quebec Pension Plan (C/QPP)**, **Old Age Security (OAS)**, **Guaranteed Income Supplement (GIS)**, and private employer pensions and **Registered Retirement Savings Plans (RRSPs)**.

sandwich generation A within-family "generation" that is simultaneously faced with caregiving for both a young dependent child and an older parent or grandparent.

self-care The self-determined, everyday actions of lay persons (e.g., not guided by professionals) that promote their personal health, prevent disease, and help them manage symptoms and illnesses.

self-fulfilling prophecy A phenomenon in which a false belief or prediction only becomes true through some change of behaviour or events that the prophecy itself invokes.

social capital A concept that emphasizes the connections between individuals' participation within their communities and the sense of cohesion, trust, security, and reciprocity among community members that promotes and is further generated by this participation.

social clocks See **age norms**.

social constructionism An interpretive theoretical and methodological approach that highlights the processes through which humans create meaning and interpret their world through language and social interaction.

social determinants of health Environmental or external factors or life circumstances that influence the health of individuals and populations.

social exclusion A lack of integration into all aspects of society (e.g., relational, cultural, material, civic, basic services), resulting from systemic social processes (e.g., political, economic conditions, inequalities) that operate as barriers to this integration. See also **social inclusion**.

social gerontology The interdisciplinary study of the social aspects of aging.

social gradient A population-level phenomenon in which higher socio-economic status is associated with better health and longer life expectancy.

social inclusion Integration into all aspects of society (e.g., relational, cultural, material, civic, basic services). See also **social exclusion**.

social institutions In a broad sense, refers to durable features of societies that structure our daily lives in particular ways. This is distinct from the more limited term *institution*, which tends to refer to a kind of building or organization that structures a particular form of group living, such as a mental institution, prison, or personal care home.

social integration The extent to which individuals are incorporated within the structural bonds generated by the collective/group. See also **social inclusion**.

social isolation A lack of connections, relationships, and interactions with others. Feelings of loneliness may or may not result from social isolation.

social labelling A social psychological theory of deviant behaviour in which the non-conforming behaviours or acts are viewed as generated by societal tendencies to stereotype particular individuals, and the tendency among individuals to internalize these labels in their self-identities.

social learning A social psychological theory explaining how behaviours are learned through observing and modelling from others in the social environment.

social network At the individual level, this refers to the total number of people with which one has contact and/or connection in some way (i.e., through ongoing acquaintance and/or the exchange of resources). At a broader level, this refers to the entire web of particular kinds of dyadic relationships and connections that are a form of social structure.

social norms Explicit or implicit standards for appropriate behaviours and ways of being that group members learn and internalize within their individual identities through processes of socialization in particular social groups.

social order Constantly self-reproducing social structural arrangements, institutions, and practices that maintain relatively stable systems of inequality, control, and power.

social participation Individual involvement in social, leisure, civic, or voluntary activities; membership in formal and informal groups in the community or broader society.

social reproduction The ways in which existing systems of inequality tend to regenerate the conditions necessary for their existence, over time and within new generations of individuals.

social safety net Publicly funded government services and benefit programs designed to act as a buffer for disadvantaged groups and to alleviate some of the negative effects of poverty.

social structure The ways in which a society is organized at a given point in history, including its distribution of wealth, political and economic system, cultural patterns, dominant social roles, and power relations between groups.

social support The functional content of our social networks, including various kinds of assistance and resources that are exchanged between network members.

socialization A complex and lifelong process through which individuals learn the social norms, habits, lifestyles, values, ways of thinking, and other aspects of their culture, and internalize these as important parts of their own personal identities. This process occurs as a result of their interactions and experiences with a variety of influential forces in their lives, such as family, peers, teachers, the media, and so on. Note: the term refers to more than just friends interacting with each other in an informal way.

sociological perspective A perspective that views individual behaviours, experiences, and decisions, and micro-level events and practices, as explained by macro-level social and historical conditions, structures, and systems.

status levelling Socio-economic inequality is reduced within cohorts as they age.

status maintenance Socio-economic inequality remains stable within cohorts as they age.

stereotypes Distorted (e.g., oversimplified or exaggerated) and rigid typifications applied to an entire social category of persons that often legitimate discriminatory behaviour towards that group.

stigmatization When the imagined or actual traits or characteristics of a person (such as their perceived group membership or deviant behaviour) serve to label and identify them as an undesirable element and as distinct from the rest of society, resulting in spoiled identities and a loss of power.

structural functionalism A theoretical perspective within sociology that focuses on how different structural components of society (e.g., social roles and norms, socialization processes, social institutions, social control mechanisms) play important functions that help to maintain a balance in the social system. This perspective tends to minimize the existence of conflict and inequality.

structural lag The mismatch created when certain social trends (changing demographics or historical conditions) generate new realities that are not yet accounted for by changes in broader structural features such as policies, practices, regulations, structural opportunities, roles, or norms.

structured dependency Dependency that is generated by established social actions, practices, and policies, such as when ageist stereotypes are internalized by individuals, or when nursing homes do not encourage older residents to move around or keep active.

symbolic interactionism A sociological theory that seeks to explain the complex social rules and symbolic meanings involved in everyday, face-to-face interactions between individuals.

symbolic meanings Shared, subjective interpretations of the broader significance, connotations, and implications of particular actions, behaviours, gestures, events, or statements.

technogenarians Older persons who actively utilize and adapt innovative and everyday technologies to maintain independence and manage illness.

timing of transitions principle The causes and consequences of any particular key change or event in our lives depend partly on when it occurs to us in our life.

total dependency ratio The proportion of dependent older adults and children compared or relative to the proportion of the working-age population. See also **old-age dependency ratio**.

total institutions Enclosed, formally administered places, such as prisons, boarding schools, or mental health facilities, designed for the residence of a large number of individuals, who are removed from the population for some duration of time and resocialized into new, often strictly organized ways of life and identities.

trajectories Patterns or pathways of particular **transitions** over time.

transitions Changes of social position, status, or role (e.g., marriage, retirement).

transnational families Families in which one or more members live in a separate country.

References

Aboderin, I. (2004). Modernisation and ageing theory revisited: Current explanations of recent developing world and historical Western shifts in material family support for older people. *Ageing and Society, 24*(1), 29–50.

Achenbaum, W. A., & Bengtson, V. L. (1994). Re-engaging the disengagement theory of aging: On the history and assessment of theory development in gerontology. *The Gerontologist, 34*(6), 756–763.

Addis, S., Davies, M., Greene, G., MacBride-Stewart, S., & Shepherd, M. (2009). The health, social care and housing needs of lesbian, gay, bisexual and transgender older people: A review of the literature. *Health and Social Care in the Community, 17*(6), 647–658.

Age UK. (2011). *Grey matters—A survey of ageism across Europe: EU briefing and policy recommendations.* Retrieved from http://www.ageuk.org/documents/en-gb/for-professionals/international/ageism_across_europe_report.pdf?dtrk=true

Ajrouch, K. J., Antonucci, T. C., & Janevic, M. R. (2001). Social networks among Blacks and Whites: The interaction between race and age. *Journals of Gerontology, 56B*(2), S112–S118.

Alan, S., Atalay, K., & Crossley, T. F. (2008). The adequacy of retirement savings: Subjective survey reports by retired Canadians. *Canadian Public Policy, 34,* 95–118.

Albert, K. (2014). Erasing the social from social science: The intellectual costs of boundary-work and the Canadian Institute of Health Research. *Canadian Journal of Sociology, 39*(3), 393–420.

Algars, M., Santtila, P., Varjonen, M., Witting, K., Johansson, A., Jern, P., & Sandnabba, N. K. (2009). The adult body: How age, gender, and body mass index are related to body image. *Journal of Aging and Health, 21*(8), 1112–1132.

Allan, L. J., & Johnson, J. A. (2009). Undergraduate attitudes toward the elderly: The role of knowledge, contact and aging anxiety. *Educational Gerontology, 35*(1), 1–14.

Alley, D. E., Putney, N. M., Rice, M., & Bengtson, V. L. (2010). The increasing use of theory in social gerontology: 1990–2004. *Journals of Gerontology, 65B*(5), 583–590.

Ambachtsheer, K. (2008). Why we need a pension revolution. *Canadian Public Policy, 34*(4), 7–14.

Andersen, E. (2009). Working in long-term residential care: A qualitative meta summary encompassing roles, working environments, work satisfaction, and factors affecting recruitment and retention of nurse aides. *Global Journal of Health Science, 1*(2), 2–41.

Anderson, J. M., Blue, C., & Lau, A. (1998). Women's perspectives on chronic illness: Ethnicity, ideology and restructuring of life. In D. Coburn, C. D'Arcy, & G. Torrance (Eds.), *Health and Canadian society: Sociological perspectives* (pp. 163–186). Toronto, ON: University of Toronto Press.

Anderson, J. M., Tang, S., & Blue, C. (2007). Health care reform and the paradox of efficiency: "Writing in" culture. *International Journal of Health Services, 37*(2), 291–320.

Andrew, M. K. (2005). Social capital, health, and care home residence among older adults: A secondary analysis of the Health Survey for England 2000. *European Journal of Ageing, 2*(2), 137–148.

Andrews, G. J., Gavin, N., Begley, S., & Brodie, D. (2003). Assisting friendships, combating loneliness: Users' views on a "befriending" scheme. *Ageing and Society, 23*(3), 349–362.

Ankri, J., Andrieu, S., Beaufils, B., Grand, A., & Henrard, J. C. (2005). Beyond the global score of the Zarit Burden Inventory: Useful dimensions for clinicians. *International Journal of Geriatric Psychiatry, 20*(3), 254–260.

Antonucci, T. C., Birditt, K. S., Sherman, C. W., & Trinh, S. (2011). Stability and change in the intergenerational family: A convoy approach. *Ageing and Society, 31*(7), 1084–1106.

Aronson, J. (1992). Women's sense of responsibility for the care of old people: "But who else is going to do it?" *Gender and Society, 6*(1), 8–29.

Aronson, J. (1998). Women's perspectives on informal care of the elderly: Public ideology and personal experience of giving and receiving care. In D. Coburn, C. D'Arcy, & G. Torrance (Eds.), *Health and Canadian society: Sociological perspectives* (pp. 399–416). Toronto, ON: University of Toronto Press.

Aronson, J. (2002a). Elderly people's accounts of home care rationing: Missing voices in long-term care policy debates. *Ageing & Society, 22*(4), 399–418.

Aronson, J. (2002b). Frail and disabled users of home care: Confident consumers or disentitled citizens? *Canadian Journal on Aging, 21*(1), 11–25.

Aronson, J. (2006). Silenced complaints, suppressed expectations: The cumulative effects of home care rationing. *International Journal of Health Services, 36*(3), 535–556.

Aronson, J., & Neysmith, S. M. (1996). "You're not just in there to do the work": Depersonalizing policies and the exploitation of home care workers' labor. *Gender and Society, 10*(1), 59–77.

Aronson, J., & Neysmith, S. M. (2001). Manufacturing social exclusion in the home care market. *Canadian Public Policy, 27*(2), 151–165.

Asakawa, K., Feeny, D., Senthilselvan, A., Johnson, J. A., & Rolfson, D. (2009). Do the determinants of health differ between people living in the community and in institutions? *Social Science and Medicine, 69*(3), 345–353.

Atchley, R. C. (1989). A continuity theory of normal aging. *The Gerontologist, 29*(2), 183–190.

Attias-Donfut, C., & Segalen, M. (2002). The construction of grandparenthood. *Current Sociology, 50*(2), 281–294.

Auger, J. A., & Tedford-Litle, D. (2002). *From the inside looking out: Competing ideas about growing old.* Halifax, NS: Fernwood Publishing.

Austin, W., Lemermeyer, G., Goldberg, L., Bergum, V., & Johnson, M. S. (2005). Moral distress in healthcare practice: The situation of nurses. *HEC Forum, 17*(1), 33–68.

Avlund, K., Lund, R., Holstein, B. E., Due, P., Sakari-Rantala, R., & Heikkinen, R. L. (2004). The impact of structural and functional characteristics of social relations as determinants of functional decline. *Journals of Gerontology, 59B,* 44–51.

Baars, J., Dannefer, D., Phillipson, C., & Walker, A. (2006). Introduction: Critical perspectives in social gerontology. In J. Baars, D. Dannefer, C. Phillipson, & A. Walker (Eds.), *Aging, globalization and inequality: The new critical gerontology* (pp. 1–16). Amityville, NY: Baywood.

Baars, J., & Phillipson, C. (2013). Connecting meaning with social structure: Theoretical foundations. In J. Baars, J. Dohmen, A. Grenier, & C. Phillipson (Eds.), *Ageing, meaning and social structure: Connecting critical and humanistic gerontology* (pp. 11–30). Chicago, IL: Policy Press.

Baines, C., Evans, P., & Neysmith, S. (1998). Women's caring: Work expanding, state contracting. In C. Baines, P. Evans, & S. Neysmith (Eds.), *Women's caring: Feminist perspectives on social welfare* (pp. 3–22). Toronto, ON: Oxford University Press.

Baker, M., Benjamin, D., & Fan, E. (2009). *Public policy and the economic wellbeing of elderly immigrants.* Canadian Labour Market and Skills Researcher Network, Working Paper No. 52. Vancouver, BC: University of British Columbia. Retrieved from http://www.clsrn.econ.ubc.ca/workingpapers.php

Baker, M., Gruber, J., & Milligan, K. (2003). The retirement incentive effects of Canada's income security programs. *Canadian Journal of Economics, 36*(2), 261–290.

Baldassar, L. (2007). Transnational families and aged care: The mobility of care and the migrancy of ageing. *Journal of Ethnic and Migration Studies, 33*(2), 275–297.

Baldassar, L. (2008). Missing kin and longing to be together: Emotions and the construction of co-presence in transnational relationships. *Journal of Intercultural Studies, 29*(3), 247–266.

Baldock, C. V. (2000). Migrants and their parents: Caregiving from a distance. *Journal of Family Issues, 21*(2), 205–224.

Baldwin, B. (2009). *Research study on the Canadian retirement income system.*

Ministry of Finance, Government of Ontario. Retrieved from http://www.fin.gov.on.ca/en/consultations/pension/dec09report.html

Ball, M. M., Lepore, M. L., Perkins, M. M., Hollingsworth, C., & Sweatman, M. (2009). "They are the reasons I come to work": The meaning of resident-staff relationships in assisted living. *Journal of Aging Studies, 23*, 37–47.

Baltes, M. M., & Carstensen, L. L. (1996). The process of successful ageing. *Ageing and Society, 16*, 397–422.

Banerjee, A., Daly, T., Armstrong, P., Szebehely, M., Armstrong, H., & Lafrance, S. (2012). Structural violence in long-term, residential care for older people: Comparing Canada and Scandinavia. *Social Science and Medicine, 74*(3), 390–398.

Barer, M. L., Evans, R. G., & Hertzman, C. (1995). Avalanche or glacier? Health care and the demographic rhetoric. *Canadian Journal on Aging, 14*(2), 193–224.

Bassett, R. (2012). Fragmented performances: Ageism and the health of older women. In E. A. Gibbon (Ed.), *Oppression: A social determinant of health* (pp. 62–72). Winnipeg, MB: Fernwood.

Beatty, B. B., & Berdahl, L. (2011). Health care and Aboriginal seniors in urban Canada: Helping a neglected class. *The International Indigenous Policy Journal, 2*(1). Retrieved from http://ir.lib.uwo.ca/iipj/vol2/iss1/10

Beaujot, R. (1990). The family and demographic change in Canada: Economic and cultural interpretations and solutions. *Journal of Comparative Family Studies, 21*(1), 25–38.

Beck, U., & Beck-Gernsheim, E. (2001). *Individualization: Institutionalized individualism and its social and political consequences*. London, UK: Sage.

Béland, D., & Shinkawa, T. (2007). Public and private policy change: Pension reform in four countries. *Policy Studies Journal, 35*(3), 349–371.

Bell, S., & Menec, V. (2013, January 6). "You don't want to ask for the help": The imperative of independence: Is it related to social exclusion? *Journal of Applied Gerontology*. Published online before print. doi:10.1177/0733464812469292

Bellah, R. N., Madsen, R., Sullivan, W. M., Swidler, A., & Tipton, S. M. (1985). *Habits of the heart: Individualism and commitment in American life*. Berkeley, CA: University of California Press.

Bengtson, V. L. (1996). Teaching concepts and theories in the sociology of aging. In V. Minichiello, N. Chappell, & H. Kendig (Eds), *Sociology of ageing: Proceedings of the 1995 International Sociological Association Research on Ageing Intercongress Meeting*. Melbourne: International Sociological Association.

Bengtson, V. L. (2001). Beyond the nuclear family: The increasing importance of multigenerational bonds. *Journal of Marriage and Family, 63*(1), 1–16.

Bengtson, V. L., Burgess, E. O., & Parrott, T. M. (1997). Theory, explanation, and a third generation of theoretical development in social gerontology. *Journals of Gerontology, 52B*(2), 72–88.

Bengtson, V. L., Dowd, J. J., Smith, D. H., & Inkeles, A. (1975). Modernization, modernity, and perceptions of aging: A cross-cultural study. *Journal of Gerontology, 30*(6), 688–695.

Bengtson, V. L., Elder, G. H., Jr., & Putney, N. M. (2005). The lifecourse perspective on ageing: Linked lives, timing, and history. In M. L. Johnson (Ed.), *The Cambridge handbook of age and ageing* (pp. 493–501). New York, NY: Cambridge University Press.

Bengtson, V. L., Lowenstein, A., Putney, N. M., & Gans, D. (2003). Global aging and the challenge to families. In V. L. Bengtson & A. Lowenstein (Eds.), *Global aging and challenges to families* (pp. 1–24). New York, NY: Walter de Gruyter.

Biggs, S., & Powell, J. L. (2003). Older people and family in social policy. In V. L. Bengtson & A. Lowenstein (Eds.), *Global aging and challenges to families* (pp. 103–119). New York, NY: Walter de Gruyter.

Billeter-Koponen, S., & Ereden, L. (2005). Long-term stress, burnout and patient-nurse relations: Qualitative interview study about nurses' experiences. *Scandinavian Journal of Caring Sciences, 19*, 20–27.

Binney, E. A., & Estes, C. L. (1988). The retreat of the state and its transfer of responsibility: The intergenerational war. *International Journal of Health Services, 18*(1), 83–96.

Binstock, R. H. (2003). The war on "anti-aging medicine." *The Gerontologist, 43*(1), 4–14.

Binstock, R. H. (2004). Anti-aging medicine and research: A realm of conflict and profound societal implications. *Journals of Gerontology, 59B*(6), 523–533.

Blane, D. (2002). The life course, the social gradient, and health. In M. Marmot & R. G. Wilkinson (Eds.), *Social determinants of health* (pp. 64–80). Oxford, UK: Oxford University Press.

Blieszner, R., & Hamon, R. R. (1992). Filial responsibility: Attitudes, motivators, and behaviors. In J. W. Dwyer & R. T. Coward (Eds.), *Gender, families and elder care* (pp. 105–119). Thousand Oaks, CA: Sage.

Bode, I. (2007). From the citizen's wage to self-made pensions? The changing culture of old age provision in Canada and Germany. *Current Sociology, 55*(5), 696–717.

Bolaria, B. S. (1994). Lifestyles, material deprivation, and health. In B. S. Bolaria & R. Bolaria (Eds.), *Racial minorities, medicine and health* (pp. 67–84). Halifax, NS: Fernwood.

Bond, J. (1992). The medicalization of dementia. *Journal of Aging Studies, 6*(4), 397–403.

Bone, D. (2002). Dilemmas of emotion work in nursing under market-driven health care. *International Journal of Public Sector Management, 15*(2), 140–150.

Bould, S. (1993). Familial caretaking: A middle-range definition of family in the context of social policy. *Journal of Family Issues, 14,* 133–151.

Bourdieu, P. (1977). *Outline of a theory of practice.* Cambridge, UK: Cambridge University Press.

Bourdieu, P. (1984). *Distinction: A social critique of the judgment of taste.* Cambridge, MA: Harvard University Press.

Bourgeault, I. L., Armstrong, P., Armstrong, H., Choiniere, J., Lexchin, J., Mykhalovsky, E., Peters, S., & White, J. (2001). Everyday experiences of implicit rationing: Comparing the voices of nurses in California and British Columbia. *Sociology of Health and Illness 23*(5), 633–653.

Bourgeault, I. L., Atanackovic, J., Parpia, R., Denton, M., McHale, J., Winkup, J., . . . Rashid, A. (2009). *The role of immigrant care workers in an aging society: The Canadian context & experience.* Retrieved from https://www.compas.ox.ac.uk/research/labourmarkets/migrantcareworkers/

Bourgeault, I. L., Atanackovic, J., Rashid, A., & Parpia, R. (2010). Relations between immigrant care workers and older persons in home and long-term care. *Canadian Journal on Aging, 29*(Special Issue 1), 109–118.

Bourgeault, I. L., Lindsay, S., Mykhalovsky, E., Armstrong, P., Armstrong, H., Choiniere, J., . . . White, J. (2004). At first you will not succeed: Negotiating for care in the context of health reform. *Research in the Sociology of Health Care, 22,* 261–276.

Bourgeault, I. L., Parpia, R., & Atanackovic, J. (2010). Canada's Live-In Caregiver program: Is it an answer to the growing demand for elderly care? *Journal of Population Ageing, 3*(1–2), 83–102.

Bowling, A., Banister, D., Sutton, S., Evans, O., & Windsor, J. (2002). A multidimensional model of the quality of life in older age. *Aging and Mental Health, 6*(4), 355–371.

Brackley, M. E., & Penning, M. J. (2009). Home-care utilization within the year of death: Trends, predictors and changes in access equity during a period of health policy reform in British Columbia, Canada. *Health and Social Care in the Community, 17*(3), 283–294.

Braun, K. L., Browne, C. V., Kaʻopua, L. S., Kim, B. J., & Mokuau, N. (2014). Research on indigenous elders: From positivistic to decolonizing methodologies. *The Gerontologist, 54*(1), 117–126.

British Columbia Law Institute & Canadian Centre for Elder Law (2010). *Care/work: Law reform to support family caregivers to balance paid work and unpaid caregiving* (BCLI/CCEL Study Paper No. 4). Retrieved from www.bcli.org/projects/family-caregiving

Brittain, K. R., & Shaw, C. (2007). The social consequences of living with and dealing with incontinence: A carers perspective. *Social Science and Medicine, 65*(6), 1274–1283.

Brookman, C., Holyoke, P., Toscan, J., Bender, D., & Tapping, E. (2011). *A guide to the promising practices and indicators for caregiver education and support programs.* Markham, ON: Saint Elizabeth.

Brooks, A. T. (2010). Aesthetic anti-ageing surgery and technology: Women's friend or foe? *Sociology of Health and Illness, 32*(2), 238–257.

Brothers, D., & de Jong Gierveld, J. (2011). Challenges and opportunities for relationships in the era of the third age. In D. C. Carr & K. Komp (Eds.), *Gerontology in the era of the third age* (pp. 189–205). New York, NY: Springer.

Brotman, S., Ryan, B., & Cormier, R. (2003). The health and social service needs of gay and lesbian elders and their families in Canada. *The Gerontologist, 43*(2), 192–202.

Brown, R. L. (2001). Impacts on economic security programs of rapidly shifting demographics. *North American Actuarial Journal, 5*(1), 12–31.

Brown, R. L. (2011). Economic security in an aging Canadian population. *Canadian Journal on Aging, 30*(3), 391–399.

Brown, S. L., Lee, G. R., & Bulanda, J. R. (2006). Cohabitation among older adults: A national portrait. *Journals of Gerontology, 61B*(2), S71–S79.

Browne, C. V., & Braun, K. L. (2008). Globalization, women's migration, and the long-term-care workforce. *The Gerontologist, 48*(1), 16–24.

Bruce, E. (2004). Social exclusion (and inclusion) in care homes. In A. Innes, C. Archibald, & C. Murphy (Eds.), *Dementia and social inclusion: Marginalised groups and marginalised areas of dementia research, care and practice* (pp. 123–136). London, UK: Jessica Kingsley Publishers.

Brym, R. J. (2014). Politics and social movements. In R. J. Brym (Ed.), *New Society* (7th ed.) (pp. 429–450). Toronto, ON: Nelson.

Buchignani, N., & Armstrong-Esther, C. (1999). Informal care and older Native Canadians. *Ageing and Society, 19*(1), 3–32.

Buettner, D. (2012, October 24). The island where people forget to die. *New York Times.* Retrieved from http://www.nytimes.com/2012/10/28/magazine/the-island-where-people-forget-to-die.html?pagewanted=all&_r=0

Buffel, T., Verté, D., De Donder, L., De Witte, N., Dury, S., Vanwing, T., &

Bolsenbroek, A. (2012). Theorising the relationship between older people and their immediate social living environment. *International Journal of Lifelong Education, 31*(1), 13–32.

Burnett, J. (2010). *Generations: The time machine in theory and practice.* Surrey, UK: Ashgate Press.

Burns, V. F., Lavoie, J.-P., & Rose, D. (2012). Revisiting the role of neighbourhood change in social exclusion and inclusion of older people. *Journal of Aging Research, 2012,* 1–11.

Bushnik, T. (2006). Child care in Canada. *Children and Youth Research Paper Series* (Catalogue No. 89-599-MIE—No. 003). Ottawa, ON: Statistics Canada, Minister of Industry.

Butler, R. (1969). Ageism: Another form of bigotry. *The Gerontologist, 9,* 243–246.

Butler, R. (1975). *Why survive? Being old in America.* New York, NY: Harper & Row.

Bury, M. (1995). Ageing, gender and sociological theory. In S. Arber & J. Ginn (Eds.), *Connecting gender and ageing: A sociological approach* (pp. 15–30). Buckingham, UK: Open University Press.

Bytheway, B., & Johnson, J. (1990). On defining ageism. *Critical Social Policy, 10*(29), 27–39.

Cagle, J. G., & Munn, J. C. (2012). Long-distance caregiving: A systematic review of the literature. *Journal of Gerontological Social Work, 55*(8), 682–707.

Caissie, L. (2011). The raging grannies: Narrative construction of gender and aging. In G. Kenyon, E. Bohlmeijer, & W. L. Randall (Eds.), *Storying later life: Issues, investigations, and interventions in narrative gerontology* (pp. 126–142). Don Mills, ON: Oxford University Press.

Calasanti, T. (2005). Ageism, gravity, and gender: Experiences of aging bodies. *Generations, 29*(3), 8–12.

Calasanti, T. (2009). Theorizing feminist gerontology, sexuality, and beyond: An intersectional approach. In V. L. Bengtson, D. Gans, N. M. Putney, & M. Silverstein (Eds.), *Handbook of theories of aging* (2nd ed.) (pp. 471–486). New York, NY: Springer.

Calasanti, T. M., & Slevin, K. F. (2001). *Gender, social inequalities, and aging.* Walnut Creek, CA: AltaMira Press.

Calasanti, T. M., Slevin, K. F., & King, N. (2006). Ageism and feminism: From "et cetera" to center. *NWSA Journal, 18*(1), 13–30.

Callahan, D. (1987). *Setting limits: Medical goals in an aging society.* New York, NY: Simon and Schuster.

Callahan, M., Brown, L., MacKenzie, P., & Whittington, B. (2004). Catch as catch can: Grandmothers raising their grandchildren and kinship care policies. *Canadian Review of Social Policy, 54,* 58–78.

Canadian Association of Retired Persons (2009). Ageism poll analysis. Retrieved from http://www.carp.ca/2009/05/28/ageism-poll-analysis/

Canadian Home Care Association. (2008). *Home care: The next essential service.* Ottawa, ON: Author. Retrieved from http://www.cdnhomecare.ca/

Canadian Hospice Palliative Care Association. (2004). *Transforming policy: Strategic policy directions on the role of informal caregivers in palliative and end-of-life Care.* Ottawa, ON. Retrieved from http://www.chpca.net/informal_care-givers/role_of_informal_caregivers.html

Canadian Institute for Health Information. (2011). *Health care in Canada, 2011: A focus on seniors and aging.* Ottawa, ON: Author. Retrieved from https://secure.cihi.ca/free_products/HCIC_2011_seniors_report_en.pdf

Canadian Institute for Health Information. (2013). *When a nursing home is home: How do Canadian nursing homes measure up on quality?* Ottawa, Ontario: Author.

Canadian Press. (2013, November 26). Seniors living in poverty on the rise in Canada, OECD says. *CBC News.* Retrieved from http://www.cbc.ca/news/business/seniors-living-in-poverty-on-the-rise-in-canada-oecd-says-1.2440714

Cantor, M. H. & Brennan, M. (2000). *Social care of the elderly: The effects of ethnicity, class and culture.* New York, NY: Springer.

Carrière, Y. (2000). Population aging and hospital days: Will there be a problem? In E. Gee & G. Gutman (Eds.), *The overselling of population aging: Apocalyptic demography, intergenerational challenges, and social policy* (pp. 26–44). Toronto, ON: Oxford University Press.

Carrière, Y., & Galarneau, D. (2012). How many years to retirement? *Insights on Canadian society* (Catalogue No. 75-006-X). Ottawa, ON: Statistics Canada, Minister of Industry. Retrieved from http://www.statcan.gc.ca/pub/75-006-x/2012001/article/11750-eng.htm

Carrière, Y., Keefe, J., Légaré, J., Lin, X., & Rowe, G. (2007). Population aging and immediate family composition: Implications for future home care services. *Genus, 63*(1/2), 11–31.

Carstairs, S., & Keon, W. J. (2009). *Canada's aging population: Seizing the opportunity: Special Senate Committee on Aging final report.* Ottawa, ON: The Senate. Retrieved from http://www.parl.gc.ca/content/sen/committee/402/agei/subsite/aging_report_home-e.htm

Caspar, S., Cooke, H. A., O'Rourke, N., & Macdonald, S. W. S. (2013). Influence of individual and contextual character-istics on the provision of individualized care in long-term care facilities. *The Gerontologist, 53*(5), 790–800.

Cattan, M., White, M., Bond, J., & Learmouth, A. (2005). Preventing social isolation and loneliness among older people: A systematic review of health promotion interventions. *Ageing and Society, 25*(1), 41–67.

CBC News. (2014, March 31). Canada Pension Plan reform could bene-fit Canada, study found. *CBC News.* Retrieved from http://www.cbc.ca/news/business/canada-pension-plan-reform-could-benefit-canada-study-found-1.2592866

Ceci, C. (2006). Impoverished practice: Analysis of effects of economic dis-courses in home care case management practice. *Canadian Journal of Nursing Leadership, 19*(1), 56–68.

Chappell, N. L. (1993). Implications of shifting health care policy for caregiving in Canada. *Journal of Aging and Social Policy, 5*(1–2), 39–55.

Chappell, N. L. (2011). *Population aging and the evolving care needs of older Canadians: An overview of the policy challenges* (IRPP Study No. 21). Montreal, QC: Institute for Research on Public Policy.

Chappell, N. L., & Funk, L. M. (2010). Social capital: Does it add to the health inequalities debate? *Social Indicators Research, 99*(3), 357–373.

Chappell, N. L., & Funk, L. M. (2011). Social support, caregiving, and aging. *Canadian Journal on Aging, 30*(3), 355–370.

Chappell, N. L., Gee, E., McDonald, L., & Stones, M. (2003). *Aging in contemporary Canada*. Toronto, ON: Prentice Hall.

Chappell, N. L., & Penning, M. L. (2005). Family caregivers: Increasing demands in the context of 21st-century globalization? In M. L. Johnson (Ed.), *The Cambridge handbook of age and ageing* (pp. 455–462), New York, NY: Cambridge University Press.

Charpentier, M., Quéniart, A., & Jacques, J. (2008). Activism among older women in Quebec, Canada: Changing the world after age 65. *Journal of Women and Aging, 20*(3–4), 343–360.

Cheal, D. (2000). Aging and demographic change. *Canadian Public Policy, 26*(Suppl. 1), S109–S122.

Cherry, R. L. & Magnuson-Martinson, S. (1981). Modernization and the status of aged in China: Decline or equalization? *The Sociological Quarterly, 22*(2), 253–261.

Chief Public Health Officer of Canada. (2010). *Report on the state of public health in Canada, 2010: Growing older—Adding life to years*. Ottawa: Her Majesty the Queen in Right of Canada. Retrieved from http://publichealth.gc.ca/CPHOreport

Chivers, S. (2011). *The silvering screen: Old age and disability in cinema*. Toronto, ON: University of Toronto Press.

Clarke, A. E., Shim, J. K., Mamo, L., Fosket, J. R., & Fishman, J. R. (2003). Biomedicalization: Technoscientific transformations of health, illness, and U.S. biomedicine. *American Sociological Review, 68*(2), 161–194.

Cloutier-Fisher, D., Kobayashi, K., & Smith, A. (2011). The subjective dimension of social isolation: A qualitative investigation of older adults' experiences in small social support networks. *Journal of Aging Studies, 25*(4), 407–414.

Cloutier-Fisher, D. & Skinner, M. W. (2006). Levelling the playing field? Exploring the implications of managed competition for voluntary sector providers of long-term care in small town Ontario. *Health and Place, 12*(1), 97–109.

Coburn, D., & Eakin, J. (1998). The sociology of health in Canada. In D. Coburn, C. D'Arcy, & G. Torrance (Eds.), *Health and Canadian society: Sociological perspectives* (pp. 619–634). Toronto, ON: University of Toronto Press.

Cochrane, J. J., Goering, P. N., & Rogers, J. M. (1997). The mental health of informal caregivers in Ontario: An epidemiological survey. *American Journal of Public Health, 87*(12), 2002–2007.

Coleman, M., Ganong, L. H., Hans, J. D., Sharp, E. A., & Rothrauff, T. C. (2005). Filial obligations in post-divorce stepfamilies. *Journal of Divorce and Remarriage, 43*(3–4), 1–27.

Colombo, F., Nozal-Llena, A., Mercier, J., & Tjadens, F. (2011). *Help wanted? Providing and paying for long-term care*. OECD health policy studies, Paris: OECD Publishing. Retrieved from http://www.oecd.org/els/health-systems/helpwantedprovidingandpayingforlong-termcare.htm

Comondore, V. R., Devereaux, P. J., Zhou, Q., Stone, S. B., Busse, J. W., Ravindran, N. C., . . . Guyatt, G. (2009). Quality of care in for-profit and not-for-profit nursing homes: Systematic review and meta-analysis. *British Medical Journal, 339*. doi:http://dx.doi.org/10.1136/bmj.b2732

Conference Board of Canada. (2013). Elderly poverty. Retrieved from http://www.conferenceboard.ca/hcp/details/society/elderly-poverty.aspx

Connidis, I. A. (2001). *Family ties and aging*. Thousand Oaks, CA: Sage.

Connidis, I. A. & McMullin, J. A. (2002). Sociological ambivalence and family ties: A critical perspective. *Journal of Marriage and Family, 64*(3), 558–567.

Cooke, M. (2006). Policy changes and the labour force participation of older workers: Evidence from six countries. *Canadian Journal on Aging, 25*(4), 387–400.

Cooney, T. M., & Dunne, K. (2001). Intimate relationships in later life: Current realities, future prospects. *Journal of Family Issues, 22*(7), 838–858.

Coontz, S. (2000). Historical perspectives on family studies. *Journal of Marriage and Family, 62*(2), 283–297.

Cornwell, B., Laumann, E. O., & Schumm, L. P. (2008). The social connectedness of older adults: A national profile. *American Sociological Review, 73*(2), 185–203.

Coupland, J. (2007). Gendered discourses on the "problem" of ageing: Consumerized solutions. *Discourse and Communication, 1*(1), 37–61.

Covey, H. C. (1981). A reconceptualization of continuity theory: Some preliminary thoughts. *The Gerontologist, 21*(6), 628–633.

Cowgill, D. O. (1974). Aging and modernization: A revision of the theory. In J. F. Gubrium (Ed.), *Late life: Communities and environmental policy* (pp. 123–146). Springfield, IL: Charles C. Thomas.

Cowgill, D. O. & Holmes, L. D. (1972). *Aging and modernization.* New York, NY: Appleton-Century-Crofts.

Crews, J. E., & Campbell, V. A. (2004). Vision impairment and hearing loss among community-dwelling older Americans: Implications for health functioning. *American Journal of Public Health, 94*(5), 823–829.

Crosato, K. E., Ward-Griffin, C., & Leipert, B. (2007). Aboriginal women caregivers of the elderly in geographically isolated communities. *Rural and Remote Health, 7*(796). Retrieved from http://www.rrh.org.au

Crystal, S., & Shea, G. (2002). Prospects for retirement resources in an aging society. In S. Crystal, D. Shea, & W. Schaie (Eds.), *Economic outcomes in later life: Public policy, health and cumulative advantage* (pp. 271–281). Annual Review of Gerontology and Geriatrics, 22. New York, NY: Springer.

Cuddy, A. J. C., Norton, M. I., & Fiske, S. T. (2005). This old stereotype: The pervasiveness and persistence of the elderly stereotype. *Journal of Social Issues, 61*(2), 267–285.

Cumming, E. (1963). Further thoughts on the theory of disengagement. *International Social Science Journal, 15*, 377–393.

Cumming, E., & Henry, W. E. (1961). *Growing old: The process of disengagement.* New York, NY: Basic Books.

Curl, A. L., & Hokenstad, M. C. (2006). Reshaping retirement policies in post-industrial nations: The need for flexibility. *Journal of Sociology and Social Welfare, 33*(2), 85–106.

Cutler, S. J., & Hendricks, J. (2000). Age differences in voluntary association memberships: Fact or artifact? *Journals of Gerontology, 55B*(2), 98–107.

Daatland, S. O., Herlofson, K., & Lima, I. A. (2011). Balancing generations: On the strength and character of family norms in the West and East of Europe. *Ageing and Society, 31*(7), 1159–1179.

Daatland, S. O., & Lowenstein, A. (2005). Intergenerational solidarity and the family-welfare state balance. *European Journal of Ageing, 2*(3), 174–182.

Daly, T., & Szebehely, M. (2012). Unheard voices, unmapped terrain: Care work in long-term residential care for older people in Canada and Sweden. *International Journal of Social Welfare, 21*, 139–148.

Dannefer, D. (2003). Cumulative advantage/disadvantage and the life course: Cross-fertilizing age and social science theory. *Journals of Gerontology, 58B*(6), S327–S337.

Dannefer, D. (2011). Long time coming, not here yet: The possibilities of the social in age and life course studies. In R. A. Settersten Jr. & J. L. Angel (Eds.), *Handbook of sociology of aging* (pp. 633–638). New York, NY: Springer.

Daskalopoulos, M., & Kakouros, A. (2006). Perspectives on elder abuse in Greece. *Journal of Elder Abuse and Neglect, 18*(2/3), 87–104.

Davidson, K. (2001). Late life widowhood, selfishness and new partnership choices: A gendered perspective. *Ageing and Society, 21*(3), 297–317.

Davidson, K. (2002). Gender differences in new partnership choices and constraints for older widows and widowers. *Ageing International, 27*(4), 43–60.

Davidson, K. (2011). Sociological perspectives on ageing. In I. Stuart-Hamilton (Ed.), *An introduction to gerontology* (pp. 226–250). New York, NY: Cambridge University Press.

Davies, S., & Denton, M. (2002). The economic well-being of older women who become divorced or separated in mid- or later life. *Canadian Journal on Aging, 21*(4), 477–493.

Davies, S., & Nolan, M. (2006). "Making it better": Self-perceived roles of family caregivers of older people living in care homes: A qualitative study. *International Journal of Nursing Studies, 43*(3), 281–291.

de Jong Gierveld, J., & Peeters, A. (2003). The interweaving of repartnered older adults' lives with their children and siblings. *Ageing and Society, 23*(2), 187–205.

de Medeiros, K. (2005). The complementary self: Multiple perspectives on the aging person. *Journal of Aging Studies, 19*(1), 1–13.

Denton, F. T., Feaver, C. H., & Spencer, B. G. (1998). The future population of Canada, its age distribution and dependency relations. *Canadian Journal on Aging, 17*(1), 83–109.

Denton, F. T., & Spencer, B. G. (2009). What is retirement? A review and assessment of alternative concepts and measures. *Canadian Journal on Aging, 28*(1), 63–76.

Denton, M., & Boos, L. (2007). The gender wealth gap: Structural and material constraints and implications for later life. *Journal of Women and Aging, 19*(3–4), 105–120.

Denton, M. A., Zeytinoglu, I. U., & Davies, S. (2002). Working in clients' homes: The impact on the mental health and well-being of visiting home care workers. *Home Health Care Services Quarterly, 21*(1), 1–27.

Denton, M., Zeytinoglu, I. U., Davies, S., & Lian, J. (2002). Job stress and job dissatisfaction of home care workers in the context of health care restructuring. *International Journal of Health Services, 32*(2), 327–357.

Denton, M., Zeytinoglu, I., Kusch, K., & Davies, S. (2007). Market-modelled home care: Impact on job satisfaction and propensity to leave. *Canadian Public Policy, 33*(Suppl. 1), 81–99.

Devereaux, P. J., Choi, P. T. L., Lacchetti, C., Weaver, B., Scunemann, H. J., Haines, T., . . . Guyatt, G. H. (2002). A systematic review and meta-analysis of studies comparing mortality rates of private for-profit and private not-for profit hospitals. *Canadian Medical Association Journal, 166*(11), 1399–1406.

Diamond, T. (1983). Nursing homes as trouble. *Journal of Contemporary Ethnography, 12*(3), 269–286.

Diamond, T. (1992). *Making gray gold: Narratives of nursing home care.* Chicago, IL: University of Chicago Press.

Dickens, A. P., Richards, S. H., Greaves, C. J., & Campbell, J. L. (2011). Interventions targeting social isolation in older people: A systematic review. *BMC Public Health, 11*(647). doi:10.1186/1471-2458-11-647

Dobbs, D., Eckert, J. K., Rubinstein, B., Keimig, L., Clark, L., Frankowski, A. C., & Zimmerman, S. (2008). An ethnographic study of stigma and ageism in residential care or assisted living. *The Gerontologist, 48*(4), 517–526.

Dodson, L., & Zincavage, R. M. (2007). "It's like a family": Caring labor, exploitation, and race in nursing homes. *Gender and Society, 21*(6), 905–928.

Dong, X., Simon, M., & Gorbien, M. (2007). Elder abuse and neglect in an urban Chinese population. *Journal of Elder Abuse & Neglect, 19*, 79–96.

Dowd, J. J. (1975). Aging as exchange: A preface to theory. *Journal of Gerontology, 30*(5), 584–594.

Dowd, J. J. (1987). The reification of age: Age stratification and the passing of the autonomous subject. *Journal of Aging Studies, 1*(4), 317–335.

Dowd, J. J. (2012). Aging and the course of desire. *Journal of Aging Studies, 26*(3), 285–295.

Dumas, A., Laberge, S., & Straka, S. M. (2005). Older women's relations to bodily appearance: The embodiment of social and biological conditions of existence. *Ageing and Society, 25*(6), 883–902.

Dumas, A., & Turner, B. S. (2007). The life-extension project: A sociological critique. *Health Sociology Review, 16*(1), 5–17.

Dumas, A., & Turner, B. S. (2013). Statecraft and soulcraft: Foucault on prolonging life. In W. C. Cockerham (Ed.), *Medical sociology on the move* (pp. 61–81). Houten, Netherlands: Springer.

Dyer, S., McDowell, L., & Batnitzky, A. (2008). Emotional labour/body work: The caring labours of migrants in the UK's National Health Service. *Geoforum, 39*(6), 2030–2038.

Dykstra, P. A. (2010). *Intergenerational family relationships in ageing societies.* Geneva, Switzerland: United Nations Economic Commission for Europe.

Dykstra, P. A., & Hagestad, G. O. (2007). Roads less taken: Developing a nuanced view of older adults without children. *Journal of Family Issues, 28*(10), 1275–1310.

Ehni, H. J., & Marckmann, G. (2009). Social justice, health inequalities and access to new age-related interventions. *Medicine Studies, 1*, 281–295.

Ekerdt, D. J. (2009). Frontiers of research on work and retirement. *Journals of Gerontology, 65B*(1), 69–80.

Ekerdt, D. J., & Deviney, S. (1990). On defining persons as retired. *Journal of Aging Studies, 4*(3), 211–229.

Elder, G. H. (1994). Time, human agency and social change: Perspectives on the life course. *Social Psychology Quarterly, 57*(1), 4–15.

Elder, G. H. (1998). The life course as developmental theory. *Child Development, 69*(1), 1–12.

Elder, G. H. (1999). *Children of the Great Depression: Social change and life experience.* Boulder, CO: Westview Press. (Original work published 1974)

Elgersma, S. (2010). *Immigrant seniors: Their economic security and factors affecting their access to benefits* (No. 07-45-E). In Brief. Ottawa, ON: Library of Parliament. Retrieved from http://www.parl.gc.ca/content/lop/researchpublications/07-45-e.htm

Ellaway, A., & Macintyre, S. (2007). Is social participation associated with cardiovascular disease risk factors? *Social Science and Medicine, 64*(7), 1384–1391.

Ellis, S. R., & Morrison, T. G. (2005). Stereotypes of ageing: Messages promoted by age-specific paper birthday cards available in Canada. *The International Journal of Aging and Human Development, 61*(1), 57–73.

Ekström, H., Ivanoff, S. D., & Elmståhl, S. (2008). Restriction in social participation and lower life satisfaction among fractured in pain: Results from the population study "Good Aging in Skåne." *Archives of Gerontology and Geriatrics, 46*(3), 409–424.

Employment and Social Development Canada. (2012). *Summative Evaluation of the Old Age Security Program—April 2012* (Cat. No. HS28-203/2012E). Ottawa, ON: Author. Retrieved from http://www.esdc.gc.ca/eng/publications/evaluations/income/2012/april.shtml

Estes, C. L. (1979). *The aging enterprise.* San Francisco, CA: Jossey-Bass.

Estes, C. L. (1999a). Critical gerontology and the new political economy of aging. In M. Minkler & C. L. Estes (Eds.), *Critical gerontology: Perspectives from political and moral economy* (pp. 17–36). Amityville, NY: Baywood.

Estes, C. L. (1999b). The aging enterprise revisited. In M. Minkler & C. L. Estes (Eds.), *Critical gerontology: Perspectives from political and moral economy* (pp. 135–146). Amityville, NY: Baywood.

Estes, C. L. (2006). Critical feminist perspectives, aging, and social policy. In J. Baars, D. Dannefer, C. Phillipson, & A. Walker (Eds.), *Aging, globalization and inequality* (pp. 81–101). Amityville, NY: Baywood.

Estes, C. L. (2011). Crises and old age policy. In R. A. Settersten Jr. & J. L. Angel (Eds.), *Handbook of sociology of aging* (pp. 297–320). New York, NY: Springer.

Estes, C. L., & Binney, E. A. (1989). The biomedicalization of aging: Dangers and dilemmas. *The Gerontologist, 29*(5), 587–596.

Estes, C. L., & Phillipson, C. (2002). The globalization of capital, the welfare state, and old age policy. *International Journal of Health Services, 32*(2), 279–297.

Estes, C. L., Swan, J. H., & Gerard, L. E. (1982). Dominant and competing paradigms in gerontology: Towards a political economy of ageing. *Ageing and Society, 12*, 151–164.

Estes, C. L., Wallace, S. P., Linkins, K. W., & Binney, E. A. (2001). The medicalization and commodification of aging and the privatization and rationalization of old age policy. In Estes, C. L. (Ed.), *Social policy and aging: A critical perspective* (pp. 45–60). Thousand Oaks, CA: Sage.

Evans, R. G., McGrail, K. M., Morgan, S. G., Barer, M. L., & Hertzman, C. (2001). Apocalypse no: Population aging and the future of health care systems. *Canadian Journal on Aging, 20*(Suppl. S1), 160–191.

Evans, R. G., & Stoddart, G. L. (1994). Producing health, consuming health care. In R. G. Evans, M. L. Barer, & T. R. Marmor (Eds.), *Why are some people healthy and others not? The determinants of health of populations* (pp. 27–66). New York, NY: Aldine de Gruyter.

Everard, K. M., Lach, H. W., Fisher, E. B., & Baum, M. C. (2000). Relationship of activity and social support to the functional health of older adults. *Journals of Gerontology, 55B*(4), 208–212.

Eyerman, R., & Turner, B. S. (1998). Outline of a theory of generations. *European Journal of Social Theory, 1,* 91–106.

Eyetsemitan, F., Gire, J. T., Khaleefa, O., & Satiardama, M. P. (2003). Influence of the cross-cultural environment on the perception of aging and adult develop-ment in the developing world: A study of Bahrain, Brazil and Indonesia. *Asian Journal of Social Psychology, 6,* 51–60.

Fast, J., & Keating, C. (2000). Family caregiving and consequences for carers: Toward a policy research agenda. *Canadian Policy Research Network Discussion Paper,* F10.

Ferraro, K. F. (2014). The time of our lives: Recognizing the contributions of Mannheim, Neugarten, and Riley to the study of aging. *The Gerontologist, 54*(1), 127–133.

Ferraro, K. F., & Shippee, T. P. (2009). Aging and cumulative inequality: How does inequality get under the skin? *The Gerontologist, 49*(3), 333–343.

Field, D., & Johnson, I. (1993). Satisfaction and change: A survey of volunteers in a hospice organisation. *Social Science and Medicine, 36*(12), 1625–1633.

Finch, J., & Mason, J. (1993). *Negotiating family responsibilities.* London, UK: Tavistock/Routledge.

Findlay, R. A. (2003). Interventions to reduce social isolation amongst older people: Where is the evidence? *Ageing and Society, 23*(5), 647–658.

Fine, M., & Glendinning, C. (2005). Dependence, independence, or inter-dependence? Revisiting the concepts of "care" and "dependency." *Ageing and Society, 25*(4), 601–621.

Finley, N., Roberts, M. D., & Banahan, B. (1988). Motivators and inhibitors of attitudes of filial obligation toward aging parents. *The Gerontologist, 28*(1), 73–78.

Fischer, L. R., Rogne, L., & Eustis, N. N. (1990). Support systems for the family-less elderly: Care without commitment. In J. F. Gubrium and A. Sankar (Eds.), *The home care experience: Ethnography and policy* (pp. 129–143). Newbury Park, CA: Sage.

Fitzpatrick, M. (2012, February 8). Old Age Security sustainable, says budget watchdog. *CBC News.* Retrieved from http://www.cbc.ca/news/politics/ story/2012/02/08/pol-old-age-security.html

Foner, A. (2000). Age integration or age conflict as society ages? *The Gerontologist, 40*(3), 272–276.

Foot, D. K., & Venne, R. A. (2011). The long goodbye: Age, demographics, and flexibility in retirement. *Canadian Studies in Population, 38*(3–4), 59–74.

Forbes, D., Ward-Griffin, C., Kloseck, M., Mendelsohn, M., St-Amant, O., DeForge, R., & Clark, K. (2011). "Her world gets smaller and smaller with nothing to look forward to": Dimensions of social inclusion and exclusion among rural dementia care networks. *Online Journal of Rural Nursing and Health Care, 11*(2), 27–42.

Fries, J. (1980). Aging, natural death and the compression of morbidity. *New England Journal of Medicine 303,* 130–135.

Funk, L. M. (2002). *Autonomy, in context: Understanding preferences for involvement in decision-making among long-term care facility residents.* Unpublished Masters thesis, University of Victoria, British Columbia, Canada.

Funk, L. M. (2004). Who wants to be involved? Decision-making preferences among residents of long-term care facili-ties. *Canadian Journal on Aging, 23*(1), 47–58.

Funk, L. M. (2010). The interpretive dynamics of filial and collective respon-sibility for aging parents. *Canadian Review of Sociology, 47*(1), 71–92.

Funk, L. M. (2011). [Review of the book *Generations: The Time Machine in Theory and Practice,* by J. A. Burnett]. *Canadian Journal on Aging, 30*(2), 303–306.

Funk, L. M. (2012a). *Manitoba caregiver consultation final report.* Prepared for the Seniors and Healthy Aging Secretariat, Ministry of Health Living, Seniors and Consumer Affairs. Winnipeg, MB. Retrieved from http://www.gov.mb.ca/ shas/publications/index.html

Funk, L. M. (2012b). "Returning the love," not "balancing the books": Talk about delayed reciprocity in supporting age-ing parents. *Ageing and Society, 32*(4), 634–654.

Funk, L. M., & Kobayashi, K. (2014). From motivations to accounts: An interpretive analysis of "Living Apart Together" relationships in mid- to late-life. *Journal of Family Issues.* Advance online publication. doi:10.1177/0192513X14529432

Funk, L. M., Stajduhar, K. I., Cohen, R., Heyland, D. K., & Williams, A. (2012). Legitimising and rationalising in talk about satisfaction with formal healthcare among bereaved family members. *Sociology of Health and Illness, 34*(7), 1010–1024.

Funk, L. M., Waskiewich, S., & Stajduhar, K. I. (2013–2014). Meaning-making and managing difficult feelings: Providing front-line end-of-life care. *Omega: Journal of Death and Dying, 68*(1), 23–43.

Gagnon, É., & Sévigny, A. (2000). Permanence et mutations du monde bénévole. *Recherches Sociographiques, 41,* 529–544.

Galabuzi, G. E. (2009). Social exclusion. In D. Raphael (Ed.), *Social determinants of health: Canadian perspectives* (2nd ed.) (pp. 252–268). Toronto, ON: Canadian Scholars' Press.

Ganong, L., & Coleman, M. (2006). Obligations to stepparents acquired in later life: Relationship quality and acuity of needs. *Journals of Gerontology, 61B*(2), 80–88.

Ganong, L., Coleman, M., McDaniel, A. K., & Killian, T. (1998). Attitudes regarding obligations to assist an older parent or stepparent following later-life remarriage. *Journal of Marriage and Family, 60*(3), 595–610.

Garnham, B. (2013). Designing "older" rather than denying ageing: Problematizing anti-ageing discourse in relation to cosmetic surgery undertaken by older people. *Journal of Aging Studies, 27*(1), 38–46.

Gaugler, J. E. (2005). Family involvement in residential long-term care: A synthesis and critical review. *Aging and Mental Health, 9*(2), 105–118.

Gaymu, J., Busque, M.-A., Légaré, J., Décarie, Y., Vézina, S., & Keefe, J. (2010). What will the family composition of older persons be like tomorrow? A comparison of Canada and France. *Canadian Journal on Aging, 29*(1), 57–71.

Gazso, A. (2005). The poverty of unattached senior women and the Canadian retirement income system: A matter of blame or contradiction?
Journal of Sociology and Social Welfare, 32(2), 41–62.

Gee, E. M. (2000). Population and politics: Voodoo demography, population aging, and social policy. In Gee, E. M., & Gutman, G. (Eds.), *The overselling of population aging: Apocalyptic demography, intergenerational challenges, and social policy* (pp. 5–25). Toronto, ON: Oxford University Press.

Gee, E. M. (2002). Misconceptions and misapprehensions about population ageing. *International Journal of Epidemiology, 31*(4), 750–753.

Gilleard, C. (2005). Cultural approaches to the ageing body. In M. L. Johnson (Ed.), *The Cambridge handbook of age and ageing* (pp. 156–164). New York, NY: Cambridge University Press.

Gilleard, C., & Higgs, P. (1998). Ageing and the limiting conditions of the body. *Sociological Research Online, 3*(4). Retrieved from http://www.socresonline.org.uk/3/4/4.html

Gilleard, C., & Higgs, P. (2005). *Contexts of ageing: Class, cohort and community.* Malden, MA: Policy Press.

Gilmour, H. (2012). Social participation and the health and well-being of Canadian seniors (Statistics Canada Catalogue No. 82-003-X). *Health Reports, 23*(4). Ottawa, ON: Minister of Industry.

Glass, T. A., Mendes de Leon, C., Bassuk, S. S., & Berkman, L. F. (2006). Social engagement and depressive symptoms in late life: Longitudinal findings. *Journal of Aging and Health, 18*(4), 604–628.

Goffman, E. K. (1961). *Asylums.* New York, NY: Doubleday.

Goffman, E. K. (1963). *Stigma: Notes on the management of spoiled identity.* Englewood Cliffs, NJ: Prentice-Hall.

Gollom, M. (2012, February 1). Is Old Age Security truly unsustainable? *CBC News.* Retrieved from http://www.cbc.ca/news/business/taxes/is-old-age-security-truly-unsustainable-1.1145910

Granzoi, S. L., & Koehler, V. (1998). Age and gender differences in body attitudes: A comparison of young and elderly adults. *The International Journal of Aging and Human Development, 47*(1), 1–10.

Gray, A. (2005). The changing availability of grandparents as carers and its implications for childcare policy in the UK. *Journal of Social Policy, 34*(4), 557–577.

Gray, A. (2009). The social capital of older people. *Ageing and Society, 29*(1), 5–31.

Green, S. P., & Pritchard, M. E. (2003). Predictors of body image dissatisfaction in adult men and women. *Social behavior and personality: An international journal, 31*(3), 215–222.

Grenier, A. (2012). *Transitions and the life course: Challenging the constructions of "growing old."* Chicago, IL: Policy Press.

Grenier, A. M., & Guberman, N. (2009). Creating and sustaining disadvantage: The relevance of a social exclusion framework. *Health and Social Care in the Community, 17*(2), 116–124.

Grenier, A., & Hanley, J. (2007). Older women and "frailty": Aged, gendered and embodied resistance. *Current Sociology, 55*(2), 211–228.

Grenier, A., & Phillipson, C. (2013). Rethinking agency in late life: Structural and interpretive approaches. In J. Baars, J. Dohmen, A. Grenier, & C. Phillipson (Eds.), *Ageing, meaning and social structure: Connecting critical and humanistic gerontology* (pp. 55–79). Chicago, IL: Policy Press.

Groger, L., & Mayberry, P. S. (2001). Caring too much? Cultural lag in African Americans' perceptions of filial responsibilities. *Journal of Cross-Cultural Gerontology, 16*(1), 21–39.

Grundy, E. (2010). Family support for older people: Determinants and consequences. In S. Tuljapurkar, N. Ogawa, & A. H. Gauthier (Eds.), *Ageing in Advanced Industrial States,* (pp. 197–222). International Studies in Population, Volume 8. Netherlands: Springer.

Guberman, N., Lavoie, J.-P., Blein, L., & Olazabal, I. (2012). Baby boom caregivers: Care in the age of individualization. *The Gerontologist, 52*(2), 210–218.

Guberman, N., Lavoie, J.-P., & Olazabal, J. I. (2011). Baby-boomers and the "denaturalisation" of care-giving in Quebec. *Ageing and Society, 31*(7), 1141–1158.

Gubrium, J. F. (1988). Family responsibility and caregiving in the qualitative analysis of the Alzheimer's disease experience. *Journal of Marriage and Family, 50,* 197–207.

Gubrium, J. F., & Holstein, J. A. (1999). The nursing home as a discursive anchor for the ageing body. *Ageing and Society, 19*(5), 519–538.

Gubrium, J. F., & Holstein, J. A. (2003). The everyday visibility of the aging body. In C. A. Faircloth (Ed.), *Aging bodies: Images and everyday experience* (pp. 205–227). Walnut Creek, CA: AltaMira Press.

Guerriere, D. N., Wong, A. Y. M., Croxford, R., Leong, V. W., McKeever, P., & Coyte, P. (2008). Costs and determinants of privately financed home-based health care in Ontario, Canada. *Health and Social Care in the Community, 16*(2), 126–136.

Guiaux, M., van Tilburg, T., & Broese van Groenou, M. (2007). Changes in contact and support exchange in personal networks after widowhood. *Personal Relationships, 14*(3), 457–473.

Gutman, G. M. (2010). Population ageing and apocalyptic demography: Separating fact from fiction. In L. B. Knudsen & A. Lindhart Olsen (Eds.), *Our demographic future: A challenge* (pp. 3–27). Aalborg, DK: Aalborg University Press and Nordic Demographic Society.

Hagestad, G. O., & Uhlenberg, P. (2005). The social separation of old and young: A root of ageism. *Journal of Social Issues, 61*(2), 343–360.

Hagestad, G. O., & Uhlenberg, P. (2006). Should we be concerned about age segregation? Some theoretical and empirical explorations. *Research on Aging, 28*(5), 638–653.

Hale, B., Barrett, P., & Gauld, R. (2010). *The age of supported independence: The voices of in-home care.* London, UK: Springer.

Haley, W. E., West, C. A., Wadley, V. G., Ford, G. R., White, F. A., Barrett, J. J., . . . Roth, D. L. (1995). Psychological, social and health impact of caregiving: A comparison of Black and White dementia family caregivers and non-caregivers. *Psychology and Aging, 10*(4), 540–552.

Hall, C. (2013, December 18). Analysis: Why Jim Flaherty is turning his back on CPP reform. *CBC News.* Retrieved from http://www.cbc.ca/news/politics/why-jim-flaherty-is-turning-his-back-on-cpp-reform-1.2468066

Hall, S. S. (2013, May). On beyond 100. *National Geographic,* 28–50.

Hand, C., Law, M., Hanna, S., Elliott, S., & McColl, M. A. (2012). Neighbourhood influences on participation in activities among older adults with chronic health conditions. *Health and Place, 18*(4), 869–876.

Hank, K., & Buber, I. (2009). Grandparents caring for their grandchildren: Findings from the 2004 Survey of Health, Ageing and Retirement in Europe. *Journal of Family Issues, 30*(1), 53–73.

Hanlon, N., Rosenberg, M., & Clasby, R. (2007). Offloading social care responsibilities: Recent experiences of local voluntary organizations in a remote urban centre in British Columbia, Canada. *Health and Social Care in the Community, 15*(4), 343–351.

Happ, M. B., Williams, C. C., Strumpf, N. E., & Burger, S. G. (1996). Individualized care for frail elders: Theory and practice. *Journal of Gerontological Nursing, 22*(3), 6–14.

Harbison, J., & Morrow, M. (1998). Re-examining the social construction of "elder abuse and neglect": A Canadian perspective. *Ageing and Society, 18*, 691–711.

Hartke, R. J., & King, R. B. (2003). Telephone group intervention for older stroke caregivers. *Topics in Stroke Rehabilitation, 9*(4), 65–81.

Haskey, J. & Lewis, J. (2006). Living-Apart-Together in Britain: Context and meaning. *International Journal of Law in Context, 2*, 37–48.

Hasson, H., & Arnetz, J. E. (2008). Nursing staff competence, work strain, stress and satisfaction in elderly care: A comparison of home-based care and nursing homes. *Journal of Clinical Nursing, 17*(4), 468–481.

Hay, D. (1994). Social status and health status: Does money buy health? In B. S. Bolaria & R. Bolaria (Eds.), *Racial minorities, medicine and health* (pp. 9–52). Halifax, NS: Fernwood.

Hayflick, L. (2000). The future of aging. *Nature, 408*, 267–269.

Hayslip, B., & Kaminski, P. L. (2005). Grandparents raising their grandchildren: A review of the literature and suggestions for practice. *The Gerontologist, 45*(2), 262–269.

Health Council of Canada. (2013). *Canada's most vulnerable: Improving health care for First Nations, Inuit, and Métis seniors.* Retrieved from http://www.healthcouncilcanada.ca/content_ab.php?mnu=2&mnu1=48&mnu2=30&mnu3=55

Heaton, J. (1999). The gaze and visibility of the carer: A Foucauldian analysis of the discourse of informal care. *Sociology of Health and Illness 21*, 759–777.

Heikennen, S. J. (2011). Exclusion of older immigrants from the former Soviet Union to Finland: The meaning of inter-generational relationships. *Journal of Cross-Cultural Gerontology, 26*, 379–395.

Heilbronn, L. K., & Ravussin, E. (2003). Caloric restriction and aging: Review of literature and implications for studies in humans. *American Journal of Clinical Nutrition, 78*, 361–369.

Heinz, W. R. & Krüger, H. (2001). Life course: Innovations and challenges for social research. *Current Sociology, 49*(2), 29–45.

HelpAge International. (n.d.). The Madrid Plan (MIPAA). Retrieved from http://www.helpage.org/what-we-do/rights/the-madrid-plan-mipaa/

Henderson, J., & Forbat, L. (2002). Relationship-based social policy: Personal and policy constructions of "care." *Critical Social Policy, 22*, 669–687.

Henkens, K., & van Solinge, H. (2002). Spousal influences on the decision to retire. *International Journal of Sociology, 32*(2), 55–74.

Hertzberg, A., Ekman, S. L., & Axelsson, K. (2001). Staff activities and behavior are the source of many feelings: Relatives' interactions and relationships with staff in nursing homes. *Journal of Clinical Nursing, 10*(3), 380–388.

Hertzman, C., Frank, J., & Evans, R. G. (1994). Heterogeneities in health status and the determinants of population health. In R. G. Evans, M. L. Barer, & T. R. Marmor (Eds.), *Why are some people healthy and others not? The determinants of health of populations* (pp. 67–92). New York, NY: Aldine de Gruyter.

Higgs, P., & Jones, I. R. (2009). *Medical sociology and old age: Towards a sociology of health in later life.* London, UK: Routledge.

Hinterlong, J., & Ryan, S. (2008). Creating grander families: Older adults adopting younger kin and nonkin. *The Gerontologist, 48*(4), 527–536.

Hochschild, A. (1983). *The managed heart: Commercialization of human feeling.* Berkeley, CA: University of California Press.

Hochschild, A. R. (1975). Disengagement theory: A critique and proposal. *American Sociological Review, 40,* 553–569.

Hooyman, N. R. (1990). Women as caregivers of the elderly: Implications for social welfare policy and practice. In D. E. Biegel & A. Blum (Eds.), *Aging and caregiving: Theory, research and policy* (pp. 221–241). London, UK: Sage.

Hooyman, N. R., & Gonyea, J. (1995). *Feminist perspectives on family care: Policies for gender justice.* Thousand Oaks, CA: Sage.

House, J., Lepkowski, J. M., Kinney, A. M., Mero, R. P., Kessler, R. C., & Herzog, A. R. (1994). The social stratification of aging and health. *Journal of Health and Social Behavior, 35,* 213–234.

Huang, C.-S. (2013). Undergraduate students' knowledge about aging and attitudes toward older adults in East and West: A socio-economic and cultural exploration. *The International Journal of Aging and Human Development, 77*(1), 59–76.

Hurd Clarke, L. (2000). Older women's body image and embodied experience: An exploration. *Journal of Women and Aging, 12*(3/4), 77–97.

Hurd Clarke, L., & Griffin, M. (2007). The body natural and the body unnatural: Beauty work and aging. *Journal of Aging Studies, 21*(3), 187–201.

Hurd Clarke, L., & Griffin, M. (2008). Visible and invisible ageing: Beauty work as a response to ageism. *Ageing and Society, 28*(5), 653–674.

Hurd Clarke, L., Griffin, M., & Maliha, K. (2009). Bat wings, bunions and turkey wattles: Body transgressions and older women's strategic clothing choices. *Ageing and Society, 29*(5), 709–726.

Hurd Clarke, L., & Korotchenko, A. (2011). Aging and the body: A review. *Canadian Journal on Aging, 30*(3), 495–510.

Hutchinson, S. L., & Wexler, B. (2007). Is "raging" good for health? Older women's participation in the raging grannies. *Health Care for Women International, 28*(1), 88–118.

Hyyppä, M. T., Mäki, J., Impivaara, O., & Aromaa, A. (2007). Individual-level measures of social capital as predictors of all-cause and cardiovascular mortality: A population-based prospective study of men and women in Finland. *European Journal of Epidemiology, 22*(9), 589–597.

Ibarra, M. (2002). Emotional proletarians in a global economy: Mexican immigrant women and elder care work. *Urban Anthropology and Studies of Cultural Systems and World Economic Development, 31*(3/4), 317–350.

Ibbott, P., Kerr, D., & Beaujot, R. (2006). Probing the future of mandatory retirement in Canada. *Canadian Journal on Aging, 25*(2), 161–178.

Ilcan, S., & Basok, T. (2004). Community government: Voluntary agencies, social justice, and the responsibilization of citizens. *Citizenship Studies, 8*(2), 129–144.

Illich, I. (1975). *Medical nemesis: The expropriation of health.* New York, NY: Pantheon Books.

Isaksen, L.W. (2002). Toward a sociology of (gendered) disgust: Images of bodily decay and the social organization of care work. *Journal of Family Issues, 23*(7), 791–811.

Jarvis, M. J., & Wardle, J. (2002). Social patterning of individual health behaviours: The case of cigarette smoking. In M. Marmot & R. G. Wilkinson (Eds.), *Social determinants of health* (pp. 240–255). Oxford, UK: Oxford University Press.

Johnson, M. J., Jackson, N. C., Arnette, J. K., & Koffman, S. D. (2005). Gay and lesbian perceptions of discrimination in retirement care facilities. *Journal of Homosexuality, 49*(2), 83–102.

Johnson, R. W., Toohey, D., & Wiener, J. (2007). *Meeting the long-term care needs of the baby boomers: How changing families will affect paid helpers and institutions* (Discussion Paper No. 07-04). The Retirement Project. Washington, DC: Urban Institute.

Johnston, J. (2014). Globalization. In R. J. Brym (Ed.), *New Society* (7th ed.). (pp. 451–477). Toronto, ON: Nelson.

Johnstone, M.-J., & Kanitsaki, O. (2009). Population ageing and the politics of demographic alarmism: Implications for the nursing profession. *Australian*

Journal of Advanced Nursing, 26(3), 86–110.

Johri, M., Damschroder, L. J., Zikmund-Fisher, B. J., & Ubel, P. A. (2005). The importance of age in allocating health care resources: Does intervention-type matter? *Health Economics, 14*(7), 669–678.

Jones, I. R. & Higgs, P. F. (2010). The natural, the normal and the normative: Contested terrains in ageing and old age. *Social Science and Medicine, 71*(8), 1513–1519.

Joyce, K., & Loe, M. (2010). A sociological approach to ageing, technology and health. *Sociology of Health and Illness, 32*(2), 171–180.

Kaaslainen, S., Brazil, K., Ploeg, J., & Martin, L.S. (2007). Nurses' perceptions around providing palliative care for long-term care residents with dementia. *Journal of Palliative Care, 23*(3), 173–80.

Kaida, L., & Boyd, M. (2011). Poverty variations among the elderly: The roles of income security policies and family co-residence. *Canadian Journal on Aging, 30*(1), 83–100.

Kail, B. L., Quadagno, J., & Keene, J. R. (2009). The political economy perspective of aging. In V. L. Bengtson, D. Gans, N. M. Putney, & M. Silverstein (Eds.), *Handbook of theories of aging* (2nd ed.) (pp. 555–595). New York, NY: Springer.

Kalache, A. (2012). Human rights in older age. In J. Beard, S. Biggs, D. Bloom, L. Fried, P. Hogan, A. Kalache, & J. Olshansky (Eds.), *Global population ageing: Peril or promise?* (pp. 89–92). Program on the Global Demography of Ageing, Working Paper No. 89. Retrieved from http://www.hsph.harvard.edu/pgda/working.htm

Kälvemark, S., Höglund, A. T., Hansson, M. G., Westerholm, P., & Arnetz, B. (2004). Living with conflicts: Ethical dilemmas and moral distress in the health care system. *Social Science and Medicine, 58*(6), 1075–1084.

Kaminski, P. L., & Hayslip, B., Jr. (2006). Gender differences in body esteem among older adults. *Journal of Women and Aging, 18*(3), 19–35.

Kampf, A., & Bothelo, L. A. (2009). Anti-aging and biomedicine: Critical studies on the pursuit of maintaining, revitalizing and enhancing aging bodies. *Medicine Studies, 1,* 187–195.

Kane, R. A. (2003). Definition, measurement, and correlates of quality of life in nursing homes: Toward a reasonable practice, research, and policy agenda. *The Gerontologist, 43*(Suppl. 2), 28–36.

Kane, R. A., Freeman, I. C., Caplan, A. L., Aroskar, M. A., & Urv-Wong, E. K. (1990). Everyday autonomy in nursing homes. *Generations,* 14(Suppl.), 69–71.

Kane, R. L., & Kane, R. A. (2005). Ageism in healthcare and long-term care. *Generations, 29*(3), 49–54.

Karlsson, S. G., & Borell, K. (2002). Intimacy and autonomy, gender and ageing: Living apart together. *Ageing International, 27*(4), 11–26.

Karlsson, S. G., & Borell, K. (2005). A home of their own: Women's boundary work in LAT-relationships. *Journal of Aging Studies, 19*(1), 73–84.

Kass, L. R. (2001). L'chaim and its limits: Why not immortality? *First Things, 13,* 17–24.

Katz, S. (1992). Alarmist demography: Power, knowledge, and the elderly population. *Journal of Aging Studies, 6*(3), 203–225.

Katz, S. (2012). [Review of the book *The silvering screen: Old age and disability in cinema,* by S. Chivers]. *Canadian Journal on Aging, 31*(2), 254–255.

Katz, S., & Marshall, B. (2003). New sex for old: Lifestyle, consumerism, and the ethics of aging well. *Journal of Aging Studies, 17*(1), 3–16.

Kaufman, S. R. (1994). The social construction of frailty: An anthropological perspective. *Journal of Aging Studies, 8*(1), 45–58.

Kaufman, S. R. (2000). The ageless self. In J. F. Gubrium & J. A. Holstein (Eds.), *Aging and everyday life* (pp. 103–111). Malden, MA: Blackwell. (Original work published 1986)

Kaufman, S. R., Shim, J. K., & Russ, A. J. (2004). Revisiting the biomedicalization of aging: Clinical trends and ethical challenges. *The Gerontologist, 44*(6), 731–738.

Kaufman, S. R., Shim, J. K., & Russ, A. J. (2006). Old age, life extension, and the character of medical choice. *Journals of Gerontology, 61B*(4), S175–184.

Keating, N., Swindle, J., & Fletcher, S. (2011). Aging in rural Canada: A retrospective and review. *Canadian Journal on Aging, 30*(3), 323–338.

Keefe, J. (2011). *Supporting caregivers and caregiving in an aging Canada* (IRPP Study No. 23). Montreal, QC: Institute for Research on Public Policy.

Keefe, J., & Fancey, P. (2000). The care continues: Responsibility for elderly relatives before and after admission to a long term care facility. *Family Relations, 49*(3), 235–244.

Keefe, J., Légaré, J., Charbonneau, P., & Décarie, Y. (2012). Intergenerational support to older Canadians by their adult children: Implications for the future. In G. De Santis (Ed.), *The family, the market or the state?* (pp. 141–158). International Studies in Population, Volume 10. Netherlands: Springer.

Keefe, J., & Rajnovich, B. (2007). To pay or not to pay: Examining underlying principles in the debate on financial support for family caregivers. *Canadian Journal on Aging, 26*(Suppl. S1), 77–89.

Kemp, C. L. (2005). Dimensions of grandparent-adult grandchild relationships: From family ties to intergenerational friendships. *Canadian Journal on Aging, 24*(2), 161–177.

Kemp, C. L., & Denton, M. (2003). The allocation of responsibility for later life: Canadian reflections on the roles of individuals, government, employers and families. *Ageing and Society, 23*(6), 737–760.

Kiecolt-Glaser, J. K., Preacher, K. J., MacCallum, R. C., Atkinson, C., Malarkey, W. B., & Glaser, R. (2003). Chronic stress and age-related increases in the proinflammatory cytokine IL-6. *Proceedings of the National Academy of Sciences of the United States of America, 100*(15), 9090–9095.

Kontos, P. C. (2005). Embodied selfhood in Alzheimer's disease: Rethinking person-centred care. *Dementia, 4*(4), 553–570.

Labonte, R., & Penfold, S. (1981). Canadian perspectives in health promotion: A critique. *Health Education, 19*, 4–9.

Lai, D. (2011). Abuse and neglect experienced by aging Chinese in Canada. *Journal of Elder Abuse and Neglect, 23*(4), 326–347.

Lamoureux, H. (2002). Le danger d'un détournement de sens: Portée et limites du bénévolat. *Nouvelles Pratiques Sociales, 15*(2), 77–86.

Lan, P. C. (2002). Subcontracting filial piety: Elder care in ethnic Chinese immigrant families in California. *Journal of Family Issues, 23*(7), 812–835.

Lanting, S., Crossley, M., Morgan, D., & Cammer, A. (2011). Aboriginal experiences of aging and dementia in a context of sociocultural change: Qualitative analysis of key informant group interviews with Aboriginal seniors. *Journal of Cross-Cultural Gerontology, 26*, 103–117.

LaPierre, T. A., & Hughes, M. E. (2009). Population aging in Canada and the United States. In P. Uhlenberg (Ed.), *International handbook of population aging* (pp. 191–230). Springer Netherlands.

Lasby, D. M. & Embuldeniya, D. K. (2002). *Voluntary health organizations in Canada: Public involvement and support.* Toronto, ON: Canadian Centre for Philanthropy.

Lashewicz, B., Manning, G., Hall, M., & Keating, N. (2007). Equity matters: Doing fairness in the context of family caregiving. *Canadian Journal on Aging, 26*(Suppl. S1), 91–102.

Laurin, A., Milligan, K., & Schirle, T. (2012). *Comparing nest eggs: How CPP reform affects retirement choices* (Working Paper No. 352). C. D. Howe Institute Commentary Pension Paper (pp. 1–8). Toronto, ON: C. D. Howe Institute. Retrieved from http://papers.ssrn.com/sol3/papers.cfm?abstract_id=2088947

Lawton, J. (1998). Contemporary hospice care: The sequestration of the unbounded body and "dirty dying." *Sociology of Health and Illness, 20*(2), 121–143.

Laz, C. (1998). Act your age. *Sociological Forum, 13*(1), 85–113.

Laz, C. (2003). Age embodied. *Journal of Aging Studies, 17*, 503–519.

Lee, S., Colditz, G. A., Berkman, L. F., & Kawachi, I. (2003a). Caregiving and risk of coronary heart disease in U.S. women: A prospective study. *American Journal of Preventive Medicine, 24*(2), 113–119.

Lee, S., Colditz, G., Berkman, L., & Kawachi, I. (2003b). Caregiving to children and grandchildren and risk of coronary heart disease in women. *American Journal of Public Health, 93*(11), 1939–1944.

Lemon, B. W., Bengtson, V. L., & Peterson, J. A. (1972). An exploration of the activity theory of aging: Activity types and life satisfaction among in-movers to a retirement community. *Journal of Gerontology, 27*(4), 511–523.

Levin, I. (2004). Living apart together: A new family form. *Current Sociology, 52*(2), 223–240.

Levy, B. R., Chung, P. H., Bedford, T., & Navrazhina, K. (2014). Facebook as a site for negative age stereotypes. *The Gerontologist, 54*(2), 172–176. doi:10.1093/geront/gns194

Lewinter, M. (2003). Reciprocities in caregiving relationships in Danish elder care. *Journal of Aging Studies, 17*(3), 357–377.

Lewis, D. C., Medvedev, K., & Seponski, D. M. (2011). Awakening to the desires of older women: Deconstructing ageism within fashion magazines. *Journal of Aging Studies, 25*(2), 101–109.

Lilly, M. B. (2008). Medical versus social work-places: Constructing and compensating the personal support worker across health care settings in Ontario, Canada. *Gender, Place and Culture, 15*(3), 285–299.

Link, B. G., & Phelan, J. C. (1995). Social conditions as fundamental causes of disease. *Journal of Health and Social Behavior, 35*(Extra issue), 80–94.

Link, B. G., & Phelan, J. C. (1996). Understanding socioeconomic differences in health: The role of fundamental social causes [Editorial]. *American Journal of Public Health, 86*, 471–473.

Logue, B. J. (1990). Modernization and the status of the frail elderly: Perspectives on continuity and change. *Journal of Cross-Cultural Gerontology, 5*(4), 345–374.

Long, S. O. (2012). Bodies, technologies, and aging in Japan: Thinking about old people and their silver products. *Journal of Cross-Cultural Gerontology, 27,* 119–137.

Longino, C. F., Jr., & Kart, C. S. (1982). Explicating activity theory: A formal replication. *Journal of Gerontology, 27*(6), 713–722.

Longino, C. F., Jr., & Powell, J. L. (2009). Toward a phenomenology of aging. In V. L. Bengtson, D. Gans, N. M. Putney, & M. Silverstein (Eds.), *Handbook of theories of aging* (2nd ed.) (pp. 375–387). New York, NY: Springer.

Lui, C.-W., Warburton, J., Winterton, R., & Bartlett, H. (2011). Critical reflections on a social inclusion approach for an ageing Australia. *Australian Social Work, 64*(3), 266–282.

Lundgren, A. S., & Ljuslinder, K. (2011a). "The baby-boom is over and the ageing shock awaits": Populist media imagery in news-press representations of population ageing. *International Journal of Ageing and Later Life, 6*(2), 39–71.

Lundgren, A. S., & Ljuslinder, K. (2011b). Problematic demography: Representations of population ageing in the Swedish Daily Press. *Journal of Population Ageing, 4*(3), 165–183.

Lunt, N. (2009). Older people within transnational families: The social policy implications. *International Journal of Social Welfare, 18*(3), 243–251.

Lupton, D. (1993). Risk as moral danger: The social and political functions of risk discourse in public health. *International Journal of Health Services, 23*, 425–435.

Lyman, K. A. (1989). Bringing the social back in: A critique of the biomedicalization of dementia. *The Gerontologist, 29*(5), 597–605.

Lynott, R. J., & Lynott, P. P. (1996). Tracing the course of theoretical development in the sociology of aging. *The Gerontologist, 36*(6), 749–760.

MacCourt, P., & Krawczyk, M. (2012). *Supporting the caregivers of seniors through policy: The caregiver policy lens.* Vancouver, BC: British Columbia Psychogeriatric Association.

Macionis, J. J., & Gerber, L. M. (2011). *Sociology* (7th Canadian ed.). Toronto, ON: Pearson.

MacKenzie, P., Brown, L., Callahan, M., & Whittington, B. (2011). Spinning the family web: Grandparents raising grandchildren in Canada. In C. Benoit & H. Hallgrímsdóttir (Eds.), *Valuing intimate labour: Gender and work in economic and non-economic organizations* (pp. 193–212). Toronto, ON: University of Toronto Press.

MacRae, H. (1992). Fictive kin as a component of the social networks of older people. *Research on Aging, 14*(2), 226–247.

Mannheim, K. (1963). The problem of generations. *Psychoanalytic Review, 57*, 378–404.

Marier, P., & Skinner, S. (2008). The impact of gender and immigration on pension outcomes in Canada. *Canadian Public Policy, 34*(4), 59–78.

Marmor, T. R., Barer, M. L., & Evans, R. G. (1994). The determinants of a population's health: What can be done to improve a democratic nation's health status? In R. G. Evans, M. L. Barer, & T. R. Marmor (Eds.), *Why are some people healthy and others not? The determinants of health of populations* (pp. 219–230). New York, NY: Aldine de Gruyter.

Marshall, B. L. (2009). Rejuvenation's return: Anti-aging and re-masculinization in biomedical discourse on the "aging male." *Medicine Studies, 1,* 249–265.

Marshall, B. L. (2012). Medicalization and the refashioning of age-related limits on sexuality. *Journal of Sex Research, 49*(4), 337–343.

Marshall, B. L., & Katz, S. (2012). The embodied life course: Post-ageism or the renaturalization of gender? *Societies, 2*(4), 222–234.

Marshall, V. W. (1994). A critique of Canadian aging and health policy. In V. W. Marshall & B. McPherson (eds.), *Aging: Canadian perspectives* (pp. 232–244). Peterborough, Ontario: Broadview Press.

Marshall, V. W., & Bengtson, V. L. (2011). Theoretical perspectives on the sociology of aging. In R. A. Settersten Jr. & J. L. Angel (Eds.), *Handbook of sociology of aging* (pp. 17–33). New York, NY: Springer.

Marshall, V. W., & Marshall, J. G. (2003). Ageing and work in Canada: Firm policies. *The Geneva papers on risk and insurance: Issues and practice, 28*(4), 625–639.

Marshall, V. W., Matthews, S. H., & Rosenthal, C. J. (1993). Elusiveness of family life: A challenge for the sociology of aging. *Annual Review of Gerontology and Geriatrics, 13*(1), 39–72.

Marshall, V. W., & Mueller, M. M. (2003). Theoretical roots of the life-course perspective. In W. R. Heinz & V. W. Marshall (eds.), *Social dynamics of the life course: Transitions, institutions, and interrelations* (pp. 3–32). New York, NY: Aldine de Gruyter.

Marshall, V. W., & Taylor, P. (2005). Restructuring the lifecourse: Work and retirement. In M. L. Johnson (Ed.),

The Cambridge handbook of age and ageing (pp. 572–582). New York, NY: Cambridge University Press.

Martens, A., Goldenberg, J. L., & Greenberg, J. (2005). A terror management perspective on ageism. *Journal of Social Issues, 61*(2), 223–239.

Martin, R., Williams, C., & O'Neill, D. (2009). Retrospective analysis of attitudes to ageing in the *Economist*: Apocalyptic demography for opinion formers. *British Medical Journal, 339,* b4914.

Martin-Matthews, A., & Campbell, L. D. (1995). Gender roles, employment and informal care. In S. Arber & J. Ginn (Eds.), *Connecting gender and ageing: A sociological approach* (pp. 129–143). Buckingham, UK: Open University Press.

Martinson, M., & Minkler, M. (2006). Civic engagement and older adults: A critical perspective. *The Gerontologist, 46*(3), 318–324.

Matier, C. (2012, February 8). *Federal fiscal sustainability and elderly benefits.* Ottawa, ON: Office of the Parliamentary Budget Officer. Retrieved from http://pbo-dpb.gc.ca/files/files/Publications/Sustainability_OAS.pdf

Mayer, K. U. (2004). Whose lives? How history, societies and institutions define and shape life courses. *Research in Human Development, 3,* 161–187.

McBride, A. M. (2006). Civic engagement, older adults, and inclusion. *Generations, 30*(4), 66–71.

McDaniel, S. A. (1987). Demographic aging as a guiding paradigm in Canada's welfare state. *Canadian Public Policy, 13*(3), 330–336.

McDaniel, S. A. (2000). "What did you ever do for me?": Intergenerational linkages in a restructuring Canada. In E. Gee & G. Gutman (Eds.), *The overselling of population aging: Apocalyptic demography, intergenerational challenges, and social policy* (pp. 130–153). Toronto, ON: Oxford University Press.

McDaniel, S. A. (2001). Born at the right time? Gendered generations and webs of entitlement and responsibility. *Canadian Journal of Sociology, 26*(2), 193–214.

McDaniel, S. A. (2003). Toward disentangling policy implications of economic and demographic changes in Canada's aging population. *Canadian Public Policy, 29*(4), 491–509.

McDaniel, S. A. (2004). Generationing gender: Justice and the division of welfare. *Journal of Aging Studies, 18,* 27–44.

McDaniel, S. (2007). Population aging: Better than the alternative. In J. Leonard, C. Ragan & F. St-Hilaire (Eds.), *A Canadian priorities agenda: Policy choices to improve economic and social well-being* (pp. 223–232). Institute for Research on Public Policy. Montreal, QC.

McDonald, L., & Donahue, P. (2011). Retirement lost? *Canadian Journal on Aging, 30*(3), 401–422.

McDonald, L., Donahue, P. & Marshall, V. W. (2000). The economic consequences of unexpected early retirement. In F. Denton, D. Fretz, & B. Spencer (Eds.), *Independence and economic security in old age* (pp. 267–292). Vancouver, BC: UBC Press.

McDonald, L., Donahue, P., & Moore, B. (2000). The poverty of retired widows. In F. Denton, D. Fretz, & B. Spencer (Eds.), *Independence and economic security in old age* (pp. 328–345). Vancouver, BC: UBC Press.

McDonald, L., & Robb, A. L. (2004). The economic legacy of divorce and separation for women in old age. *Canadian Journal on Aging, 23*(Supplement), 83–97.

McGrail, K. M., Broemeling, A. M., McGregor, M. J., Salomons, K., Ronald, L. A., & McKendry, R. (2008). *Home health Services in British Columbia: A portrait of users and trends over time.* Vancouver, BC: UBC Centre for Health Services and Policy Research. Retrieved from http://www.chspr.ubc.ca/pubs/report/home-health-services-british-columbia

McGrail, K. M., McGregor, M., Cohen, M., Tate, R. B., & Ronald, L. A. (2007). For-profit versus not-for-profit delivery of long term care. *Canadian Medical Association Journal, 176*(1), 57–58.

McGregor, M. J. & Ronald, L. A. (2011). *Residential long-term care for Canadian seniors: Nonprofit, for-profit or does it matter?* (IRPP Study No. 14). Montreal, QC: Institute for Research on Public Policy. Retrieved from http://irpp.org/research-studies/residential-long-term-care-for-canadas/

McHugh, K. E. (2003). Three faces of ageism: Society, image and place. *Ageing and Society, 23*(2), 165–185.

McHugh, M. C. (2012). Aging, agency, and activism: Older women as social change agents. *Women and Therapy, 35*(3–4), 279–295.

McMullin, J. A. (2000). Diversity and the state of sociological aging theory. *The Gerontologist, 40*(5), 517–530.

McMullin, J. A., & Marshall, V. W. (2001). Ageism, age relations, and garment industry work in Montreal. *The Gerontologist, 41*(1), 111–122.

McMullin, J. A., & Duerden Comeau, T. (2011). Aging and age discrimination in IT firms. In J. A. McMullin (Ed.), *Age, gender and work: Small IT firms in the new economy* (pp. 133–158). Vancouver, BC: UBC Press.

Mégret, F. (2011). The human rights of older persons: A growing challenge. *Human Rights Law Review, 11*(1), 37–66.

Mellow, M. (2011). Voluntary caregiving? Constraints and opportunities for hospital volunteers. In C. Benoit & H. Hallgrímsdóttir (Eds.), *Valuing care work: Comparative perspectives* (pp. 215–235). Toronto, ON: University of Toronto Press.

Mendes de Leon, C., Glass, T. A., & Berkman, L. F. (2003). Social engagement and disability in a community population of older adults. *American Journal of Epidemiology, 157*(7), 633–642.

Menec, V. H. (2003). The relation between everyday activities and successful aging: A 6-year longitudinal study. *Journals of Gerontology, 58B*(2), 74–82.

Mental Health Commission of Canada. (2012). *Changing directions, changing lives: The mental health strategy for Canada.* Calgary, AB: Author. Retrieved from http://strategy.mentalhealthcommission.ca/

Mhatre, S. L., & Deber, R. B. (1998). From equal access to health care to equitable access to health: A review of Canadian provincial health commissions and reports. In D. Coburn, C. D'Arcy, & G. Torrance (Eds.), *Health and Canadian society: Sociological perspectives* (pp. 459–484). Toronto, ON: University of Toronto Press.

Milan, A., & Peters, A. (2003, Summer). Couples living apart. *Canadian Social*

Trends, 69 (Statistics Canada Catalogue No. 11-008) (pp. 2–6). Ottawa ON: Statistics Canada.

Miller, B., Glasser, M., & Rubin, S. (1992). A paradox of medicalization: Physicians, families and Alzheimer's disease. *Journal of Aging Studies, 6*(2), 135–148.

Miller, B., & Montgomery, A. (1990). Family caregivers and limitations in social activities. *Research on Aging, 12*(1), 72–93.

Milligan, K. (2008). The evolution of elderly poverty in Canada. *Canadian Public Policy, 34*(4), S79–S94.

Mills, C. W. (1959). *The sociological imagination.* New York, NY: Oxford University Press.

Mikkonen, J., & Raphael, D. (2010). *Social determinants of health: The Canadian facts.* Toronto, ON: York University School of Health Policy and Management.

Mitchell, B. A. (2003). Would I share a home with an elderly parent? Exploring ethnocultural diversity and intergenerational support relations during young adulthood. *Canadian Journal on Aging, 22*(1), 69–82.

Mitteness, L. S., & Barker, J. C. (1995). Stigmatizing a "normal" condition: Urinary incontinence in late life. *Medical Anthropology Quarterly, 9*(1), 188–210.

Mo, L., Légaré, J., & Stone, L. O. (2006). *Diversification and the privatization of the sources of retirement income in Canada.* SEDAP Research paper, No. 159. Hamilton, ON: SEDAP Research Program, McMaster University.

Moffatt, S., & Glasgow, N. (2009). How useful is the concept of social exclusion when applied to rural older people in the United Kingdom and the United States? *Regional Studies, 43*(10), 1291–1303.

Moody, H. R. (2001–2002, Winter). Who's afraid of life extension? *Generations, 25*(4), 33–37.

Moore, K. D., Robson, W. B. P., & Laurin, A. (2010). *Canada's looming retirement challenge: Will future retirees be able to maintain their living standards upon retirement?* C. D. Howe Institute Commentary Pension Paper (No. 317). Retrieved from http://papers.ssrn.com/sol3/papers.cfm?abstract_id=1749542

Moreira, T., May, C., & Bond, J. (2009). Regulatory objectivity in action: Mild cognitive impairment and the collective production of uncertainty. *Social Studies of Science, 39*(5), 665–690.

Morell, C. M. (2003). Empowerment and long-living women: Return to the rejected body. *Journal of Aging Studies,17*(1), 69–85.

Morgan, L. A., & Kunkel, S. R. (2011). *Aging, society, and the life course* (4th ed.). New York, NY: Springer.

Morgan, S., & Cunningham, C. (2011). Population aging and the determinants of healthcare expenditures: The case of hospital, medical and pharmaceutical care in British Columbia, 1996 to 2006. *HealthCare Policy, 7*(1), 68–79.

Morissette, R. (2002). Pensions: Immigrants and visible minorities. *Perspectives on labour and income, 3*(6), 13–18 (Catalogue No. 75-001-XIE). Ottawa, ON: Statistics Canada.

Morris, R. (2012). *Exploring the caregiving attitudes of adult stepchildren and the expectations of older stepparents.* Unpublished Masters thesis, University of Victoria, British Columbia, Canada.

Moss, M. S., Moss, S. Z., Rubinstein, R. L., & Black, H. K. (2003). The metaphor of "family" in staff communication about dying and death. *The Journals of Gerontology, 58*(5), 290–296.

Muise, A., & Desmarais, S. (2010). Women's perceptions and use of "anti-aging" products. *Sex Roles, 63*(1–2), 126–137.

Murphy, B., Zhang, X., & Dionne, C. (2012). Low income in Canada: A multi-line and multi-index perspective. *Income Research Paper Series* (Catalogue No. 75F0002M—No.001). Ottawa, ON: Statistics Canada. Retrieved from http://www.statcan.gc.ca/pub/75f0002m/75f0002m2012001-eng.htm

Murray, M., & Crummett, A. (2010). "I don't think they knew we could do these sorts of things": Social representations of community and participation in community arts by older people. *Journal of Health Psychology, 15*(5), 777–785.

Musaiger, A. O., & D'Souza, R. (2009). Role of age and gender in the perception of aging: A community-based survey in Kuwait. *Archives of Gerontology and Geriatrics, 48*(1), 50–57.

Mykytyn, C. E. (2010). A history of the future: The emergence of contemporary anti-ageing medicine. *Sociology of Health and Illness, 32*(2), 181–196.

Myles, J. (2000). The maturation of Canada's retirement income system: Income levels, income inequality and low income among older persons. *Canadian Journal on Aging, 19*(3), 287–316.

Narushima, M. (2004). A gaggle of raging grannies: The empowerment of older Canadian women through social activism. *International Journal of Lifelong Education, 23*(1), 23–42.

National Advisory Council on Aging. (2005a). *Seniors on the margins: Aging in poverty in Canada* (Catalogue No. H88-5/3-2005). Ottawa, ON: Minister of Public Works and Government Services Canada.

National Advisory Council on Aging. (2005b). *Seniors on the margins: Seniors from ethnocultural minorities* (Catalogue No. H88-5/1-2005E). Ottawa, ON: Minister of Public Works and Government Services Canada.

National Institute on Aging & National Institutes of Health. (2007). *Why population aging matters: A global perspective* (Publication No. 07-6134). US Department of Health and Human Services. Retrieved from http://www.nia.nih.gov/research/publication/why-population-aging-matters-global-perspective

National Seniors Council. (2009). *Report of the National Seniors Council on low income among seniors* (Cataloge No. HS1-9/2008). Gatineau, QC: Government of Canada. Retrieved from http://www.seniorscouncil.gc.ca/eng/research_publications/low_income/2009/hs1_9/page05.shtml

National Seniors Council. (2011). *Report on the labour force participation of seniors and near seniors, and intergenerational relations* (Catalogue No. HS4-111/2011). Gatineau, QC: Government of Canada. Retrieved from http://www.seniorscouncil.gc.ca/eng/research_publications/labour_force/page00.shtml

Neilson, B. (2003). Globalization and the biopolitics of aging. *CR: The New Centennial Review, 3*(2), 161–186.

Nett, E. M. (1981). Canadian families in social-historical perspective. *Canadian Journal of Sociology, 6*(3), 239–260.

Neugarten, B. L. (1974). Age groups in American society and the rise of the young-old. *The ANNALS of the American Academy of Political and Social Science, 415*(1), 187–198.

Neugarten, B. L., Moore, J. W., & Lowe, J. C. (1965). Age norms, age constraints, and adult socialization. *American Journal of Sociology, 70*(6), 710–717.

Nieminen, T., Martelin, T., Koskinen, S., Simpura, J., Alanen, E., Härkänen, T., and Aromaa, A. (2008). Measurement and socio-demographic variation of social capital in a large population-based survey. *Social Indicators Research, 85*(3), 405–423.

Ng, E., Lai, D. W. L., Rudner, A. T., & Orpana, H. (2012). *What do we know about immigrant seniors aging in Canada? A demographic, socio-economic and health profile.* CERIS Working Paper Series. Toronto, ON: CERIS—The Ontario Metropolis Centre. Retrieved from http://ceris.ca/wp-content/uploads/virtual-library/Ng_et_al_2012.pdf

Northcott, H. C. (1994). Public perceptions of the population aging "crisis." *Canadian Public Policy, 20*(1), 66–77.

O'Connor, D. L. (2007). Self-identifying as a caregiver: Exploring the positioning process. *Journal of Aging Studies, 21*(2), 165–174.

Office of the Chief Actuary. (2014, October 28). *Registered Pension Plan (RPP) and Retirement Savings Coverage (Canada).* Ottawa: Office of the Superintendent of Financial Institutions Canada. Retrieved from http://www.osfi-bsif.gc.ca/eng/oca-bac/fs-fr/pages/fs_rpp_2014.aspx

Ogg, J. (2005). Social exclusion and insecurity among older Europeans: The influence of welfare regimes. *Ageing and Society, 25*(1), 69–90.

Olsen, G. M. (1998). Locating the Canadian welfare state: Family policy and health care in Canada, Sweden, and the United States. In D. Coburn, C. D'Arcy, & G. Torrance (Eds.), *Health and Canadian society: Sociological perspectives* (3rd edition) (pp. 580–596). Toronto, ON: University of Toronto Press.

Olshansky, S. J., Biggs, S., Achenbaum, W. A., Davison, G. C., Fried, L., Gutman, G., . . . Butler, R. (2011). The Global Agenda Council on the Ageing Society: Policy principles. *Global Policy, 2*(1), 97–105.

Ontario Human Rights Commission. (2001). *Time for action: Advancing human rights for older Ontarians*. Retrieved from http://www.ohrc.on.ca/sites/default/files/attachments/Time_for_action%3A_Advancing_human_rights_for_older_Ontarians.pdf

Ontario Human Rights Commission. (2007). *Policy and guidelines on discrimination because of family status*. Retrieved from www.ohrc.on.ca

O'Rand, A. M. (1996a). The cumulative stratification of the life course. In R. H. Binstock & L. K. George (Eds.), *Handbook of aging and the social sciences* (4th ed.) (pp. 188–205). San Diego, CA: Academic Press.

O'Rand, A. M. (1996b). The precious and the precocious: Understanding cumulative disadvantage and cumulative advantage over the life course. *The Gerontologist, 36*(2), 230–238.

Organisation for Economic Co-operation and Development [OECD]. (2013). *Pensions at a Glance 2013: OECD and G20 Indicators*. OECD Publishing. Retrieved from http://dx.doi.org/10.1787/pension_glance-2013-en

O'Rourke, N., Cappeliez, P., & Guindon, S. (2003). Depressive symptoms and physical health of caregivers of persons with cognitive impairment: Analysis of reciprocal effects over time. *Journal of Aging and Health, 15*(4), 688–712.

Osberg, L. (2001). Poverty among senior citizens: A Canadian success story. In: *The state of economics in Canada: Festschrift in honour of David Slater* (pp.151–182). Ottawa, ON: Centre for the Study of Living Standards. Retrieved from http://ideas.repec.org/h/sls/secfds/08.html

Ostir, G. V., Ottenbacher, K. J., Fred, L. P., & Guralnik, J. M. (2007). The effect of depressive symptoms on the association between functional status and social participation. *Social Indicators Research, 80*, 379–392.

Outcalt, L. (2013). Paid companions: A private care option for older adults. *Canadian Journal on Aging, 32*(1), 87–102.

Palmore, E. B., & Manton, K. (1974). Modernization and status of the aged: International correlations. *Journal of Gerontology, 29*(2), 205–210.

Partridge, B., Lucke, J., Bartlett, H., & Hall, W. (2011). Public attitudes towards

human life extension by intervening in ageing. *Journal of Aging Studies, 25*, 73–83.

Patterson, M., & Malley-Morrison, K. (2006). A cognitive-ecological approach to elder abuse in five cultures: Human rights and education. *Educational Gerontology, 32*(1), 73–82.

Paxton, P. (1999). Is social capital declining in the United States? A multiple indicator assessment. *American Journal of Sociology, 105*(1), 88–127.

Pedersen, A. W. (2004). The privatization of retirement income? Variation and trends in the income packages of old age pensioners. *Journal of European Social Policy, 14*(1), 5–23.

Penning, M. J. (2002). Hydra revisited: Substituting formal for self and informal in-home care among older adults with disabilities. *The Gerontologist, 42*, 4–16.

Penning, M. J., Brackley, M. E., & Allan, D. E. (2006). Home care and health reform: Changes in home care utilization in one Canadian province, 1990–2000. *The Gerontologist, 46*(6), 744–758.

Penning, M. J., & Keating, N. C. (1999). Self, informal and formal care: Partnerships in community-based and residential care settings. *Canadian Journal on Aging 19*, 75–100.

Persson, T., & Wästerfors, D. (2009). "Such trivial matters": How staff account for restrictions of residents' influence in nursing homes. *Journal of Aging Studies, 23*(1), 1–11.

Petersen, D. (2002). The potential of social capital measures in the evaluation of comprehensive community-based health initiatives. *American Journal of Evaluation, 23*(1), 55–64.

Pfefferle, S. G., & Weinberg, D. B. (2008). Certified nursing assistants making meaning of direct care. *Qualitative Health Research, 18*(7), 952–961.

Phelan, E. A, Anderson, L. A., Lacroix, A. Z., & Larson, E. B. (2004). Older adults' views of "successful aging": How do they compare with researchers' definitions? *Journal of the American Geriatrics Society, 52*, 211–216.

Phillips, J., Ajrouch, K., & Hillcoat-Nallétamby, S. (2010). *Key concepts in social gerontology*. Los Angeles, CA: Sage.

Phillips, J., & Marks, G. (2008). Ageing lesbians: Marginalising discourses and social exclusion in the aged care industry. *Journal of Gay and Lesbian Social Services, 20*(1–2), 187–202.

Phillipson, C. (2005). The political economy of old age. In Johnson, M. L. (Ed.), *The Cambridge handbook of age and ageing* (pp. 502–509). New York, NY: Cambridge University Press.

Phillipson, C. (2007). The "elected" and the "excluded": Sociological perspectives on the experience of place and community in old age. *Ageing and Society, 27*(3), 321–342.

Phillipson, C. (2010). Globalisation, global ageing and intergenerational change. In M. Izuhara (Ed.), *Ageing and intergenerational relations: Family reciprocity from a global perspective* (pp. 13–28). Bristol, UK: Polity Press.

Pilcher, J. (1994). Mannheim's sociology of generations: An undervalued legacy. *British Journal of Sociology, 45*, 481–495.

Pilkington, P. D., Windsor, T. D., & Crisp, D. A. (2012). Volunteering and subjective well-being in midlife and older adults: The role of supportive social networks. *Journals of Gerontology, 67B*(2), 249–260.

Pinquart, M., & Sorensen, S. (2000). Influences of socioeconomic status, social network, and competence on subjective wellbeing in later life: A meta-analysis. *Psychology and Aging, 15*(2), 187–224.

Ploeg, J., Campbell, L., Denton, M., Joshi, A., & Davies, S. (2004). Helping to build and rebuild secure lives and futures: Financial transfers from parents to adult children and grandchildren. *Canadian Journal on Aging, 23*(Suppl.1), 113–135.

Podnieks, E. (2006). Social inclusion: An interplay of the determinants of health—New insights into elder abuse. *Journal of Gerontological Social Work, 46*(3–4), 57–79.

Powell, J. L., & Hendricks, J. (2009). The sociological construction of ageing: Lessons for theorising. *International Journal of Sociology and Social Policy, 29*(1/2), 84–94.

Prince, M. J. (2000). Apocalyptic, opportunistic and realistic demographic discourse: Retirement income and social policy or chicken littles, nest-eggies, and humpty dumpties. In E. Gee & G. Gutman (Eds.), *The overselling of population aging: Apocalyptic demography, intergenerational challenges, and social policy* (pp. 100–114). Toronto, ON: Oxford University Press.

Provis, C., & Stack, S. (2004). Caring work, personal obligation and collective responsibility. *Nursing Ethics, 11*, 5–14.

Prus, S. G. (2002). Changes in income within a cohort over the later life course: Evidence for income status convergence. *Canadian Journal on Aging, 21*(4), 495–504.

Prus, S. G. (2000). Income inequality as a Canadian cohort ages. *Research on Aging, 15*(4), 481–485.

Rankin, J. (2001). Texts in action: How nurses are doing the fiscal work of health care reform. *Studies in Cultures, Organizations and Societies, 7*(2), 251–267.

Ranzijn, R. (2010). Active ageing: Another way to oppress marginalized and disadvantaged elders? Aboriginal elders as a case study. *Journal of Health Psychology, 15*(5), 716–723.

Raphael, D. (2009). *Social determinants of health: Canadian perspectives* (2nd ed.). Toronto, ON: Canadian Scholars' Press Inc.

Renaud, M. (1994). The Future: Hygeia versus panakeia? In R. G. Evans, M. L. Barer, & T. R. Marmor (Eds.), *Why are some people healthy and others not? The determinants of health of populations* (pp. 317–334). New York, NY: Aldine de Gruyter.

Revera & International Federation on Ageing. (2012). *Revera report on ageism.* Retrieved from http://www.reveraliving.com/About-Us/Media-Centre/Revera-Report-on-Ageism/docs/Report_Ageism.aspx

Rhoads, E. C. (1984). Reevaluation of the aging and modernization theory: The Samoan evidence. *The Gerontologist, 24*(3), 243–250.

Richard, L., Gauvin, L., Gosselin, C., & Laforest, S. (2009). Staying connected: Neighbourhood correlates of social participation among older adults living in an urban environment in Montréal, Québec. *Health Promotion International, 24*(1), 46–57.

Riley, M. W. (1971). Social gerontology and the age stratification of society. *The Gerontologist, 11*(1 part 1), 79–87.

Riley, M. W., Kahn, R. L., & Foner, A. (1994). *Age and structural lag: Society's failure to provide meaningful opportunities in work, family, and leisure.* New York, NY: Wiley.

Riley, M. W., Kahn, R. L., Foner, A., & Mack, K. A. (1994). Introduction: The mismatch between people and structures. In M. W. Riley, R. L., Kahn, & A. Foner (Eds.), *Age and structural lag: Society's failure to provide meaningful opportunities in work, family, and leisure* (pp. 1–12). New York: Wiley.

Riley, M. W., & Riley, J. W. (1999). Sociological research on age: Legacy and challenge. *Ageing and Society, 19,* 123–132.

Riley, M. W., & Riley, J. W. (2000). Age integration: Conceptual and historical background. *The Gerontologist, 40*(3), 266–270.

Robertson, A. (1990). The politics of Alzheimer's disease: A case study in apocalyptic demography. *International Journal of Health Services, 20*(3), 429–442.

Robertson, A. (1997). Beyond apocalyptic demography: Towards a moral economy of interdependence. *Ageing and Society, 17*(4), 425–446.

Robertson, A. (1999). Beyond apocalyptic demography: Toward a moral economy of interdependence. In M. Minkler, & C. L. Estes (Eds.), *Critical gerontology: Perspectives from political and moral economy* (pp. 75–90). Amityville, NY: Baywood.

Robertson, A., & Minkler, M. (1994). New health promotion movement: A critical examination. *Health Education Quarterly, 21,* 295–312.

Room, G. (1995). *Beyond the threshold: The measurement and analysis of social exclusion.* Bristol, UK: The Policy Press.

Roos, N. P, & Havens, B. (1998). Predictors of successful aging: A twelve-year study of Manitoba elderly. In D. Coburn, C. D'Arcy, & G. Torrance (Eds.), *Health and Canadian society: Sociological perspectives* (pp. 295–307). Toronto, ON: University of Toronto Press.

Rose, H., & Bruce, E. (1995). Mutual care but differential esteem: Caring between older couples. In S. Arber & J. Ginn (Eds.), *Connecting gender and ageing: A sociological approach* (pp. 114–128). Buckingham: Open University Press.

Rosenthal, C. J., Denton, M., Martin-Matthews, A., & French, S. E. (2000). Changes in work and family over the life course: Implications for economic security of today's and tomorrow's older women. In F. T. Denton, D. Fretz, & B. G. Spencer (Eds.), *Independence and economic security in old age* (pp. 86–111). Vancouver, BC: UBC Press.

Rowe, J. W., & Kahn, R. L. (1997). Successful aging. *The Gerontologist, 37,* 433–440.

Roy, C. (n.d.). The original raging grannies: Using creative and humorous protests for political education [Online research paper]. Retrieved from http://raging-grannies.org/herstory/

Roy, M., & Payette, H. (2012). The body image construct among Western seniors: A systematic review of the literature. *Archives of Gerontology and Geriatrics, 55*(3), 505–521.

Rozanova, J., Keating, N., & Eales, J. (2012). Unequal social engagement for older adults: Constraints on choice. *Canadian Journal on Aging, 31*(1), 25–36.

Russell, C. (1987). Ageing as a feminist issue. *Women's Studies International Forum, 10,* 125–132.

Ryan, T., Nolan, M., Enderby, P., & Reid, D. (2004). "Part of the family": Sources of job satisfaction amongst a group of community-based dementia care workers. *Health and Social Care in the Community, 12*(2), 111–118.

Salter, C. I., Howe, A., McDaid, L., Blacklock, J., Lenaghan, E., & Shepstone, L. (2011). Risk, significance and biomedicalisation of a new population: Older women's experience of osteoporosis screening. *Social Science and Medicine, 73*(6), 808–815.

Sass, J. S. (2000). Emotional labor as cultural performance: The communication of caregiving in a nonprofit nursing home. *Western Journal of Communication, 64*(3), 330–358.

Sawchuk, D. (2009). The Raging Grannies: Defying stereotypes and embracing aging through activism. *Journal of Women and Aging, 21*(3), 171–185.

Scharf, T., & Bartlam, B. (2008). Ageing and social exclusion in rural communities. In N. Keating (Ed.), *Rural ageing: A good place to grow old?* (pp. 97–108). Bristol, UK: Polity Press.

Scharf, T., Phillipson, C., Kingston, P., & Smith, A. E. (2001). Social exclusion and older people: Exploring the connections. *Education and Ageing, 16*(3), 303–320.

Scharf, T., Phillipson, C., & Smith, A. E. (2005). Social exclusion of older people in deprived urban communities of England. *European Journal of Ageing, 2*(2), 76–87.

Schirle, T. (2010). Health, pensions, and the retirement decision: Evidence from Canada. *Canadian Journal on Aging, 29*(4), 519–527.

Schmeekle, M., Giarrusso, R., Feng, D., & Bengtson, V. L. (2006). What makes someone family? Adult children's perceptions of current and former stepparents. *Journal of Marriage and Family, 68*(3), 595–610.

Segall, A., & Chappell, N. (2000). *Health and health care in Canada.* Toronto: Prentice Hall.

Seltzer, M. M., & Li, L. W. (2000). The dynamics of caregiving: Transitions during a three-year prospective study. *The Gerontologist, 40*(2), 165–178.

Settersten, R. A., Jr., & Angel, J. L. (2011). Trends in the sociology of aging: Thirty year observations. In R. A. Settersten Jr. & J. L. Angel (Eds.), *Handbook of sociology of aging* (pp. 3–13). New York, NY: Springer.

Sharman, Z., McLaren, A. T., Cohen, M., & Ostry, A. (2008). "We only own the hours": Discontinuity of care in the British Columbia home support system. *Canadian Journal on Aging, 27*(1), 89–99.

Shaw, F. (2002). Is the ageing population the problem it is made out to be? *Foresight, 4*(3), 4–11.

Shaw, M., Dorling, D., & Davey Smith, G. (2002). Poverty, social exclusion, and minorities. In M. Marmot & R. G. Wilkinson (Eds.), *Social determinants of health,* (pp. 211–239). Oxford, UK: Oxford University Press.

Sheng, X., & Settles, B. H. (2006). Intergenerational relationships and elderly care in China: A global perspective. *Current Sociology, 54*(2), 293–313.

Shim, J. K., Russ, A. J., & Kaufman, S. R. (2006). Risk, life extension and the pursuit of medical possibility. *Sociology of Health and Illness, 28*(4), 479–502.

Shookner, M. (2002). *The Inclusion Lens: Workbook for looking at social and economic exclusion and inclusion.* Population Health Research Centre, Dalhousie University, for the Population and Public Health Branch, Atlantic Regional Office, Health Canada.

Sinding, C. (2003). Disarmed complaints: Unpacking satisfaction with end-of-life care. *Social Science and Medicine, 57,* 1375–1385.

Smith, P. (1993). Family responsibility and the nature of obligation. In D. Tietjens Meyers, K. Kipnis, & C. F. J. Murphy (Eds.), *Kindred matters: Rethinking the philosophy of the family* (pp. 41–58). Ithaca, NY: Cornell University Press.

Smith, R., Magee, L., Robb, A. L., & Burbidge, J. B. (2000). The independence and economic security of older women living alone. In F. Denton, D. Fretz, & B. Spencer (Eds.), *Independence and economic security in old age* (pp. 293–327). Vancouver, BC: UBC Press.

Sohal, R. S., & Forster, M. J. (2014). Caloric restriction and the aging process: A critique. *Free Radical Biology and Medicine, 73,* 366–382.

Spindler, M., & Streubel, C. (2009). The media and anti-aging medicine: Witchhunt, uncritical reporting, or fourth estate? *Medicine Studies, 1,* 229–247.

Spitze, G., & Gallant, M. P. (2004). "The bitter with the sweet": Older adults' strategies for handling ambivalence in relations with their adult children. *Research on Aging, 26*(4), 387–412.

Stacey, C. L. (2005). Finding dignity in dirty work: The constraints and rewards of low-wage home care labour. *Sociology of Health and Illness, 27*(6), 831–854.

Stahl, S. M., & Feller, J. R. (1990). Old equals sick: An ontogenic fallacy. In S. M. Stahl (Ed.), *The legacy of longevity* (pp. 21–34). Newbury Park, CA: Sage.

Starr, J. M. (1982–1983). Toward a social phenomenology of aging: Studying the self process in biographical work. *The International Journal of Aging and Human Development, 16*(4), 255–270.

Statistics Canada. (2010). Population and demography. In Statistics Canada, *Canada year book 2010* (pp. 313–326) (Catalogue no. 11-402-X). Retrieved from http://www.statcan.gc.ca/pub/11-402-x/2010000/pdf/population-eng.pdf

Statistics Canada. (2011a). *Income compos-
ition in Canada* (Catalogue No. 99-014-
S2011001). Ottawa, ON: Minister of
Industry.

Statistics Canada. (2011b). *Portrait of
Canada's labour force: National household
survey, 2011* (Catalogue No. 99-012-
X2011002). Ottawa, ON: Minister of
Industry.

Statistics Canada. (2012). *Portrait of families
and living arrangements in Canada:
Families, households and marital status,
2011 Census of Population* (Catalogue
No. 98-312-X2011001). Ottawa, ON:
Minister of Industry.

Statistics Canada. (2013, November 25).
Canada's population estimates: Age
and sex, 2013. *The Daily*, Component
of Statistics Canada (Catalogue No.
11-001-X). Retrieved from http://www.
statcan.gc.ca/daily-quotidien/131125/
dq131125a-eng.pdf

Status of Women Canada. (2015, February
25). Fact sheet: Economic security.
Retrieved from http://www.swc-cfc.
gc.ca/initiatives/wesp-sepf/fs-fi/es-se-
eng.html#fnb3

Stein, C. H., Wemmerus, V. A., Ward,
M., Gaines, M. E., Freeberg, A. L., &
Jewell, T. C. (1998). "Because they're
my parents": An intergenerational study
of felt obligations and parental caregiving. *Journal of Marriage and Family,
60*(3), 611–622.

Stewart, M., Craig, D., MacPherson, K., &
Alexander, S. (2001). Promoting positive affect and diminishing loneliness
of widowed seniors through a support
intervention. *Public Health Nursing,
18*(1), 54–63.

Stewart, M. J., Neufeld, A., Harrison,
M. J., Spitzer, D., Hughes, K., &
Makwarimba, E. (2006). Immigrant
women family caregivers in Canada:
Implications for policies and pro-
grammes in health and social sectors.
*Health and Social Care in the Community,
14*(4), 329–340.

Stewart, M., Shizha, E., Makwarimba, E.,
Spitzer, D., Khalema, E. N., & Nsaliwa,
C. D. (2011). Challenges and barriers
to services for immigrant seniors in
Canada: "You are among others but
you feel alone." *International Journal of
Migration, Health and Social Care, 7*(1),
16–32.

Strain, L. A., Grabusic, C. C., Searle, M.
S., & Dunn, N. J. (2002). Continuing
and ceasing leisure activities in later life:
A longitudinal study. *The Gerontologist,
42*(2), 217–223.

Strohm, C. Q., Seltzer, J. A., Cochran,
S. D., & Mays, V. M. (2009). "Living
Apart Together" relationships in the
United States. *Demographic Research, 21,*
178–214.

Szinovacz, M. E., DeViney, S., & Davey,
A. (2001). Influences of family obliga-
tions and relationships on retirement:
Variations by gender, race, and marital
status. *Journals of Gerontology, 56B*(1),
S20–S27.

Talley, R. C., & Crews, J. E. (2007).
Framing the public health of caregiving.
American Journal of Public Health, 97(2),
224–228.

Tam, S., & Neysmith, S. (2006). Disrespect
and isolation: Elder abuse in Chinese
communities. *Canadian Journal on
Aging, 25*(2), 141–151.

Tang, K.-L., & Lee, J.-J. (2006). Global
social justice for older people: The case
for an International Convention on the
Rights of Older People. *British Journal of
Social Work, 36*(7), 1135–1150.

Taylor, P. (2013). Introduction: Older work-
ers in an ageing society. In P. Taylor
(Ed.), *Older workers in an ageing society:
Critical topics in research and policy.*
Cheltenham, UK: Edward Elgar.

Taylor, P. S. (2013, November 25). Pay up,
grandma. *Maclean's, 126*(46), 18–21.

Theurer, K., & Wister, A. (2010). Altruistic
behaviour and social capital as predictors
of well-being among older Canadians.
Ageing and Society, 30(1), 157–181.

Thompson, E. H., Futterman, A. M.,
Gallagher-Thompson, D., Rose, J. M., &
Lovett, S. B. (1993). Social support and
caregiving burden in family caregivers
of frail elders. *Journals of Gerontology,
48B*(5), 245–254.

Tiggemann, M. (2004). Body image across
the adult life span: Stability and change.
Body Image, 1(1), 29–41.

Torrance, G. M. (1998). Socio-historical
overview: The development of the
Canadian health system. In D. Coburn,
C. D'Arcy, & G. Torrance (Eds.),
*Health and Canadian society: Sociological
perspectives* (pp. 3–22). Toronto, ON:
University of Toronto Press.

Torres, S. (2012). International migration: Patterns and implications for exclusion in old age. In T. Scharf & N. Keating (Eds.), *From exclusion to inclusion in old age: A global challenge* (pp. 33–50). Bristol, UK: The Policy Press.

Trottier, H., Martel, L., Houle, C., Berthelot, J. M., & Légaré, J. (2000). Living at home or in an institution: What makes the difference for seniors? *Health Reports, 11*(4), 49–61. Ottawa, ON: Statistics Canada, Canadian Centre for Health Information.

Tulle, E. (2004). Introduction. In E. Tulle (Ed.), *Old age and agency.* New York, NY: Nova Science Publishers.

Tunaley, J. R., Walsh, S., & Nicolson, P. (1999). "I'm not bad for my age": The meaning of body size and eating in the lives of older women. *Ageing and Society, 19*(6), 741–759.

Turcotte, M. (2013, March). Living apart together. *Insights on Canadian society* (Catalogue No. 75-006-X). Ottawa, ON: Statistics Canada, Minister of Industry.

Turcotte, M., & Schellenberg, G. (2007). *A portrait of seniors in Canada* (Catalogue No. 89-519-XIE). Ottawa, ON: Statistics Canada, Minister of Industry. Retrieved from http://www.statcan.gc.ca/pub/89-519-x/2006001/4122091-eng.htm

Twigg, J. (2000). Carework as a form of bodywork. *Ageing and Society, 20*(4), 389–411.

Twigg, J. (2004). The body, gender, and age: Feminist insights in social gerontology. *Journal of Aging Studies, 18*(1), 59–73.

Twigg, J. (2007). Clothing, age and the body: A critical review. *Ageing and Society, 27*(2), 285–305.

Twigg, J., Wolkowitz, C., Cohen, R. L., & Nettleton, S. (2011). Conceptualising body work in health and social care. *Sociology of Health and Illness* [Special issue], *33*(2), 171–188.

Ungerson, C. (1997). Social politics and the commodification of care. *Social Politics, 4*, 362–381.

United Nations. (2002). Political Declaration and Madrid International Plan of Action on Ageing. *Second World Assembly on Ageing, Madrid, Spain, 8–12 April 2002.* New York, NY: Author.

Utz, R. L. (2011). Like mother, (not) like daughter: The social construction of menopause and aging. *Journal of Aging Studies, 25*(2), 143–154.

Utz, R. L., Carr, D., Nesse, R., & Wortman, C. B. (2002). The effect of widowhood on older adults' social participation: An evaluation of activity, disengagement, and continuity theories. *The Gerontologist, 42*(4), 522–533.

van den Hoonaard, D. K. (1997). Identity foreclosure: Women's experiences of widowhood as expressed in autobiographical accounts. *Journal of Aging Studies, 17*(5), 533–551.

van den Hoonaard, D. K. (2002). Attitudes of older widows and widowers in New Brunswick, Canada towards new partnerships. *Ageing International, 27*(4), 79–92.

van Tilburg, T. (1998). Losing and gaining in old age: Changes in personal network size and social support in a four-year longitudinal study. *Journals of Gerontology, 53B*(6), S313–S323.

Veenstra, G. (2000). Social capital, SES and health: An individual-level analysis. *Social Science and Medicine, 50*(5), 619–629.

Veenstra, G. (2005). Location, location, location: Contextual and compositional health effects of social capital in British Columbia, Canada. *Social Science and Medicine, 60*(9), 2059–2071.

Venn, S., Davidson, K., & Arber, S. (2011). Gender and aging. In R. A. Settersten Jr. & J. L. Angel (Eds.), *Handbook of sociology of aging* (pp. 71–81). New York, NY: Springer.

Vezina, M., & Turcotte, M. (2010). Caring for a parent who lives far away: The consequences. *Canadian Social Trends* (Statistics Canada Catalogue No. 11-008-X). Ottawa, ON: Statistics Canada.

Vincent, J. A. (2006). Ageing contested: Anti-ageing science and the cultural construction of old age. *Sociology, 40*(4), 681–698.

Vincent, J. A. (2008). The cultural construction of old age as a biological phenomenon. *Journal of Aging Studies, 22*(4), 331–339.

Vincent, J. A. (2009). Ageing, anti-ageing, and anti-anti-ageing: Who are the progressives in the debate on the future of human biological ageing? *Medicine Studies, 1*(3), 197–208.

Walker, A. (1981). Towards a political economy of old age. *Ageing and Society, 7*, 73–94.

Walker, A. (2005). Towards an international political economy of ageing. *Ageing and Society, 25*(6), 815–839.

Walker, A. (2012). The new ageism. *The Political Quarterly, 83*(4), 812–819.

Wang, D. (2004). Ritualistic coresidence and the weakening of filial practice in rural China. In C. Ikels (Ed.), *Filial piety: Practice and discourse in contemporary East Asia* (pp. 16–33). Stanford, CA: Stanford University Press.

Wannell, T. (2007). Young pensioners. *Perspectives on labour and income, 8*(2), 5–15.

Ward-Griffin, C., Bol, N., Hay, K., & Dashnay, I. (2003). Relationships between families and registered nurses in long-term care facilities: A critical analysis. *Canadian Journal of Nursing Research, 35*(4), 150–174.

Ward-Griffin, C., & Marshall, V. (2004). Reconceptualizing the relationship between "public" and "private" elder-care. *Journal of Aging Studies 17*(2), 189–208.

Waskiewich, S., Funk, L. M., & Stajduhar, K. I. (2012). End of life in residential care from the perspective of care aides. *Canadian Journal on Aging, 31*(4), 411–21.

Waskul, D. D., & Vannini, P. (2006). Introduction: The body in symbolic interaction. In D. D. Waskul & P. Vannini (Eds.), *Body/embodiment: Symbolic interaction and the sociology of the body* (pp. 1–18). Burlington, VT: Ashgate Publishing.

Webster, J., & Tiggemann, M. (2003). The relationship between women's body satisfaction and self-image across the life span: The role of cognitive control. *The Journal of Genetic Psychology, 164*(2), 241–252.

Wellin, C. (2010). Growing pains in the sociology of aging and the life course: A review essay on recent textbooks. *Teaching Sociology, 38*(4), 373–382.

Wheelcock, J., & Jones, K. (2002). "Grandparents are the next best thing": Informal childcare for working parents in urban Britain. *Journal of Social Policy, 31*(3), 441–463.

Whitaker, A. (2010). The body as existential midpoint: The aging and dying body of nursing home residents. *Journal of Aging Studies, 24*(2), 96–104.

Whitfield, K., & Wismer, S. (2006). Inclusivity and dementia: Health services planning with individuals with dementia. *Healthcare Policy, 1*(2), 120–134.

Whyte, M. K. (2004). Filial obligations in Chinese families: Paradoxes of modernization. In C. Ikels (Ed.), *Filial piety: Practice and discourse in contemporary East Asia* (pp. 106–127). Stanford, CA: Stanford University Press.

Wilcox, S. (1997). Age and gender in relation to body attitudes: Is there a double standard of aging? *Psychology of Women Quarterly, 21*(4), 549–565.

Wilkinson, R. G. (2002). Putting the picture together: Prosperity, redistribution, health, and welfare. In M. Marmot & R. G. Wilkinson (Eds.), *Social determinants of health* (pp. 256–274). Oxford, UK: Oxford University Press.

Williams, A. P., Deber, R., Baranek, P., & Gildiner, A. (2001). From medicare to home care: Globalization, state retrenchment, and the profitization of Canada's health-care system. In P. Armstrong, H. Armstrong, & D. Coburn (Eds.), *Unhealthy times: Political economy perspectives on health and care* (pp. 7–30). Don Mills, ON: Oxford University Press.

Williams, C. (2005). The sandwich generation. *Canadian Social Trends* (Catalogue No. 11-008) (pp. 16–21). Ottawa, ON: Statistics Canada.

Williams, S. W., Zimmerman, S., & Williams, C. S. (2012). Family caregiver involvement for long-term care residents at the end of life. *Journals of Gerontology, S67*(4), 595–604.

Wilson, D., Truman, C. D., Huang, J., Sheps, S., Thomas, R., & Noseworthy, T. (2004). The possibilities and the realities of home care. *Canadian Journal of Public Health, 96*(5), 385–389.

Wilson, K., Rosenberg, M. W., Abonyi, S., & Lovelace, R. (2010). Aging and health: An examination of differences between older aboriginal and non-aboriginal people. *Canadian Journal on Aging, 29*(3), 369–382.

Wolfson, M. (2011). *Projecting the adequacy of Canadians' retirement incomes: Current prospects and possible reform options.* IRPP Study 17. Montreal, QC: Institute for Research on Public Policy.

World Health Organization. (1948). *Preamble to the Constitution of the World Health Organization as adopted by the International Health Conference, New York, 19–22 June, 1946* (Official Records of the World Health Organization, No. 2, p. 100). Retrieved from http://www.who.int/about/definition/en/

Wray, S. (2003). Women growing older: Agency, ethnicity and culture. *Sociology, 37*(3), 511–527.

Yan, E., & Tang, C. (2001). Prevalence and psychological impact of Chinese elder abuse. *Journal of Interpersonal Violence, 16*(11), 1158–1174.

Yip, W., Subramanian, S. V., Mitchell, A. D., Lee, D. T. S., Wang, J., & Kawachi, I. (2007). Does social capital enhance health and well-being? Evidence from rural China. *Social Science and Medicine, 64*(1), 35–49.

Young, A., Russell, A., & Powers, J. (2004). The sense of belonging to a neighbourhood: Can it be measured and is it related to health and well being in older women? *Social Science and Medicine, 59*(12), 2627–2637.

Zarit, S. H., Reever, K. E., & Bach-Peterson, J. (1980). Relatives of the impaired elderly: Correlates of feelings of burden. *The Gerontologist, 20*(6), 649–655.

Zechner, M. (2008). Care of older persons in transnational settings. *Journal of Aging Studies, 22*(1), 32–44.

Zhan, H. J. (2004a). Socialization or social structure: A study of one-child generation students' willingness to accept filial responsibilities in urban China. *The International Journal of Aging and Human Development, 59*(2), 105–125.

Zhan, H. J. (2004b). Willingness and expectations: Intergenerational differences in attitudes toward filial responsibility. *Marriage and Family Review, 36*(1–2), 175–200.

Zhang, Y. B., Harwood, J., Williams, A., Ylänne-McEwen, V., Wadleigh, P. M., & Thimm, C. (2006). The portrayal of older adults in advertising: A cross-national review. *Journal of Language and Social Psychology, 25*(3), 264–282.

Zhou, Y. R. (2012). Space, time, and self: Rethinking aging in the contexts of immigration and transnationalism. *Journal of Aging Studies, 26*(3), 232–242.

Index